Literary Feuds

ALSO BY ANTHONY ARTHUR

Deliverance at Los Baños
Bushmasters
The Tailor-King

Literary Feuds

A Century of Celebrated Quarrels —from Mark Twain to Tom Wolfe

ANTHONY ARTHUR

THOMAS DUNNE BOOKS

ST. MARTIN'S PRESS

NEW YORK

THOMAS DUNNE BOOKS.
An imprint of St. Martin's Press.

LITERARY FEUDS. Copyright © 2002 by Anthony Arthur. All rights reserved.
Printed in the United States of America. No part of this book may be used or
reproduced in any manner whatsoever without written permission except in
the case of brief quotations embodied in critical articles or reviews. For information, address St. Martin's Press, 175 Fifth Avenue, New York, N.Y. 10010.

www.stmartins.com

ISBN 0-312-27209-X

First Edition: December 2002

10 9 8 7 6 5 4 3 2 1

For Nell and Duncan, who are hardly ever quarrelsome

Contents

ACKNOWLEDGMENTS ix

PREFACE xi

1 Partners No More: Mark Twain and Bret Harte 1

2 The Boy with the Interested Eyes: Ernest Hemingway and Gertrude Stein 23

3 The Slap Heard 'Round the World: Sinclair Lewis, Theodore Dreiser, and the Nobel Prize 49

4 Not Always a "Pleasant Tussle": The Difficult Friendship of Edmund Wilson and Vladimir Nabokov 77

5 The Battle of the "Two Cultures": C. P. Snow and F. R. Leavis 109

6 "Now *There's* a Play": Lillian Hellman and Mary McCarthy 135

7 *Les Enfants Terribles:* Truman Capote and Gore Vidal 159

8 Not-So-Dry Bones: Tom Wolfe, John Updike, and the Perils of Literary Ambition 187

NOTES 209

INDEX 231

Acknowledgments

Friends whose careful readings of all or parts of this book as it was in preparation, and to whom I am most grateful, include John Broesamle, Barbara Kelly, Peter Brier, Jackson Bryer, John Clendenning, and Sidney Richman. Naturally, they are innocent of any of its flaws. I also wish to thank the following students for their thoughtful essays on some of these writers and their quarrels: Shelley Armstrong, Shira Brown, Allison Conant, James Filippini, Wendy Hector, Mandy Kuntz, Brenda Lavin, Jennifer Lockwood, Christopher Paquette, Nancy Peterson, Cheryl Spatz, Robert Sicanoff, Nora Strickland, Melissa Weaver, Melodie Williamson, and Karen Woiwode.

What demons drove Truman Capote to the miserable death that Vidal called a "good career move"?

Final answers to these questions are impossible: Real people are much harder to figure out than fictional ones. But posing the questions at least leads us to think usefully about the writers and their works. For example, I am struck by how unyielding, how committed to unconditional victory most of the feuding writers have been: Nothing—not money, not fame, not popular adulation, not critical approbation, much less the disapproval of friends or even threats of lawsuits—ever persuaded them simply to shrug off offenses that either were not worth fighting about or were impossible to fix.

It may be that such compulsiveness is what gives writers much of their force, as Sigmund Freud argues in *Art and Neurosis*. When it's merely personal, the force often emerges as destructive or mean. When it's channeled into a more creative context, it becomes more positive.

The feuds, when seen in this light, provide a natural counterpoint to the novels, the plays, and the criticism written by the authors described here, and not a contradiction to them. They are not irrelevant distractions or sideshows but avenues of greater insight into the literature that the feuding writers have created for us.

crime, poverty, sex, social upheavals, national and international politics, and, of course, literary art. It is no coincidence that many of them, most notably Mark Twain, Edmund Wilson, Ernest Hemingway, and Tom Wolfe, were originally journalists. They feuded with other writers most often over literary matters—Wilson savaging Vladimir Nabokov's English translation of Pushkin, Wolfe responding to Updike's negative review of *A Man in Full*. But their concept of literature included a strong admixture of politics and public affairs—Mary McCarthy opposing Lillian Hellman as a Stalinist, C. P. Snow and F. R. Leavis debating the idea of culture, Gore Vidal unrolling his revisionist history of the United States while scorning Truman Capote as a frivolous poseur. These disputes, then, do not simply turn around personalities and gossip. Rather, they provide insight into the social and intellectual history of the twentieth century.

Writing about social issues and about literature encourages at least a degree of reasoned argument. But the second broad theme of these stories is not social; it is psychological. What fascinates most of us about literature is that it helps us understand why people do the things they do. How is it, then, that writers who can accomplish this feat in their work can behave so oddly in their personal relationships, often at such variance with their better selves?

Granted, some of the participants here seem more sinned against than sinning—Snow, Lewis, perhaps Harte. And a few seem to know exactly what they are doing—Wolfe, Vidal, and McCarthy all have a calculated edge to their attacks. But what could have driven Edmund Wilson to betray his friend Nabokov as he did? Why did Mark Twain go to such lengths to ruin Bret Harte's reputation? Where did Leavis think his character assassination of Snow would take him? How could a man so celebrated, so revered as Hemingway let himself be upset by an old woman who had once been his teacher and his friend?

Preface

Can good writers be bad people? Three literary reviewers seem to think so, particularly when writers are fighting with other writers. Judith Shulevitz mocks Norman Mailer, who, in his notorious *Advertisements for Myself*, "wallows in self-pity, pride and a world-historical egomania, thereby providing an accurate portrait of the mental state of most writers most of the time." Walter Kirn says, "Famous writers are critics in the same way crocodiles are carnivores—from birth, by training and by instinct. . . ." And Roger Rosenblatt calls them "a bad lot on the whole—petty, nasty, bilious, suffused with envy and riddled with fear."

Nobody gets particularly upset that some artists, composers, sculptors, and the like are rogues. But writers still labor under the burden of Matthew Arnold's definition of culture in terms of literature—that is, as "the best that has been thought and said." Logically enough, but against our better judgment and common sense, we expect literary people whose works include the classic attributes of truth and beauty to be themselves true and beautiful. When they are petty, prideful, and unpleasant, we scorn them for being just like the rest of us, as messengers unworthy of their tasks.

Paul Johnson, pursuing this idea, argues in his 1988 book, *Intellectuals*, that writers from Rousseau through Noam Chomsky have been a pack of self-serving frauds, if not compulsive liars—among whom he includes Ernest Hemingway and Lillian Hellman. But Johnson overstates his case, and I suspect that Shulevitz, Kirn, and Rosenblatt are, at bottom, condemning bad behavior more than bad character. My sense of the real reason for the widespread interest in the perceived foibles of writers is that we wonder how people who so vividly describe human failure (as well as triumph) can themselves fall short of perfection. Viewed negatively, our interest is simply *Schadenfreude*, an ignoble enjoyment of others' discomfort. Viewed positively, it is an appreciation of the degree to which writers, in their art, overcome their limitations as people.

I offer these thoughts because I want to be clear about the purpose of this book. It is not to condemn the writers for feuding, though they flay their opponents with gusto. Rather, it is to satisfy the curiosity of readers about the sometimes paradoxical relationship between these writers' lives and their works. The so-called New Critics used to disparage literary biography as an irrelevant distraction from the works themselves, calling it the "biographical fallacy." But I've taught all of the authors discussed here to college students since the 1960s, and my experience has been that the more we know about writers in general, the better able we are to appreciate and understand their work.

I am indebted to the many biographers, critics, and reviewers who have written about these feuds, and especially to John Updike and Tom Wolfe for their personal responses to my questions. I also, of course, owe much to all of my disputatious subjects for their vivid language, and for the fact that their disagreements were, in general, not over trivial matters. Two broad themes emerge from what Clausewitz called the fog of combat.

The first stems from the fact that none of these writers was reclusive or retiring by nature. All were actively engaged with the world, writing about the Big Issues of their times: race, war,

Literary Feuds

1

Partners No More

MARK TWAIN AND BRET HARTE

Here's how it started, this famous and doomed friendship: It was mid-morning, early in the summer of 1864 in San Francisco. If it was a typical morning, the pale sun was parting the fog that curled past the third floor of the *San Francisco Call* building on Commercial Street, where the offices of the United States Mint were located. Two men, both in their mid-twenties, slightly built and short, sat in friendly conversation. The younger man (though only by a year) was the host, for it was his office—that of the assistant to the district supervisor of the Mint. His guest was the recently hired beat reporter for the newspaper downstairs.

Writing, not watching over the government's money, was what interested Bret Harte. At twenty-seven, he was seen by the thriving literary set in San Francisco as a comer, even as a genius if taken at his own word, according to which he read Shakespeare at the age of six, Dickens at seven, and Montaigne at eight, though he stopped short of claiming to have read the latter in the original French.

Harte was not a native Californian—few Americans were. He had come west from Albany with his widowed mother in 1854 and worked as a tutor and at other odd jobs, many more interesting in his creative retelling than they were in actual fact. (His brief, uneventful stint with the Wells, Fargo Express Company in 1857 soon became a perilous tour of duty riding shotgun on a stagecoach; the man who preceded him was wounded by bandits and his successor was killed, he said.) He wandered through northern California, eventually finding work in Humboldt County, near the border with Oregon, as a newspaper reporter. One true story from this period reflects well on Harte as a man of generous spirit and some courage. He wrote a blistering attack on a mob massacre of about sixty Indians—one of the more notorious incidents of early California history—and barely got out of town with his own life when the lynchers came looking for him.

Returning to San Francisco in 1860, Harte won the favor of Jessie Benton Frémont, wife of the famous explorer, who hosted a literary salon in her house overlooking the bay. It was through Mrs. Frémont that Harte won his position with the Mint, more a sinecure than a real job, though he performed his simple duties capably enough. Widely published within the next few years in local newspapers and magazines, he took his first step toward national recognition by appearing in the October 1863 issue of the country's leading magazine, the *Atlantic Monthly*. In May 1864 his friend Charles Webb initiated a new literary journal, the *Californian*, with Harte as one of its main contributors and as occasional editor. Within two years Harte would publish a vast number of pieces in the *Californian*—thirty-five poems and seventy-eight prose pieces, including parodies of James Fenimore Cooper ("Muck-a-Muck"), Dickens, Dumas, and Charlotte Brontë.

Newly married, to a pretty but severe young woman named Anna Griswold, and securely if undemandingly employed, Harte was beginning to gather the material for some of the stories that in a few years would make him famous: "The Luck of Roaring Camp," about a baby born to a dying prostitute in a rough gold-mining town who makes rowdies and killers into softhearted daddies; "The Outcasts of Poker Flat," in which the righteous townsfolk send a gambler, a prostitute, and other undesirables out to die in a snowstorm; and "Tennessee's Partner," about two miners whose friendship survives even death.

An elegant if not foppish dresser, Bret Harte favored tailored suits and white broadcloth shirts set off by a diamond stickpin and a bright red necktie. Though his face was marked with smallpox scars, he was a handsome man, with curly black hair, finely chiseled features, and a luxuriant black mustache. He wasn't famous for his conversation; when he did talk, he affected a witty, sardonic pose not unlike that of his notoriously cynical friend Ambrose Bierce.

Harte's guest on that summer morning in 1864 provided a vivid study in contrasts with his elegant host. He was rumpled and bombastic, with bushy reddish eyebrows and mustache, wildly luxuriant brown hair, and an intensity of eye so like that of an eagle, Harte later wrote, that "a second lid would not have surprised me." His "general manner [was] one of supreme indifference to surroundings and circumstances." The guest's name was Sam Clemens, and he had grown up on the shores of the Mississippi River, hoping to become that most romantic and picturesque of mortals, as he later said—a steamboat pilot. He achieved his aim just in time to see it sunk by the Civil War, which closed off all river traffic and made the nation dependent on the railroad instead.

Mildly patriotic for the South, Clemens saw early and brief service as a Confederate militia volunteer. An inconsequential but bloody skirmish persuaded him that "war must be the killing of strangers against whom you feel no personal animosity," and that he was "not rightly equipped for this awful business. . . ." He went with some similarly disillusioned comrades to inform his captain that "the war was a disappointment to us and we were going to disband." In fact, he deserted.

Many years later, Twain would end his most famous novel with Huckleberry Finn's rueful observation that Tom Sawyer's

Aunt Sally was planning to "adopt me and sivilize me," a horrible prospect. Huck says, " 'I reckon I got to light out for the Territory . . . ,'" that is, the West, where a man could be free to do as he pleased. Sam Clemens, leaving behind not civilization but war, lit out in 1861 for the territory of Nevada, where his older brother, Orion, had been hired as secretary to the territorial governor. He found his calling there as a reporter for the newspaper in Virginia City, gathering material, sharpening his eye for vernacular humor, and adopting his pen name, Mark Twain. He also made a bad enemy, the husband of a woman he had smilingly insulted in print and who proposed to shoot him.

He left town in a hurry for San Francisco, taking with him a whole skin and a bag full of stories that he planned to start selling. Here was one, he told Harte a few days after their first encounter, that he thought had potential. It was about a jumping frog named Dan'l Webster, whose master, Jim Smiley, had trained him so well—*educated* him—that Dan'l could out-jump any other frog in the world. A smooth-talking stranger boasts that if he had a frog, he could make it a winner. He'd be willing to bet forty dollars. Smiley volunteers to catch a fresh frog from the nearby swamp. While he is gone the stranger pours quail shot down Dan'l's gullet. When the race begins, "the new frog hopped off lively, but Dan'l gave a heave and hysted up his shoulders—so—like a Frenchman, but it warn't no use—he couldn't budge; he was planted as solid as a church, and he couldn't no more stir than if he was anchored out." The stranger disappears with the forty dollars, and Smiley is left with a shot-filled frog and eternal renown.

Years later, Harte would remember the moment when he first heard "The Celebrated Jumping Frog of Calaveras County," which defined Mark Twain's genius and set him on his path to literary greatness. The story is still "known and laughed over wherever the English language is spoken; but it will never be as funny to any one in print as it was to me, told for the first time by the unknown Twain himself on that morning in the San Francisco Mint."

It was one of those golden moments in literary history, remembered by both men in slightly different ways. Though neither of them would stay much longer in California—it had already lost, for them, much of its earlier charm, having been turned over to economic buccaneers and civic uplifters—their paths would cross often in succeeding years.

For a while, the relationship was cordial. Harte hired the "genial humorist," as he called Mark Twain, to write weekly articles for the *Californian* and praised him generously, even as his own influence grew. Early in 1868 he became the first editor of a new magazine based in San Francisco and called the *Overland Monthly*. Under his astute guidance, the magazine became prosperous and influential, featuring his own stories as well as those of Bierce, Twain, and lesser writers. All of them, including Twain, were fortunate to have Harte as their guide and mentor. "Waves of influence" rippled out from Harte at this time, a literary historian wrote later: "indeed the literary West may be said to have founded itself upon the imagination of Bret Harte."

Harte, for his part, saw immediately that Mark Twain was "inimitable" and was one of the first to praise his genius both as writer and platform speaker. In a review of Twain's public lecture on his adventures in Hawaii, he said the young Midwesterner took his audience "by storm," in no small part because he displayed such "shrewdness and a certain hearty abhorrence of shams." Twain "can write seriously and well when he chooses, which is perhaps the best test of true humor," Harte noted; minor faults of "crudeness" and "coarseness" could not obscure the clear signs that Mark Twain was "a new star rising in this western horizon."

Harte not only published and lauded Twain's early stories, he taught the less experienced writer much about style, control, and voice while editing his magazine submissions. He "trimmed and trained and schooled me patiently," Twain said in 1870, "until he changed me from an awkward utterer of coarse grotesquenesses to a writer of paragraphs and chapters that have found a certain favor in the eyes of some of the very decentest people in the land."

But even at the height of his fame, in the early 1870s, some readers saw Harte's stories as too sentimental, too cloying. Though his own experience had taught him that the West was often vicious, Harte laid the foundation for several generations of platitudes and clichés, obscuring the truths that readers might have found too unpleasant for comfort. He was, in essence, a writer of romance. Mark Twain's reputation, by contrast, would come to be based upon puncturing sentimental hypocrisy; he thought of himself as a realist, not a romantic, and he soon regretted his identification with Harte as a local colorist celebrating the virtues of the Old West.

Moreover, Twain was by nature competitive. Like Ernest Hemingway, a Twain admirer who later spoke of himself as eager to "get into the ring" with "Mr. Proust" and "Mr. Tolstoi," he wanted above all to "shine . . . to make money, to rival and outrival those whom the public most admired." As early as 1866, Twain clearly thought of himself and Harte as competitors: "Though I am generally placed at the head of my breed of scribblers in this part of the country, the place properly belongs to Bret Harte, I think, though he denies it, along with the rest." By 1871, though, he is vowing to "top" Bret Harte or "bust."

In 1871, we should remember, the upward trajectory of Mark Twain's astounding career was barely perceptible, his critical reputation hovering somewhere between those of Dave Barry and Garrison Keillor today. He had published his first collection of stories, which included Jim Smiley's "Celebrated

Frog," in 1867, and *The Innocents Abroad*, an intermittently funny Ugly American collection about traveling in Europe and the Holy Land, in 1869; but *The Adventures of Tom Sawyer* would not appear until 1876 and his long-delayed masterpiece, *The Adventures of Huckleberry Finn,* came out in 1884. In 1871, he had done nothing to justify his later beatification as "the Lincoln of our literature" by his friend William Dean Howells, and had not even conceived of the story that would lead Hemingway to call him the father of modern American literature ("It all begins with *Huckleberry Finn*").

Today, of course, Twain is an American icon, lovingly reincarnated by Hal Holbrook as a mischievous old gent with a cigar, a hanky, and a white linen suit. The public Twain was amusingly cantankerous but essentially wise, patient, and tolerant of human foibles, in his manner if not in his words. His life is regarded as an extraordinary American success story, and his afterlife, in terms of public esteem and unflagging sales of his works, not to mention movies made from them, is a continuing triumph. He remains one of the few American authors to inspire real affection among readers and nonreaders alike.

But the late nineteenth century was full of stories about schizophrenic characters whose frightening doubles belied their public appearances. Stevenson's Jekyll and Hyde, Oscar Wilde's Dorian Gray, Dostoyevsky's underground man, Wells's invisible man are only the best known of many. Sam Clemens's most effective fictional character would be that of Mark Twain, as many of his biographers have noted—Justin Kaplan would even call his popular life of the author *Mr. Clemens and Mark Twain*. Twain himself (as most of his commentators now refer to him) was fully aware of the disparity between his public image and his private; particularly in his later years he was, in Hamlin Hill's apt words, "a man whose sense of rage at the world in which he lived grew and grew to mammoth proportions. . . ." A primary target of Twain's rage, perhaps because he was reachable—unlike the world itself—would be Bret Harte.

Bret Harte's early fame was about to fade even as Twain enviously vowed to overtake him or "bust," though he seemed to be poised for triumph. In 1871 Harte was offered a contract by the *Atlantic Monthly* for ten thousand dollars—enough money to live well on for two years. The *Atlantic Monthly* had fallen on hard times, and its energetic new editor, William Dean Howells, thought Harte's popularity would serve to rejuvenate the magazine's sagging circulation numbers. For Harte, who wanted to be a larger frog in a larger pond than was possible in San Francisco, the offer was a career-maker. All he had to do was submit a dozen usable pieces of writing within a year, and the best magazine in the country would print them.

Harte and his family, which now included two boys, seven and five years old, left San Francisco by train in February 1871 for New York. It was a leisurely and pleasant passage, marked by stops in Denver, Chicago, Syracuse, and other cities, where he was interviewed and feted as the celebrated author of the Gold Camp stories and, more recently, "Plain Language from Truthful James." The best part of this long narrative poem, published in the *Overland Monthly* in September 1870, was "The Heathen Chinee." Intended by Harte as a satire of anti-Chinese phobia in the West, it was misread by most of his audience as a humorous exposé of "the yellow peril," and it became a huge popular success. Harte had no illusions about the poem's quality, saying he had composed it in a rush to fill out the issue, and was unhappy with the misperception of his satire. But he was at the peak of his popularity and not inclined to climb down from it. He was, Mark Twain said in March 1871, "the most celebrated man in America today . . . the man whose name is on every single tongue from one end of the continent to the other"—and "Plain Language from Truthful James" was what "did it for him." One can almost hear the envy in Twain's voice as he records that Harte "crossed the continent through such a prodigious blaze of national interest and excitement that one might have supposed he was the Viceroy of India." Howells later said Harte's trip was "like the progress of a prince" in the way it prompted "universal attention and interest" in the press.

His reception in Boston was everything that Harte could have wished for. Howells met him at the train station and took him to his home for a week. He dined with the luminaries of the literary set at the Parker House, men whose dignity and reputations were symbolized by their weighty triple names: James Russell Lowell, Ralph Waldo Emerson, Oliver Wendell Holmes, Sr., Henry Wadsworth Longfellow, Richard Henry Dana. Harte had some reason to believe that he had been accepted as a member of this Olympian group. His pedigree, despite his years in the ruffianly West, was good on his mother's side, as she was descended from Revolutionary War heroes and old Knickerbockers. His literary fame, if not his actual accomplishments, led him to think himself the equal of anyone. And, indeed, he was cordially received, at first, by everyone he met—Emerson, with whom Harte spent a day walking around Walden Pond, thought him "an easy, kindly, well-behaved man."

Bernard DeVoto, whose work on Twain remains important, thought Harte had succeeded in winning over the literary establishment, mostly by obsequious flattery, in a way that Twain did not, and that this accounted for some of Twain's distrust of Harte. In DeVoto's words, doors that were "incapable of opening to Mark Twain" did so for Harte, a "schoolteacher and the son of schoolteachers," whose "sympathy, embedded in sweet tales, greatly comforted the nice people." But Gary Scharnhorst, the foremost authority on Harte, plausibly argues that Harte was regarded by Howells as merely an attractive personality and as a popular writer who could help revive the *Atlantic Monthly*, not as a writer of genius like Mark Twain. Harte "always remained an outsider" for Howells and for his charmed circle, Scharnhorst says, "a 'salaried contributor' and a 'delightful guest' " but no more.

In any event, Harte had more serious problems than social acceptance. He had been paid handsomely to do a job, and he failed miserably at it. Sadly, for a man who had worked effectively enough at the Mint, Harte had remarkably little sense of how to manage his own money; and for an editor who had lived on deadlines, he lacked self-discipline about his own writing. He frittered away most of the *Atlantic Monthly* advance in short order, and met his stipulated output for Howells only by churning out wretched hackwork for him. His contract with the *Atlantic Monthly* was not renewed and his submissions to Howells and other editors were, after grudging acceptance, meeting increased resistance.

Still famous enough to be in demand as a speaker, Harte supported himself for several years by making public appearances, reading from his own works, though often with little effort to speak clearly or emphatically; in St. Louis the local paper wrote him up as a boring dandy who, "in full dress costume with spotless linen and diamond studs," spoke with such "gentle and elegant languor" that half the audience couldn't hear him. That was when he showed up—he had a reputation for canceling engagements with little or no explanation. The content of his talks was also frequently disappointing; Harte's lecture on American humor, which should have been a natural for him, "wasn't worth listening to," according to one critic, no more than "a careless piece of hack-work, gotten up simply to be advertised on the bills."

Famous too early, Harte was living on the diminishing capital of his earlier reputation. He continued to be careless with his own money and borrowed freely from friends in anticipation of future advances on his writing. Even when he came into some money, he rarely paid it back. He became notorious as a deadbeat. One friend, putting the matter as generously as possible, said Harte was "utterly destitute of what is sometimes called 'the money sense'" and consequently "was continually involved in troubles that he might have escaped with a little more financial shrewdness." His enemies accused him of worse. On December 15, 1872, the *San Francisco Chronicle* published an article by W. A. Kendall, a poet who had contributed to the *Californian* and the *Overland Monthly* when Harte was editor of those magazines, claiming that Harte was a "loose and not infrequent borrower of sums" of money, "and then a cool ignorer of the gracious loaners." He had also been known for skimming from money supposed to be sent to contributors. For what purpose are "the whips of justice braided," Kendall cried, other than to punish such "nefarious pilferers"? Harte complained about the attack to Twain—"I don't mind his slander; that I can refute—but how am I to make this dog know he is a dog and not a man?"

Mark Twain listened to Harte's complaints—Kendall's charges were never proved—and tried to help him out, both with advice and with money. He could afford to be generous. Not only was his own writing career beginning to flourish, but he had married money in 1870: Olivia Langdon, the daughter of a wealthy industrialist from upstate New York, brought an annual income of some six thousand dollars as a dowry. In 1874, he built a house in Hartford on five acres of land that cost him more than one hundred thousand dollars, plus another twenty-one thousand for furniture, a staggering investment worth several million of today's dollars. The third floor of the mansion included Twain's combination study and billiard room.

Like many who become wealthy after growing up in humble or moderate circumstances, Twain was touchy about his new status as propertied gentleman. Harte was a frequent guest in the Hartford mansion. He teased Twain and Livy about their bourgeois tastes and their conspicuous consumption, not once but several times. Twain, who would make his reputation satirizing middle-class taste and morals, could not abide a joke at his own expense. Thirty years later he was still fuming over Harte's "smartly and wittily sarcastic" remarks about his house and his treasured wife.

But Twain cannot have been too aggrieved at the time about Harte's perceived bad manners, for in 1876 he agreed to work with Harte on a play called *Ah Sin*, about a Chinese laundryman and gambler. Neither Harte nor Twain had any gift for writing drama (though Twain was an extraordinary performer on stage), but the nineteenth-century American stage was what television and movies are today in terms of popular entertainment. There was big money for those who could satisfy popular taste for sentimental, melodramatic, and farcical fluff, and good writers like Twain and Harte were more than willing to reach for the golden ring, the money and the popularity that successful stage versions of their work might bring them.

Harte's immense success with "Plain Language from Truthful James" had already led him to attempt a comic melodrama, drawing from the same well of material, Chinese immigrants, which he called *Two Men of Sandy Bar*. The play premiered on Broadway in August 1876, to "some of the most hostile opening-night reviews in the history of American theater," in Scharnhorst's words. The kindest word it earned was "nondescript"; others included "worthless," "outrage," "garbage," "disgust[ing]," and "piti[ful]." It was, said the critic for the *New York Herald*, "an absolute outrage upon the critical reputation of the country." Harte was clearly milking his reputation—"we have never known so celebrated a writer to produce such a worthless work."

Mark Twain, however, liked Harte's play, especially the minor character of Hop Sing as played by the gifted comedian

James Parsloe. Harte responded to Twain's praise by suggesting, late in 1876, that the two of them work together on a new play built around Parsloe's Hop Sing performance. Parsloe as the star would participate with the authors in a three-way split of the proceeds. The method of the collaboration, not to mention Harte's earlier problems with putting together a play, suggests the problems to come. "Harte came down to Hartford and we talked [it] over," Twain later wrote, "and then Bret wrote it while I played billiards, but of course I had to go over it to get the dialect right. Bret never did know anything about dialect." Harte was drinking a good deal at the time—two bottles of whiskey in one December evening—and his usually dapper, if not dandified, attire had degenerated; his "ancient gray suit" was so shabby, Twain said, "that the bottoms of his trousers were frazzled to a fringe" and "his shoes were similarly out of repair and were sodden with snow-slush and mud."

Not surprisingly, the script that emerged from these desultory efforts in February 1877 satisfied neither man, and they couldn't agree on what was needed to fix it. More seriously, Harte was continuing to drink and complaining about being broke. He blamed Twain, as he would write later, for recommending to him a publisher, Elisha Bliss, who had mishandled his novel, *Gabriel Conroy*, and cost him thousands of dollars. Twain's problems with his own writing at the time, particularly difficulties in getting his interrupted manuscript of *Huckleberry Finn* back on track, made him more irritable than usual. ("A Murder, a Mystery, a Marriage," a recently discovered story written by Twain at this time, provides vivid proof of how advanced his misanthropy was already becoming.) Both men, then, were touchy and frustrated with each other, with their own work, and with their combined effort to write a play.

Twain's solution to Harte's problems and Harte's response are equally surprising. Marilyn Duckett, in her comprehensive book about their relationship, dates the estrangement of the two men from Harte's letter of March 1, 1877, to Twain. It's a response to a Twain letter (which has not survived) to Harte, in which Twain apparently declined to lend Harte any more money, but offered to hire him to begin work on yet another play with him, and to pay him twenty-five dollars a week.

Twain no doubt viewed this as a generous offer, but Harte was outraged. Duckett suggests that a short story he wrote two years later about a "gentle, trustful man" who is betrayed explains Harte's feelings at this time: Take such a man and "abuse him, show him the folly of his gentleness and kindness, prove to him that it is weakness, drive him into a corner, and you have a savage." Harte's response to Twain's offer of a salary is, if not savage, stern enough: Twain was "speculating on my poverty." Moreover, Harte said, because of Twain's role in the losses he had suffered at the hands of Elisha Bliss, he no longer felt any need to repay the $750 that he had borrowed from him. He concluded that he would manage to "struggle along" by himself—"and not write any more plays with you."

Twain responded to Harte's letter with predictable fury, tossing it aside, he claimed, after reading only "two pages of this ineffable idiotcy." The following week Harte passed Parsloe in the street and asked him how the rehearsals for *Ah Sin* were progressing. Parsloe snubbed the co-author, saying that if there was anything he needed to know, he'd tell him. Harte's face turned red with anger, Parsloe then wrote to Twain, complaining about his "annoyance with Harte." On May 7, Harte was present at the Washington premiere of *Ah Sin*, and was encouraged by the reception; Twain was absent, owing, he said, to bronchitis. On May 16, Harte sent a telegram to Twain, asking for his share of the box office receipts, "if any." There were no receipts. This would be the last direct communication between the two men.

Parsloe and Twain continued to tinker with the play, freezing Harte out entirely. By the time *Ah Sin* opened on Broadway on July 31 it was mostly Mark Twain's work, for good or ill. The reviewers' reactions were generally less harsh than they had been for Harte's first play, although one thought that "few plays of the American stamp can be mentioned whose literary execution is so bad, whose construction is so ramshackly, and whose texture is so barren of true wit." It survived long enough to go on a road trip until early November, but Twain confessed to Howells that the whole thing was "a most abject & incurable failure." It closed in Pittsburgh, "not with a bang but a whimper," as Scharnhorst says, as did the friendship of its co-authors.

By 1878 Harte was "floating on the raft made of the shipwreck of his former reputation," as a Boston newspaper put it. He had sunk to writing advertisements for soap—including a parody of Longellow's poem "Excelsior." But he still had influential friends, some of whom a year earlier had nearly persuaded the new president, Rutherford B. Hayes, to send Harte to the diplomatic mission in China. When Twain learned of this possibility, he wrote to William Dean Howells, who was related through his wife's family to the new president, urging him to tell Hayes that Harte would disgrace the nation if he were dispatched abroad. "Wherever he goes his wake is tumultuous with swindled grocers, & with defrauded innocents who have loaned him money. . . . He can lie faster than he can drivel pathos. . . . He is always steeped in whisky & brandy. . . . No man who has ever known him respects him. . . . You know that I have befriended this creature for seven years. I am even capable of doing it still—while he stays at home. But I don't want to see him sent to foreign parts to carry on his depredations." Twain's letter reached the president, either from Howells or from his wife. Hayes soon let Howells know that there was "no danger" of Harte's appointment to the China post.

Harte's other friends kept up the pressure on Hayes. On

April 5, 1878, Hayes wrote to Howells in the context of offering Harte a posting to Germany. He wanted to know if the "sinister things" that Twain said about Harte were true. Howells, perhaps feeling some compunction about his part in wrecking Harte's earlier appointment, told Hayes that while Harte was admittedly notorious for borrowing and drinking, he "never borrowed of *me*, nor drank more than I (in my presence)." Harte was in bad shape, Howells said, but "I hear he is really making an effort to reform."

As a result of—or perhaps despite—this less-than-ringing endorsement, Harte won an appointment as "commercial agent" in Krefeld, Germany, a small city near Düsseldorf. Such appointments were common rewards for well-connected writers in those days before academic sinecures—Washington Irving, Nathaniel Hawthorne, and Howells himself had received them. Harte's post would pay him three thousand dollars a year—barely half of what Livy Twain received in dividends. It was not enough for Harte to bring his wife and children (now numbering four) with him to Germany, but his relations with his wife were sufficiently strained that this drawback does not seem to have troubled him greatly. He left for his new post on June 28, 1878; he would not see his wife for more than twenty years, and he would never return to the United States.

On June 27, one day before Harte sailed, Mark Twain wrote a letter to Howells protesting the appointment, of which he had just learned. Twain was himself then in Germany, in Heidelberg, having left the country in some embarrassment a few months earlier, after making a fool of himself at a dinner in Boston in December 1877, celebrating the seventieth birthday of the great and venerable poet John Greenleaf Whittier. Most of the great American men of letters of the century were there when Twain delivered his misguided burlesque of Holmes as a tub of lard, of Lowell as a prizefighter, and of Emerson as a card shark. No one laughed, or even smiled, as Twain struggled to the end of his address, with Howells tugging at his coattails, whispering to him to sit down and shut up—he had spread something like a "black frost" around the room, Twain ruefully admitted later. But it was no joking matter, and hardly an exaggeration to say that he had literally fled the country to escape his humiliation.

Having removed himself from the arena, Twain protested to Howells but to no avail. He repeated his earlier charges, with added brio: Harte was "a liar, a thief, a swindler, a snob, a sot, a sponge, a coward . . . brim full of treachery, and he conceals his Jewish identity as carefully as if he considered it a disgrace . . . to send this nasty creature to puke upon the American name in a foreign land is too much. . . . Tell me what German town he is to filthify with his presence; then I will write the authorities there that he is a persistent borrower who never pays." Twain wanted Howells to use his influence with Hayes to have the appointment rescinded. He even wrote a letter to Hayes himself to protest the appointment.

It was too late, of course, for Twain to have any effect on the appointment. Howells, a man of considerable good sense and great talent, would later become known as "the dean of American letters." Like a good dean, he knew how to handle his squabbling faculty. He liked Harte, having found him "quite unspoiled by his great popularity" and a "thoroughly charming good-hearted fellow," though not without his faults. But he admired Twain, and wanted above all to keep the friendship of his great but irascible friend. He asked Hayes to return his letter recommending Harte, lest Twain find out about it.

Mark Twain recovered from his Whittier embarrassment and returned home two years later. He marched on from one triumph to the next, both literary and economic. In 1882 alone his expenditures came to more than $100,000—among other necessities, he acquired a direct Western Union line to his house in Hartford. His wife's large inheritance, his own bestselling books, and his speculations in the stock market all combined to make him the wealthiest working writer in the country by the time he was fifty.

Bret Harte turned fifty in 1886, a year later than Twain. He had just lost his latest government appointment as consul in Glasgow, owing, he said, to a change in administrations. In fact, as Twain might have anticipated, he had been fired from his post—not for bad debts or drunkenness, but for inattention to duty, a pattern that he had established with his first posting in Germany. His subordinate in Scotland told a visiting State Department officer truthfully that "Harte is never here. He lives in London and devotes himself to literature."

The literature to which Harte was supposedly devoting himself was self-described hackwork, none of it up to the level of his California period. But it found an audience in English and American magazines, earning Harte enough to live on and, occasionally, to send some money to Anna and their four children. He persistently discouraged any of his family from visiting him in Europe, pleading poverty. For many years he lived, in what may be called ambiguous circumstances, with a Belgian diplomat in England, Arthur Van de Velde, and his wife, Hydeline de Seigneaux, a relationship filled with Jamesian reverberations and one that caused Twain, after Van de Velde's death and Harte's continued presence in his widow's house, to charge that Harte had been the widow's "kept" man.

Mark Twain became ever more famous in his later years, even as Harte faded from the minds of American readers, but Twain never forgot his old enemy. He was particularly annoyed that Harte had twice given the toast, "To Literature," at Royal Academy Dinners and that he had been invited to lecture at Oxford and Cambridge—all this many years before Twain would receive, in 1907, his own cherished honorary degree at Oxford.

Consequently, Twain kept up a running commentary

through Harte's last years on his work and his character, revealing much about his own in the process. Twain's reference cited earlier to Harte trying to conceal his "Jewishness" is instructive. Harte's grandfather, who had left his wife when their son, Bret's father, was a year old, was a Jewish banker in New York; Harte did not conceal his Jewish ancestry from his immediate family, but in 1889 he resorted to fibbing to Havelock Ellis that "his *father* and his immediate ancestors were as distinctly English in origin" as his mother was Dutch. Harte never considered himself Jewish, and considering the widespread anti-Semitism of his time, as reflected by Twain's own comment, it is easy to see why he would not have advertised his grandfather's religion.

Twain also suggested that Harte was homosexual: he was "distinctly pretty, in spite of the fact that his face was badly pitted with smallpox"; his "dainty self-complacencies" were reflected in his walk, which was "of the mincing sort." A European scholar, Axel Nissen, follows this line of argument in his recent study *Bret Harte: Prince and Pauper*, though Gary Scharnhorst correctly, in my estimation, regards the book as "thesis ridden, its analysis marred by its search for evidence of homoeroticism in Harte's life and writings." True or not, at that time the charge alone would have been harmful to Harte's reputation.

As for his work, Twain wrote to Howells that whatever Harte wrote that was good was stolen: "I don't believe Harte ever had an idea that he came by honestly. He is the most abandoned thief that defiles the earth." Whatever of his work wasn't stolen was bad: Harte's characters typically talk "like a Bowery gutter-snipe on one page and like a courtier of Louis XV's on the very next one." On Harte's appeals to the sentimental, Twain says, "The struggle after the pathetic is more pathetic than the pathos itself; if he were to write about an Orphan Princess who lost a Peanut he would feel obliged to try to make somebody snuffle over it." Harte was not even a good literary craftsman, but "the worst literary shoe-maker I know. He is as blind as a bat. He never sees anything correctly, except Californian scenery. He is as slovenly as Thackeray, and as dull as Charles Lamb."

Harte's painful and stoically endured death from throat cancer in 1902 did not mollify Twain. "Oh, yes," he responded to a reporter who asked him for a comment on Harte and their friendship: "Say I *knew* the son of a bitch." He softened slightly a few years later, describing, in a touching and evocative passage, how he had been rereading "The Luck of Roaring Camp." He thought back on Bret Harte's subsequent triumphant "progress across the applauding continent, young & dapper & brown-haired," and how he was now dead, laid to rest, "whiteheaded & half-forgotten, in an alien land." Twain had a vision in his mind's eye of having seen Harte born, he said. And then "I saw him flit across the intervening day, as it were, & when night closed down again I saw him buried."

But Mark Twain was not yet through with Bret Harte. In 1906, four years before he died, Twain dictated his reminiscences on a variety of topics to a secretary; they were edited by Bernard DeVoto in 1940 and published under the title *Mark Twain in Eruption*. Although Harte was already nearly forgotten by 1906 and Twain was regarded as the grand old man of American letters, it may be that Twain was still concerned that the public persisted in linking them together; a 1923 American literature textbook suggests as much in its reference to Twain as a practitioner of a type of "gigantic exaggeration and calm-faced mendacity," following in the tradition of Bret Harte and "coached" by William Dean Howells.

Certainly Twain's comments seem like an effort to fix the final seal on the tomb of his rival's reputation. Harte was, Twain said, like the character in *The Man Without a Country*, albeit "in a mild and colorless way," because he lived abroad for so long. "No, not man—man is too strong a term; he was an invertebrate without a country. He hadn't any more passion for his country than an oyster has for its bed; in fact not so much and I apologize to the oyster."

It is true that Twain's final words on Harte need to be taken within the context of their time in his life. Within the past fifteen years, he had seen his fortune wiped out by imprudent investments, particularly one in a typesetting machine. A publishing venture that he had floated in order to help Ulysses S. Grant write his memoirs put him so deeply in debt, even though Grant's book was a success, that he had to spend years on the lecture circuit raising money to pay back his creditors. This he did, to the last dime, rather than take the easy but dishonorable way out by declaring bankruptcy. All this time Harte continued to rack up unpaid debts, reports of which Twain saw frequently in the newspapers. And even while Harte lived as a kept man in England and France, ignoring his wife and four children for years, Twain suffered repeated crushing losses in his family: His favorite daughter died of meningitis; another developed epilepsy; and his beloved wife, Livy, declined into invalidism before she finally died in 1904.

Quite independent of his disgust with Bret Harte, Twain was also deeply disillusioned with his country—the "United States of Lyncherdom"—and its course of empire, regarding the Spanish-American War of 1898 as a criminal enterprise. In his last years, Twain lost whatever respect he had once had for "the damned human race" to his growing conviction that "our Heavenly Father invented man because he was disappointed in the monkey." The most attractive being he could conjure up in his fiction was Satan, in *The Mysterious Stranger*, now a charmingly malevolent young man who creates and crushes human beings with equal indifference.

Bret Harte and his failings are small potatoes next to the flaws of the country, human nature, and less-than-divine providence. One wonders why the poor man remained so much on

Twain's mind. Insofar as there ever was a contest between the two writers, the winner had long been obvious. Harte's mining-camp stories can still be read with pleasure, and he is important enough in American literary history to have prompted two full-length studies in 2000 of his life and work. But Twain's literary critique of Harte's work was, while exaggerated, not wildly off target. Harte's talent was as slender as his will to succeed, and his character was deeply flawed.

Whatever his flaws, Harte never retracted his judgment of Twain's genius, which would have been foolish. More significantly, he never responded in kind to Twain's attacks on his character. It might be argued that Harte was too morally corrupt to care if his character was attacked. More charitably, we may choose to believe that he thought, as he told his daughter in later years, that Mark Twain was a sick man.

But it would be nice, even if sentimental, to think that Harte declined to respond in kind to Twain's attacks because they had once been friends—and because he was still the romantic idealist who wrote "Tennessee's Partner," and who continued to believe what he had said when their friendship first began to fray in 1877: "To be a man's 'partner,'" Harte told Twain, signified "something more than a common pecuniary or business interest; it was to be his friend through good or ill report, in adversity or fortune."

2

The Boy with the Interested Eyes

ERNEST HEMINGWAY AND GERTRUDE STEIN

Neither of them said much afterward about their first meeting, but both said other things later and many other people have also had much to say, so that one can say now what needs saying clearly and easily and, one hopes, truly.

Or so a writer today might begin who has read a great deal about and by Ernest Hemingway and Gertrude Stein and who finds himself, like so many others, sometimes open to infection by their style. Stein was forty-eight years old when they first met in February 1922, Hemingway only twenty-two; she "the Mother Goose of Montparnasse," the "queen bee of the expatriate hive," he still Archibald MacLeish's "lad with the supple look" of "a sleepy panther," a struggling newspaper reporter with only a mutual friend's recommendation and what she called his "interested eyes" to offer her.

He was interested, as all writers are interested, in setting and character and in what lies beneath the obvious. The room in which the older writer received the younger one was, Hemingway later recalled, "like one of the best rooms in the finest museum except there was a big fireplace and it was warm and comfortable and they gave you good things to eat and tea and natural distilled liqueurs made from purple plums, yellow plums or wild raspberries." No doubt he saw the portrait recently done by Pablo Picasso, one of Stein's many artist friends; she still resembled it, having not yet cut her hair to the monk-like tonsure of her later years. She had "beautiful eyes and a strong German-Jewish face." She was short and solidly built, with breasts that he (rather oddly) thought probably weighed ten pounds each. Bored by fashion, she was probably wearing the same "thick no-colored shapeless woolen clothes and honest woolen stockings knitted for her by Miss Toklas," her companion, that she wore when Katherine Anne Porter visited her, and no doubt still looked "extremely like a handsome old Jewish patriarch who had backslid and shaved off his beard."

To Hemingway, Stein's clothes, her "mobile face and her lovely, thick, alive immigrant hair" suggested not so much a rabbi as "a peasant from northern Italy." He listened intently, as he always did to those he respected, his dark brown unblinking eyes fixed on her stern but animated features. She talked volubly and at length about people she knew and places she had visited with her companion; Toklas herself, a small, thin woman with a subtly domineering manner, a hook nose, and a shadowy mustache, sat on the other side of the room, talking to Hemingway's wife, Hadley, and doing needlepoint. Only recently married and trying to economize by living in a cheap flat, the young reporter complained about needing money and Stein offered to show him how to cut his wife's hair.

A tranquil scene. Domestic, even banal. But without question one of the more suggestive moments in the literary history of the twentieth century. Old enough to be Hemingway's mother, Gertrude Stein had established herself as the doyenne of the avant-garde in Paris over the previous two decades, and, through the expertise of her brother Leo, as the champion of modern art. Painters, poets, writers, editors, and philosophers gathered at her salon, many today far more famous than she— Braque, Matisse, Cocteau, Eliot, Pound, Bertrand Russell.

Some, like Picasso and Sherwood Anderson, would be lifelong friends.

But some of her visitors were merely sycophants, especially in the postwar years when Americans found that the strong dollar would let them live more cheaply in Paris than in Kansas City or Buffalo. Many of them had artistic pretensions but little talent except for self-promotion and flattery of those who, like Stein, they thought could help them. She herself was too often inclined to accept, according to her sometime friend Robert McAlmon, "the adulation of people that a person of healthy self-confidence would dismiss at once as parasites, bores, or gigolos and pimps." Even her admiring biographer, John Malcolm Brinnin, admitted that "Throughout her life Gertrude showed very little interest in the work of artists she did not know, unless they were dead and comfortably separated from her by at least a generation." She had no idols. "She had come to be satisfied with self-adulation, knowing, as she said, that in her time she was the only one. Her affection for others was reserved for those whom she could appropriate."

James Joyce, accordingly, never visited Stein's salon; she in turn dismissed *Ulysses* and its author as "*inaccrochable*" (unacceptable)—if you mentioned Joyce's name to her more than once, Hemingway said, "you would not be invited back." Ezra Pound, an infrequent guest, not only disputed her opinions but broke a favorite chair one day by flinging himself into it too forcefully. T. S. Eliot's visit, after "The Waste Land" in 1922 had established him, along with Pound and Joyce, as one of the three great literary voices of the period, was for Stein merely an exercise in pedantry—a "solemn conversation, mostly about split infinitives and other grammatical solecisms and why Gertrude Stein used them." William Carlos Williams resented Stein's suggestion that he was a better physician than poet; her own writing reminded him, he told her, of the way children perceive experience, and that "things that children write have seemed to me so Gertrude Steinish in their repetition." She should choose the best from her vast collection of unpublished works and consign the rest to the fire. As the door closed on Williams, Stein told her maid that she was not in if he came to call again.

Stein as a writer is remembered today for her bestselling *Autobiography of Alice B. Toklas*; published in 1933, it was her own life as ostensibly told through the admiring eyes of her companion. Ordinary readers could find in it the elements of coherent narrative and character that she conscientiously excised from her serious work such as "Melanctha" and *Tender Buttons*, but it was this experimental fiction that made her reputation as a literary modernist. Her most famous Delphic utterance, "Rose is a rose is a rose is a rose," contains the essence of her appeal and of her problem. Her point was that the names of things are their essence; by repeating the word *rose*, she said, "I made poetry and what did I do I caressed completely caressed and addressed a noun." In her sentences, she had "Alice" say of her that Stein "has always been possessed by the intellectual passion for exactitude in the description of inner and outer reality." More than words and sentences—character, plot, theme, all the traditional characteristics of literature—did not interest her.

The problem was that Stein's explanation made no more sense than did "Rose is a rose is a rose is a rose" to critics who did not worship at the shrine of modernism. Alfred Kazin dismissed her as an"immense priestess of nonsense expounding her text in nonsense syllables," and Michael Gold, the American Communist editor of the *New Masses*, called her "a literary idiot." Stein could on occasion joke about her inaccessibility both to the critics and to the masses, new or old. Unable to find a commercial publisher for *Three Lives*, she turned to an American vanity press, which, upon examining the manuscript, conscientiously sent a young man to visit her in Paris to see if she could speak English. "But I am an american, said Gertrude

Stein indignantly. Yes yes I understand that perfectly now, he said, but perhaps you have not had much experience in writing."

Stein nevertheless was ambitious for wider publication. She possessed an unabashed sense of her own importance; Alice Toklas is made to declare in the *Autobiography* that she "has been privileged to know three geniuses in her lifetime: Stein, Alfred Whitehead, and Pablo Picasso." For all her self-assurance, though, Stein found herself growing "a little bitter, all her unpublished manuscripts, and no hope of publication or serious recognition." Then, she said, "Sherwood Anderson came and quite simply and directly as is his way told her what he thought of her work and what it had meant to him in his development. He told it to her then and what was even rarer he told it in print immediately after." She would always be grateful to him for his support.

It was Sherwood Anderson who would provide the impetus both for Stein and Hemingway's friendship and, in part, for their later enmity. Like Stein, he is best known today for only one book, the compelling stories that he wrote about ordinary people who lived lives of quiet desperation in the American Midwest: *Winesburg, Ohio*. Her close contemporary in age—he was born in 1876, she in 1874—Anderson was a late bloomer as a writer. His own story, as he later rather fancifully embroidered it, soon became a literary legend. A respectable husband and father in Elyria, Ohio, where he managed a paint factory, he locked his office door one day in 1912 and marched off down the railroad tracks to become a writer in Chicago. Seven years later the book that would make him famous appeared. *Winesburg, Ohio* satisfied the modernist demand that life be represented as complex, frustrated, and meaningless beneath its mundane surface. Anderson himself, friendly, engaging, and hopelessly romantic, became a celebrity in Chicago and in Paris, when he visited Europe for the first time in 1920.

Anderson met Hemingway shortly before his trip to Europe,

when the young veteran was marking time at a trade publication in Chicago before his marriage to Hadley Richardson. At twenty-eight, Hadley was much older—by eight years—than Hemingway, whose youthful energy seems to have bowled her over. She loved everything about him, she wrote breathlessly to him in a letter, from the way he could blow smoke through his nose to his skills in "boxing, fishing, writing, . . . leaving folks fall in fits of admiration about you, . . . getting war medals, playing bridge, swirling about in the black cape . . . swimming, paddling, tennis, charm, good looks, knowledge of clothes, love of women, domesticity." A female friend of Hadley's, initially dubious that such a paragon could exist, was similarly impressed: Hemingway was "beautiful," she said, with a slender, graceful body, a face marked by perfect symmetry, and a handsome mouth "that stretched from ear to ear when he smiled." His vitality was infectious: "He generated excitement because he was so intense about everything, about writing and boxing, about good food and drink. Everything we did took on new importance when he was with us."

Hadley's friend also noted how Hemingway's "focused attention [on] the person he was talking with was immensely flattering." Sherwood Anderson, a shy and modest man for all his daring break from convention, felt the warmth of the young man's personality and was convinced that he had talent. He simply *must* go to Paris, Anderson told Hemingway after he returned from his own visit. He told him about Sylvia Beach's bookstore, Shakespeare & Company, on the rue de l'Odéon, where he could meet James Joyce and Ford Madox Ford; about the quirky genius Ezra Pound, who was helping T. S. Eliot edit and revise his poems; and about the wonderful Gertrude Stein, whose literary salon allowed expatriate writers from England and America to meet.

Hemingway did not need much persuading; he wangled a post as a foreign correspondent for the *Toronto Star* and sailed from New York in December 1921. He was preceded by letters from Anderson to Pound and Stein (among others) introducing him as possessing an "extraordinary talent," as "a writer instinctively in touch with everything worthwhile going on" and as someone who was, like his wife, "delightful to know."

"Gertrude Stein and me are just like brothers," Hemingway wrote Anderson a few months later, shortly after their first meeting, in the ungrammatical patois he liked to affect in his letters, "and we see a lot of her . . . we love her." Gertrude Stein reciprocated the affection, writing Anderson to say that Ernest and Hadley were "charming. He is a delightful fellow and I like his talk."

They would often meet, during the spring of 1922 and afterwards, in the spacious Luxembourg Gardens, which lay between their apartments; eventually Hemingway was told to stop by 27, rue de Fleurus anytime to visit. Hemingway was often out of town on assignment for the *Star*—in Turkey, Greece, the Balkans, Italy, and Spain—gathering material that would also find its way into the books that were soon to come: *In Our Time, The Sun Also Rises*, and *A Farewell to Arms*. But as of their first meetings, he had published no fiction and had only a few scattered poems to show her. For all his charm, intelligence, and ambition, he was frustrated; between the burdens of incipient fatherhood and the demands of his work for the *Star*, he was accomplishing nothing. Give up newspaper work, Stein told him: "You will never see things, you will only see words and that will not do. . . ." Ultimately, he followed her advice, and always repeated it to young writers in his later years.

Her direct influence on his writing is uncertain. Hemingway would later call the first chapter of his memoir, *A Moveable Feast*, "Miss Stein Instructs." Stein herself liked to quote a professor of anatomy from her days as a medical student, who "believed in everybody developing their own technique. He also remarked, nobody teaches anybody anything, at first every student's scalpel is dull and then later every student's scalpel is sharp, and nobody has taught anybody anything."

She did offer Hemingway one famous admonishment that we know of, concerning the first draft of the great early story, "Big Two-Hearted River." Generations of English majors would later be struck by the story's quiet restraint. It depicts— apparently, for it is never spelled out—the effort of a young man who has returned from the war to take a solitary fishing trip, during which he reveals his emotionally fragile condition and begins to regain his psychic balance. The version that Hemingway showed Stein included a long section in which the young man is unmistakably a writer, concerned with establishing himself in some way at the expense of other writers, whom he seems to regard as competitors—including Joyce and E. E. Cummings. These clearly autobiographical observations were gossipy distractions. Stein said: "Hemingway, remarks are not literature." He cut out the offending passages, and the story was thereby immensely improved.

She also, rather improbably, introduced him to bullfighting, as Robert McAlmon recalled later. Stein and Toklas had been in Spain in 1915: They had pictures of themselves sitting with two famous bullfighters, and Stein had written a poem called "I Must Try to Write the History of Belmonte"; a line about Belmonte's young competitor, Gallo, suggests Hemingway's own later celebrations of the graceful, stoic courage of the great bullfighters: "I forget war and fear and courage and dancing. I forget standing and refusing. I believe choices. I choose Gallo. He is a cock. He moves plainly."

When he was out of town, on assignment in Greece and the Balkans and elsewhere, Hemingway frequently wrote postcards and letters to Stein about his "real" work, as in this note: "I've thought a lot about the things you said about working and am starting that way at the beginning. If you think of anything else I wish you'd write it to me. Am working hard about creating and keep my mind going about it all the time." His admiration for her own writing and her influence was often reflected in print, in the articles he wrote for the *Star* and the *Tribune*. She was a "sort of gauge of civilization," superior in this regard to Sinclair Lewis or H. L. Mencken. She was, moreover, "the most first rate intelligence employed in writing today," unlike D. H. Lawrence, "who writes extremely well with the intelligence of a head waiter."

Their professional and personal lives became increasingly intertwined. In March 1923, Hemingway's first child, John, was christened at St. Luke's Episcopal Church in Paris; Gertrude Stein and Alice Toklas were honored to be the godmothers of the boy, nicknamed Bumby, and assiduous in their attention to him for some time afterward. The following November marked the appearance of Hemingway's first book, *Three Stories & Ten Poems*, which included the stories "Up in Michigan," "Out of Season," and "My Old Man." Stein's appraisal in a review for the Paris edition of the *Chicago Tribune* was flattering but wrongheaded: when Hemingway "sticks to poetry and intelligence it is both poetry and intelligent," she thought, but the stories weren't much. Hemingway should "eschew the hotter emotions and the more turgid vision."

Hemingway was nevertheless grateful for Stein's attention and eager to repay the favor. Early in 1924 he persuaded Ford Madox Ford, the author of *Parade's End* and editor of the new journal *Transatlantic Review*, to publish a large chunk of her thousand-page work called *The Making of Americans*. This long book, on which Stein had been working for many years, existed only in the form of a single manuscript, so Hemingway hand-copied excerpts from it that totaled more than one hundred pages of typescript, an admirable labor of love. Later he proofread the galleys.

The book, alternately droll and perverse, often puzzling, begins this way: "Once an angry man dragged his father along the ground through his own orchard. 'Stop!' cried the groaning old man at last, 'Stop! I did not drag my father beyond this tree.'" Stein and others would later claim that Hemingway absorbed much of her peculiar style in the process of editing, copying, and proofreading *The Making of Americans*—her compound constructions (the ones English teachers call run-on sentences), and her use of gerunds, for example, as when she describes how her characters had "their own way of sleeping, their own way of resting, of loving, of talking, or keeping still, of waking, their own way of working, of having stupid being in them." Certainly this passage from a Hemingway story called "Summer People," written in 1924, suggests Stein's influence, as James R. Mellow notes in his biography of Hemingway: "It was liking, and liking the body, and introducing the body, and persuading, and taking chances, and never frightening, and assuming about the other person, and always taking never asking, and gentleness and liking, and making liking."

But Hemingway was already growing beyond Stein in 1924. "Summer People" is not a very good story—it was not even published until after his death. The significant stories from this period of his life are the extraordinary ones such as "Indian Camp" and "Big Two-Hearted River," which were collected along with twelve others in the volume he called *In Our Time*. Along with *The Sun Also Rises*, the novel that would appear in 1926, these works show that Hemingway, by the time he had reached his mid-twenties, was already a far greater writer than Stein could have ever hoped to be.

Others were beginning to take notice. Paul Rosenfeld, reviewing *In Our Time* for *The New Republic*, put his finger on Hemingway's contribution to modernism, linking his stories with "cubist painting, *Le Sacre du Printemps*, and other recent work" for their "new, tough, severe and satisfying beauty."

Even more significant for Hemingway's career, he earned the early and continuing attention of Edmund Wilson, who wrote an essay in 1939 called "Hemingway: Bourdon Gauge of Morale" that echoes (probably unintentionally) Hemingway's own earlier appraisal of Stein as a gauge of civilization in its title. Hemingway had been seriously wounded by fragments from an exploding shell during his brief service as an ambulance driver on the Italian front, and had spent months recuperating in Italian hospitals. Wilson proposed that Hemingway's wounds went much deeper than the merely physical, that he was a "wounded" artist whose genius and alienation alike derived from a deep, barely recognized trauma—a thesis that, though Hemingway himself disliked it, set the tone for a generation of serious critical consideration of his writing.

In October 1924, Wilson, only four years Hemingway's senior but already a respected critic, published his first commentary on him in a review of *Three Stories*, along with *In Our Time*, for *The Dial*. He perceptively dismissed the poems of the first collection as trivial and praised the prose, particularly the vignettes that link the stories of *In Our Time*. The focus of his review was the execution of six Greek cabinet members, the famous passage that concludes with the minister who is too sick from typhoid to stand for the firing squad: "When they fired the first volley he was sitting down in the water with his head on his knees." Wilson said Hemingway was "remarkably successful in suggesting moral values by a series of simple statements of this sort," an observation that remains at the heart of all good commentary on Hemingway's work.

Wilson also said that Hemingway showed the influence of Sherwood Anderson and that, like Anderson, he had felt "the genius of Gertrude Stein's *Three Lives*." The three writers formed "a school by themselves," one characterized by "naiveté of language, often passing into the colloquialism of the character dealt with, which serves actually to convey profound emotions and complex states of mind. . . ." But Wilson added that Hemingway was "strikingly original" and by no means "imitative" of Stein or Anderson.

Hemingway forgot Wilson's praise and chafed at the linking with writers he by now regarded as clearly inferior to him. Just twenty-five years old, he had already indicated that he had not only a firm sense of his own unique merit as a writer but, more unusual, a plan for his career as a writer. Sherwood Anderson had helped him get a three-book contract with his publisher, Boni & Liveright. Initially grateful to Anderson and happy simply to have a publisher, Hemingway was now angered by what he regarded as lazy and inept publicity for *In Our Time*. Maxwell Perkins at Scribner's was the influential editor for another of Hemingway's new friends, Scott Fitzgerald. At Fitzgerald's prompting, Perkins indicated interest in the novel Hemingway was working on about a group of dissolute British and American expatriates who travel to Pamplona for the bull-fights—the novel that he would call *The Sun Also Rises*. Scribner's was a better house than Boni & Liveright, and Perkins would, as Fitzgerald's editor, clearly be a good guide for Hemingway as well. How could he break out of the three-book contract—according to which *The Sun Also Rises* would be the third book—with Boni & Liveright? Simple enough: he would give them a demeaning parody of their star writer, Sherwood Anderson. He slapped together a fifteen-thousand-word manuscript over ten days in November 1925, and called it *The Torrents of Spring*.

Hemingway made sure that every reader would know he was talking about Anderson ("Scripps O'Neill") by beginning with the writer's own legend of his birth as an artist: "Alone, bareheaded, the snow blowing in his hair, he walked down the G. R. & I. Railway tracks. It was the coldest night he had ever known. He picked up a dead bird that had frozen and fallen onto the railroad tracks and put it inside his shirt to warm it.

The bird nestled close to his warm body and pecked at his chest gratefully. 'Poor little chap,' Scripps said. 'You feel the cold too.' Tears came into his eyes." And so on. Horace Liveright was too decent a man to allow Anderson to be insulted. He would decline to publish *Torrents*, thus releasing Hemingway from his contract and allowing his real book, the novel that would make his career, to be published by Scribner's.

Such at least is the supposition of Hemingway's biographers. He never acknowledged it as such, but a writer friend at the time, Mike Strater, had no doubt that *The Torrents of Spring* was "a cold-blooded deal breaker." At the least, it was a betrayal. John Dos Passos, when he heard Hemingway read it aloud, said that double-crossing an old friend—Anderson—wasn't a good idea. Hemingway ignored him, Dos Passos recalled—he "had a distracting way of suddenly beginning to hum while he was talking to you." Anderson, as sensitive a soul as the parody suggests, was wounded: "I keep wondering why the man feels life as he does," he wrote to Stein. "It is as though he saw it always as rather ugly. 'People have in for me. All right. I'll go for them.' There is the desire always to kill . . . he cannot bear the thought of any other men as Artists . . . [he] wants to occupy the entire field."

Stein herself was parodied, though more gently, in *Torrents*: "Ah, there was a woman! Where were her experiments in words leading her? What was at the bottom of it? All that in Paris. Ah, Paris! How far it was to Paris now. Paris in the morning. Paris in the evening. Paris at night. Paris in the morning again. Paris at noon, perhaps. Why not?" Hemingway's notes at the time to Ezra Pound confirm his malicious intent: *Torrents* was sure to "start plenty of rows," including one with Gertrude Stein, because he was exposing "all the fakes of Anderson, Gertrude, [Sinclair] Lewis, [Willa] Cather . . . and all the rest of the pretentious faking bastards . . . I don't see how Sherwood will ever be able to write again. Stuff like Gertrude isn't even worth the bother to show up. It's easier simply to quote from it."

It would take Gertrude Stein eight years to respond to Hemingway's parody of Anderson and herself—there was no overt break between them, although she told Hemingway she disapproved of his treatment of Anderson, and they met occasionally throughout this period. But his life was far too full for her to occupy more than a tiny corner of it after October 1926, when *The Sun Also Rises* was published. He underwent a remarkable double transformation in the years immediately following, culminating with the publication of *A Farewell to Arms* in 1929. He was now a bestselling writer who could live off his earnings, not an experimental modernist whose fiction appeared in little journals known only to the cognoscenti.

Hardly anyone denied Hemingway's talent, though some had grumbled that in *The Sun Also Rises* the range of his characters was narrow and the deliberate flatness of his prose was uninvolving. But a generation of readers rendered cynical by the waste and murder of the Great War—the "lost generation," as Stein had dubbed it—had no trouble responding to the understated, cryptic exchanges between Jake Barnes and his friend Bill Gorton: " 'You're an expatriate,' " Bill teases Jake. " 'You've lost touch with the soil. You get precious. Fake European standards have ruined you. You drink yourself to death. You become obsessed by sex. You spend all your time talking, not working. You're an expatriate, see? You hang around cafes.' " Hemingway's readers understood that after they hung around in cafés, sometimes punching each other out in drunken fits of pique, his heroes went to their hotel rooms and left the lights on so as not to be alone in the dark and turned their faces to the wall and wept. As Wilson explained later, they were wounded, the best of them, in terrible ways that only they—and those who were like them—could understand. Then, with *A Farewell to Arms*, the story of Frederic Henry and his doomed lover, Catherine Barkley, Hemingway melded the toughness of the earlier stories with a new vein of sentiment that expanded his readership beyond men looking for hard-boiled adventure tales.

Far more than just a popular writer, though, he was becoming an international celebrity. With the publication of *Death in the Afternoon* in 1932 and *Green Hills of Africa* in 1935, Hemingway had become a household name, featured on the cover of *Life* and *Time*, profiled in *Argosy* and *True*, his every adventure fodder for the gossip columns of Walter Winchell and Leonard Lyons. He was a six-foot, two-hundred-pound man's man, a wounded war veteran, a big-game hunter, bullfighter, and deep-sea fisherman, a boxer and a brawler, a lover and leaver of beautiful women (including Hadley), at least as handsome and photogenic as his movie-star friends Clark Gable and Gary Cooper, but with nothing of the pretend world of Hollywood about him: *This* star was the real thing. He had achieved his success based on talent—genius, some said—and hard work.

But as Hemingway became ever more successful and celebrated by the general public, his impatience with critics who faulted him personally or as a writer—and the two were hard to separate—gnawed at him. His work celebrated stoic courage in a bleak world, men and occasionally women who showed "grace under pressure" in the face of inevitable defeat. It was based on a combination of personal experience, gained from war and dangerous sports, and observation. To challenge his work was to challenge his manhood. He was particularly sensitive to criticism that he had sold out his artistic integrity for fame and money. Although he would write some of his greatest short stories in the early thirties—including "A Clean, Well-Lighted Place" and "Hills Like White Elephants"—his 1933 collection of short stories, *Winner Take Nothing*, was not favorably reviewed, and his nonfiction books about bullfighting and big-game hunting in Africa were savaged by the critics. Meanwhile, he was earning huge sums from magazines like Arnold Gingrich's *Esquire* that wanted his articles on fishing, bullfighting, and on-scene accounts of life in exotic locales that few of their readers would ever see.

Hemingway's 1936 story, "The Snows of Kilimanjaro," is about the loss of artistic integrity—a dying writer remembers how he has wasted his life and his talent, and how his friends did the same, particularly "poor Scott Fitzgerald" who let himself be ruined by his "romantic awe" of the rich. Of course, Hemingway was at that time only in his mid-thirties, and already had a body of work behind him that few writers twice his age ever achieve. But it is clear, as his many biographers show, that he was uneasy about his status as an artist, having achieved such extraordinary fame as a celebrity.

There was no shortage of critics to enhance his discomfort. Heywood Broun, the newspaper columnist, called him a "phony." Clifton Fadiman mocked him as a romantic poseur and compared him to Goethe's representation of Byron—a great poet who, when he tries to think, "is a child." Wyndham Lewis called him a "dumb ox," a "dull-witted, bovine, monosyllabic simpleton," enraging Hemingway so much that he smashed a flower vase (haplessly proving Lewis right) in Sylvia Beach's bookstore when he read Lewis's article there. Virginia Woolf said he was too "self-consciously virile." Max Eastman, following Woolf's lead, wrote a teasing article called "Bull in the Afternoon." He said that Hemingway seemed compelled to "give forth evidences of red-blooded masculinity" in his work; he wore "false hair on his chest" to hide his feelings of inadequacy and revulsion at the horrors of modern life. Perhaps he lacked "the serene confidence that he *is* a full-sized man." The next time the two men met, in Maxwell Perkins's office, Hemingway ripped open his shirt to show Eastman his fur and threw a book—Eastman's own book, in which the offending remark was written—into his face.

Even when he could not lay hands on his antagonists, Hemingway's response to criticism threatened violence. An early story in which an acquaintance, Chard Powers Smith, was depicted as effeminate and his wife as shrewish had prompted a complaining letter from Smith. His wife had since died, but he wanted the author to know how much his story had hurt them both; he called Hemingway a "contemptible worm." Hemingway replied, but only to express his "sincere and hearty contempt for you, your past, your present and your future," concluding "It will be a great pleasure to see you again in Paris and somewhat of a pleasure to knock you down a few times." He published, in the *Little Review*, a "Valentine" to a critic, a parody of the children's verse "sing a song of sixpence," rhyming "lye" with "a hope that you will die." And, responding to the New Humanists who thought his descriptions of death and mutilation exceeded the bounds of good taste, he said that they had never seen soldiers die, as he had. Parodying one of their favorite poems, Andrew Marvell's "To His Coy Mistress," he said of these supposedly effete critics, "I hope to see the finish of a few, and speculate how worms will try that long preserved sterility."

If Hemingway was a dangerous friend, as Anderson, Stein, and Fitzgerald all learned, he was a potentially homicidal enemy, hardly mellowing with age and success. Edmund Wilson, usually supportive, lamented the "arrogant, belligerent, and boastful" persona of the Hemingway articles in *Esquire* during the thirties as "certainly the worst-invented character to be found in the author's work," and wondered if his mental balance was entirely in order.

———

Gertrude Stein's annihilating remarks on Ernest Hemingway in *The Autobiography of Alice B. Toklas* would probably have bothered him less had this not been her first big success with the same public that had made him so popular. For many years Stein's works had sold in the scores of copies, if at all; now, in 1933, approaching the twilight of her life, she had in a few short weeks written a Book-of-the-Month Club bestseller that was also serialized by the *Atlantic Monthly*. Full of (mostly) genial and generous humor, it parades its famous cast of artists and writers through the salon at 27, rue de Fleurus; Gertrude Stein is like Samuel Johnson a century and a half earlier, a wise and witty force at the center of things, and Alice B. Toklas is her self-created Boswell.

Almost everyone liked the book, ordinary readers because it was chatty and familiar, critics like William Troy, in *The Nation*, because he thought it showed that she was "not nearly so isolated and eccentric a figure in American letters as is often believed." Edmund Wilson praised it for its "wisdom, its distinction and its charm." He also noted, in a passage that must have galled Hemingway as a possible veiled reference to himself, how suspicious Stein was of popular success: "Success, for her[,] seems to imply some imposture and deterioration."

Stein tells her life story chronologically, so the six pages she devotes to Hemingway don't appear until near the end; by this time, readers have had time to get used to the Stein-Toklas voice and are more likely to accept her (their?) version of the Hemingway character as the true one. The two ladies chat about the now-famous writer. Stein demurs gently, or pretends to, at some of Alice's comments. Between them, Hemingway is left with little to comfort him.

True, he is said to have been an "extraordinarily good-looking young man"—but his eyes were "passionately interested" rather than "interesting."

And it is also true that Gertrude "always says," according to

Alice, "yes sure I have a weakness for Hemingway. After all he was the first of the young men to knock at my door and he did make Ford print the first piece of The Making of Americans." But Toklas adds, "I myself have not so much confidence that Hemingway did do this. I have never known what the story is but I have always been certain that there was some other story behind it all. That is the way I feel about it."

What follows then is the series of paragraphs that most angered Hemingway. First, Stein and Sherwood Anderson talk of how Hemingway had "repudiated Sherwood Anderson and all his works," after he had "been formed by the two of them. . . ." They had, Stein implies, created a monster, "and they were both a little proud and a little ashamed of the work of their minds."

What about his originality, his uniqueness? He is a fake, taking on the guise of a modern when it suits him but an old-fashioned traditionalist at heart: "he looks like a modern and he smells of the museums."

Well, then, what about the truth that he says is the heart of all good writing, and that he strives for so mightily? Sadly, Hemingway has not told the truth: his "real story"—not the ones he writes but "the confessions of the real Ernest Hemingway"—would be "wonderful." What is the truth that he could confess? That he is a climber and a careerist above all, which will keep him from ever telling the truth: "After all, as he himself once murmured, there is the career, the career."

And the great hunter and fighter's famous courage? Alice and Gertrude are forced to "admit" that "Hemingway was yellow," a blowhard like "the flat-boat men on the Mississippi river as described by Mark Twain."

His athletic skills? Well, there was the time, Alice says, when some "young chap" whom Hemingway was teaching to box accidentally knocked him out. Of course, he wasn't very strong, Alice says: "He used to get quite worn out walking from his house to ours. But then he had been worn by the war." Alice also recalls how a "robust friend" had told Gertrude that "Ernest is very fragile, whenever he does anything sporting something breaks, his arm, his leg, or his head."

His intelligence, then—his fabled ability as a "quick study"? Gertrude admits that at least he is "such a good pupil." Alice says no, he is "a rotten pupil." Gertrude corrects her: He is the best kind of pupil, he is trainable because he listens "without understanding it, in other words he takes training and anybody who takes training is a favourite pupil."

Finally, Alice says, she got tired of having him around: "Don't you come home with Hemingway on your arm," she tells Gertrude. But he did one day, and the two sat and talked for a long time. "Finally I heard her say, Hemingway, after all you are ninety percent Rotarian. Can't you, he said, make it eighty percent. No, said she regretfully, I can't."

How seriously was Hemingway affected by Stein's cutting remarks? One of his biographers, Jeffrey Meyers, feels that "the loss of her friendship and [the] viciousness of her attack caused a profound and permanent wound." Kirk Curnutt's compilation of references to Hemingway's outrage is persuasive. Prevented from punching Stein, he fell back on the barely less aggressive substitute of charging that she was just a grumpy old lesbian gone "goofy" with her menopause—causing her, he said elsewhere, to lose her critical faculties: "she couldn't tell a good picture from a bad one, a good writer from a bad one, and it all went phtt." Her gender and her sexual orientation came in for frequent comment: What could he have expected from "a woman who isn't a woman"? Dissuaded by Perkins from calling her a "bitch" in *Green Hills of Africa*, Hemingway settled for "female," which would anger her, he joked, even more. He also declined Arnold Gingrich's invitation to attack Stein in the pages of *Esquire*, when she was visiting the United States in 1934 to promote the *Autobiography*. He didn't want, Hemingway said generously, "to slam the old bitch around" while she was on her book tour.

Most of these remarks were not made for general circulation, however, and they compose a very small percentage of what Hemingway reportedly thought and said during the twenty-eight years between the Stein and Toklas *Autobiography* in 1933 and his own death in 1961. Michael Reynolds, in his biography, *Hemingway: The American Homecoming*, concludes that Gertrude Stein, by the end of the twenties, was "no longer the writer [Hemingway] so admired" in the early years of their acquaintance. In the final volume of his biography, Reynolds calls Stein Hemingway's "literary mother." "Having had her say on Ernest" in the *Autobiography*, Reynolds wryly adds, "she made the singular mistake of leaving him alive after her passing, for he too would have his say, as he often promised."

Hemingway's revenge on Stein comes in his last book, written in 1957 and posthumously published in 1964 as *A Moveable Feast*. In this intriguing set of reminiscences, Papa Hemingway, now the old lion, king of the pride, recalls his early years in Paris. Pound, Ford, and particularly Fitzgerald come to memorable life here, but three remarkable chapters are given to his association with Gertrude Stein. The resentment and anger that boil beneath the nostalgic surface of his reminiscences suggest that Meyers's and Curnutt's reading of a festering wound in the Hemingway psyche is on target.

The first meeting, in "Miss Stein Instructs," seems at first to be rather fondly recalled. But the instruction noted is almost entirely negative or useless. It has to do with how Stein treated Hemingway and his wife "as though we were very good, well mannered and promising children"; with her misunderstanding of one of his best early stories, "Up in Michigan"; with the way her good taste in art and her strong personality persuaded

critics to "take her writing on trust"; with her admittedly profound discovery of "many truths about rhythms and the use of
words in repetition that were valid and valuable"—an admission sabotaged with the damning final clause, "and she talked
well about them"; with her "unbelievably long" work, *The
Making of Americans*, and how its undeniably brilliant passages
were undercut by endless "repetitions that a more conscientious
and less lazy writer would have put in the waste basket"; and
with her amusingly naïve attempt one day to instruct him
"about sex" and homosexuality, to which he responds with
counter-instruction about the need for a young man to carry a
knife with him when he is on the road. What Hemingway did
learn during the period of his association with Stein, he says,
came mainly from afternoons alone at the Louvre, studying
Impressionist paintings by Monet and Manet and especially
Cézanne.

This, to reiterate, is the *fond* chapter of the three—the one
that says she taught him virtually nothing. Well, then, what
about her contribution of the epigraph, "You are all a lost generation," to *The Sun Also Rises*? That single sentence provided
reviewers around the world with an irresistible hook for discussing Hemingway's novel. Surely he will give credit where
credit is due in the next chapter, "Une Génération Perdue." The
originator of the phrase was, in Hemingway's version, the
owner of the garage where Stein's car had been inadequately
serviced by a young veteran (in Stein's version, he is a hotel owner). The proprietor apologized, saying that young men become
civilized between the ages of eighteen and twenty-five. Those
who spent these formative years in the war lost the chance to
become civilized; they were doomed to waste their lives in drink
and sex and violence, to become a "*génération perdue*."

Hemingway said that Stein told him that he and his friends,
"all of you young people who served in the war," were a lost
generation. "You have no respect for anything. You drink your-

self to death. . . ." Hemingway had already parodied this assertion in *The Sun Also Rises*, in the conversation between Jake and
Bill Gorton. By the time he came to write *A Moveable Feast*, he
was sick of it. Malcolm Cowley, in *Exile's Return*, noted the original appeal of the phrase and of Hemingway's hero, Jake
Barnes: "Young men tried to get as imperturbably drunk as the
hero, young women of good family took a succession of lovers
in the same heartbroken fashion as the heroine, they all talked
like Hemingway characters, and the name"—the Lost Generation—"was fixed." At first a boast, it soon became a cliché, then
a joke, and finally a subject of ridicule.

Hemingway clearly thought that the phrase had trivialized
the tragic drama he believed was the true essence of his characters and of himself; the cause of this misunderstanding lay with
people like Gertrude Stein. Perhaps the young mechanic had
been at fault, he speculates in *A Moveable Feast*, but he imagines
a story for the young man, hauling wounded men down moun-
tain roads with burned-out brakes. He hates "all the dirty, easy
labels," he says, the "lost-generation talk." He thinks "of Miss
Stein and Sherwood Anderson and egotism and mental laziness
versus discipline and . . . who is calling who a lost generation."

So, in the first two of the three chapters, Hemingway has
shown that not only had Gertrude Stein nothing to teach him,
but that she was too emotionally and mentally lazy to learn
from him about the true nature of his generation and its response to the war. Only one prop remained to be knocked from
under her: her strength, her self-command—her dignity. In his
final, very unpleasant, chapter on Stein, "A Strange Enough
Ending," Hemingway says his visits to 27, rue de Fleurus had
diminished in frequency. He had already determined, while
trying to persuade Ford Madox Ford to publish part of *The
Making of Americans*, that "there was not much future in men
being friends with great women," and "usually even less future
with truly ambitious women writers." She pressed him to come

by: "But Hemingway, you have the run of the place. Don't you
know that?"

One "lovely spring day" he did stop by to visit. The maid let
him in and then vanished. Then he heard "someone" upstairs—
Toklas, obviously—"speaking to Miss Stein as I had never
heard one person speak to another; never, anywhere, ever. Then
Miss Stein's voice came pleading and begging, saying, 'Don't,
pussy . . . Please don't, pussy.'" "It was bad to hear and the
answers were worse," Hemingway says. He left. The friendship
was over. It ended, the reader is left to infer, not because Stein
had attacked him in her *Autobiography*—for this event predates
that book by some years. Rather, it ended because of Hemingway's pity and disgust for a poor, weak woman he could no
longer bear to see.

Stein died in 1946, long before the appearance of *A Moveable
Feast* in 1964. Hemingway died in 1961, by his own hand, at his
home in Ketchum, Idaho. The thinly (or not at all) veiled
viciousness of his comments on Stein was overshadowed by his
even more acidulous (and funny) memories of Fitzgerald, by
the genuinely touching descriptions of his early days as a writer,
struggling to define himself and to make his mark in postwar
Paris—and, not least, by the sadness of his own suicide at the
early age of sixty-two. Though both were clearly troubled by
the hostility that developed between them, neither writer's reputation seems to have been unduly damaged by the dispute.
Stein is remembered more as a literary character, perhaps her
own best creation, than as a serious writer. Hemingway, for his
part, has also become his own most memorable character, a man
in whom the creative and destructive impulses noted by Freud
seem to have been precariously balanced against each other.

As a writer, he continues to attract scholarly attention. In
1989 Jackson R. Bryer published *Sixteen Modern American*

Authors: A Survey of Research and Criticism Since 1972, one of the standard reference texts for serious students of American literature. Bruce Stark's bibliographical essay on Hemingway occupies seventy-six pages of this volume, more than are devoted to any other writer except Faulkner. Since 1989 there have been at least five more biographies and dozens of critical studies of Hemingway and his work, not to mention special panels at literary conferences. About two hundred registrants attend the Hemingway Society–sponsored international conferences every two years. Few high school students in the United States graduate without reading *The Old Man and the Sea*, and his other major titles—*In Our Time, The Sun Also Rises, A Farewell to Arms*, and *For Whom the Bell Tolls*—are staples in college courses in twentieth-century American literature.

He has also continued to be a public figure. There is an annual Hemingway look-alike contest in Key West, his home in the thirties, featuring scores of heavy men with beards who spend a lot of time drinking and arm wrestling, and the Harry's Bar Hemingway parody contest has been a popular newspaper feature for years, with United Airlines as its most recent co-sponsor. The "Ernest Hemingway Collection" offered by Thomasville Furniture Industries (one of thirteen manufacturers authorized to use the Hemingway name) includes, according to its advertisement, "96 pieces of living, dining, and bedroom furniture and accessories"; the selections are grouped according to a few of the many places that Hemingway made famous: Kenya, Key West, Havana, and Ketchum.

But all the fame and all the familiarity only make him seem more remote. As he himself seemed to sense in his last years, when he was thinking about *A Moveable Feast*, the true, now vanished Hemingway was the shy, intense boy with the "interested" eyes who sat at the feet of Gertrude Stein. He really does seem to have loved her then, not romantically but, as he joked, as a brother. But most of the many biographers and those who knew Hemingway have testified to the paradox that this power-fully creative man felt compelled to separate himself from, and sometimes to destroy, those he should have been closest to. As Donald Ogden Stewart, a friend and the model for Bill Gorton, said in an interview, "The minute he began to love you, or the minute he began to have some sort of obligation to you of love or friendship or something, then is when he had to kill you. Then you were too close to something he was protecting. He, one-by-one, knocked off the best friendships he ever had. He did it with Scott; he did it with Dos Passos—with everybody."

3

The Slap Heard 'Round the World

Sinclair Lewis, Theodore Dreiser, and the Nobel Prize

Many years after Dorothy Thompson divorced Sinclair Lewis she recalled her first impression of his extraordinary appearance: His narrow face was "roughened, red, and scarred by repeated radium and electric needle burnings," the result of vain efforts to cure his persistent skin afflictions. "There was less of the face below the hawkish nose than above it, where it broadened into a massive frontal skull, crossed by horizontal lines; reddish but almost colorless eyebrows above round, cavernously set, remarkably brilliant eyes, transparent as aquamarines and in them a strange, shy, imploring look. . . ."

It was always the eyes that people first noted. They were "[p]ale blue, clever, bulgy eyes" under invisible eyebrows and sandy lashes (the artist Peggy Bacon); they were "the eyes of a small child or a frightened animal looking through a woodpile" (the journalist Vincent Sheean); most suggestively, the eyes were for Malcolm Cowley a key to the mystery of Lewis's character and his fate. They "were very large and very round," Cowley wrote, so apparently guileless as to suggest stupidity. "They made me think of folklore. Every fairy-book hero has eyes like these; he is taken for an idiot, and mistreated by his older brothers, and sent bare-handed into the world to seek his fortune, but he proves the wiliest of them all. Invariably, he marries the King's daughter."

The privileged son of a Midwest physician who sent him to
Yale, Harry Sinclair Lewis—usually called Harry or Red, not
Sinclair—was anything but bare-handed or stupid when he set
out to make his fortune with words. In addition to his good
education, he had formidable gifts for a writer: a photographic
memory, a mind so brilliant that it was commonly called
"incandescent," a capacity for sustained and disciplined hard
work, and an all-seeing eye for the false, the pathetic, and the
absurd aspects of American middle-class life. His caustic wit
was leavened by a real sense of comedy and sufficient pathos to
suggest that he actually liked most of his victims. By the time he
was forty-one, he had written four extraordinary novels: *Main
Street* (1920), *Babbitt* (1922), *Arrowsmith* (1925), and *Elmer
Gantry* (1927). Touchstone points of reference for two generations of American readers, and still splendidly readable today,
these books about small-town ennui (the "village virus"), business boosterism, medical idealism, and religious charlatanry
made Sinclair Lewis the quintessential writer of the American
heartland in the 1920s, nearly as rich and famous as Mark
Twain had been and as Hemingway would be. In 1930 they led
to his becoming the first American author to win the Nobel
Prize for Literature.

But for all his gifts and achievements, Lewis was a deeply
troubled man, an alcoholic prone to emotional outbursts, sometimes abusive and often so gauche that we cringe with embarrassment for him. H.L. Mencken at first thought he was a
"jackass." They met at a party in 1920 in New York, where
Mencken was chatting with his friend and coeditor of the *American Mercury*, George Jean Nathan. Both men remembered the
encounter with Lewis vividly, especially Nathan: "Barely had
we taken off our hats and coats ... when the tall, skinny,
paprika-headed stranger simultaneously coiled one long arm
around Mencken's neck and the other around mine, well nigh
strangling us," and started shouting, "So you guys are critics, are

you? Well, let me tell you something. I'm the best writer in this here gottdamn country. . . ." He had a novel that was about to be published, the red-haired stranger said: "Just wait till you read the gottdamn thing. You've got a treat coming, Georgie and Hank, and don't you boys make no mistake about *that*!"

The two editors finally escaped to a tavern and stared at each other in astonishment, Mencken gasping for breath. "Of all the idiots I've ever met, that fellow is the worst!" Three days later, back home in Baltimore, Mencken had just read the galley proofs of *Main Street* that Harcourt had sent him. That idiot, Mencken wrote to Nathan, had written a masterpiece. "I begin to believe there isn't a God after all. There is no justice in the world."

Within a year of meeting Mencken, Lewis's satirical sketch of Gopher Prairie and what James D. Hart, in his study of popular American literature, calls its "smug, intolerant, unimaginatively standardized belief that whatsoever the town banker does not know and sanction is heresy, not only worthless to know but wicked to consider," had been bought by three hundred thousand people; another hundred thousand copies would be sold in the next year in hardcover—phenomenal numbers even today. In 1922 Lewis accomplished that most difficult of feats for a writer, following one success with another: *Babbitt*. George Follansbee Babbitt, Lewis's hapless "realtor," soon became a household word, literally a dictionary definition—Babbitt: "A member of the American middle class whose attachment to its ideals is such as to make of him a model of narrow-mindedness and self-satisfaction. Used disparagingly."

Lewis was too popular a writer to be entirely trusted by liberal intellectuals, who correctly perceived that he actually liked his characters and his country, even as he lampooned them. Conservative professors of literature, who assumed that anybody who was easy to read was shallow, also disdained him as clamorous and rowdy. His Nobel Prize was predictably controversial, all the more so because the award itself was—as it has remained—a natural lightning rod for controversy. The Swedish selection committee had given its first prize, in 1901, to the mediocre Sully Prudhomme, over Leo Tolstoy, and the list of other great writers who had not won the prize included Marcel Proust, Henry James, and Joseph Conrad. Now that it was finally an American's turn to win (though the committee earnestly denied that nationality ever played a role in evaluating literary art), many critics at home and abroad argued that the award should go to an indisputably great writer rather than to Lewis. Among the alternatives suggested were Sherwood Anderson, Eugene O'Neill, and Theodore Dreiser—especially Dreiser.

Lewis was painfully sensitive to slights—he had huffily rejected the Pulitzer Prize offered to him in 1926 for *Arrowsmith* because he had not won it earlier for *Main Street*—and he had good reason to believe that his work fully merited whatever recognition it got. But he was also unusually generous in recognizing the abilities of younger writers like Ernest Hemingway, who characteristically returned the favor with an insult. Lewis even went out of his way, in his acceptance speech in Stockholm, to praise his chief competitor, using Dreiser as a club to pound the conservative literary establishment: "Our American professors like their literature clear and cold and pure and very dead," he charged. They failed to recognize that the great crisis of modern America was that its material culture had outstripped its intellectual culture, and they ignored the needs of the present by concentrating on long-dead and irrelevant writers while denigrating realists such as Dreiser (and himself). It was Dreiser who,

> usually unappreciated, often hated, has cleared the trail
> from Victorian and Howellsian timidity and gentility in
> American fiction to honesty and boldness and passion of

life. Without his pioneering spirit, I doubt if any of us could, unless we liked to be sent to jail, seek to express life and beauty and terror. . . . Dreiser's first great novel, *Sister Carrie* . . . came to housebound and airless America like a great free Western wind, and to our stuffy domesticity gave us the first fresh air since Mark Twain and Whitman.

Sinclair Lewis's evocation of Mark Twain was more appropriate for himself than it was for Dreiser, whose gifts did not include satire, comedy, or stylistic finesse. Walt Whitman, however— that self-educated, windy genius who wandered through nineteenth-century America, observing lilacs and prostitutes and amputated legs "dropping horribly into pails"—does anticipate Dreiser rather nicely. Like the unconventional poet, Dreiser would sound his own "barbaric yawp" over the American literary landscape for well over forty years.

Dreiser was born in 1871 in Terre Haute, Indiana, the ninth of ten children. His mother was dreamy and devoted; his father was a surly, morose German immigrant, a failure whose fanatic religiosity drove his children into deviancy—burglary, vagrancy, semi-prostitution. Dreiser's brothers fled, and his sisters were seduced by older men. One left town with a married saloon manager, providing her brother with the germ of the plot for *Sister Carrie*. Besides Dreiser himself, only his brother Paul would survive intact the wreck of their disastrous upbringing. (Paul would change his name to Dresser and immortalize his mistress, a madam, with his song "My Gal Sal" and his state with "On the Banks of the Wabash.")

Dreiser's education was interrupted and minimal, ending with the ninth grade. He turned to journalism in his late teens, working as a reporter in Chicago, St. Louis, Cleveland, Buffalo, and New York. His most frequent beat was the police courts, giving him, as his biographer Richard Lingeman writes, insights into the world of murder, "arson, rape, sodomy, bribery, corruption, trickery and false witness in every conceivable form." In 1898 he married a former schoolteacher two years his senior. Bored almost immediately with his marriage and dissatisfied with the transiency of journalism, Dreiser began to write fiction, preparing himself by reading Balzac, Zola, and Herbert Spencer. The French naturalists provided him with useful techniques of weaving social reportage into fiction; Spencer gave him the bones of the deterministic social Darwinism that would be his overriding philosophy until he died; his newspaper experience of "arson, rape, sodomy," and various forms of corruption provided the details of real life; and his own family stood in as his characters.

The result, in 1900, was *Sister Carrie*, the trail-blazing novel that Lewis celebrated, and that nearly ended Dreiser's career even as it initiated it. The story of a poor but pretty country girl who comes to make her way in the big city of Chicago, *Sister Carrie* appears at first to be following a traditional kind of Horatio Alger plot, in which luck and pluck allow a virtuous lad or lass to win fame, fortune, and happiness against all odds—in other words, a sentimental pastiche of clichés typical of the period. Instead, Carrie is seduced by a flashy traveling salesman named Drouet who persuades her, without much difficulty, to become his mistress. She deserts Drouet for the more sophisticated George Hurstwood, modeled after the peculating saloon manager whose story Dreiser had first come across as a reporter and his own sister's story. They flee together to New York, where, after a few years, Carrie's minor but captivating talent as an actress in musical comedy allows her to thrive as Hurstwood declines into despair and suicide. Carrie's story ends. She suffers no remorse, no guilt, no punishment for adultery. Carrie is neither good nor bad. Her first chapter is called "The Magnet Attracting: A Waif Amid Forces"; she is simply, like everyone else, responding to various stimuli. We are all "chemisms," Dreiser said, seeking the sun like heliotropic plants.

As in *An American Tragedy* twenty-five years later, the real story is not so much in the plot of *Sister Carrie* as in the compelling accumulation of detail, often static, that has its own fascination, something like a Hopper painting. If you want to know what a "swell" bar looked like or how a traveling salesman dressed, Dreiser is your man. But for the wife of Dreiser's hapless publisher, Frank Doubleday, a story with no moral was immoral. She was so appalled by *Sister Carrie* that she persuaded her husband to withdraw the book from publication; fewer than five hundred copies were published in the United States before it vanished. Dreiser was outraged: "Immoral! Immoral!" he cried two years later in a protest against censorship. "Under this cloak hide the vices of wealth as well as the vast unspoken blackness of poverty and ignorance; and between them must walk the little novelist, choosing neither truth nor beauty, but some half-conceived phase of life that bears no honest relationship to either the whole of nature or to man."

It seemed for a time that Dreiser was ruined; he even had to take a job as a day laborer, apparently sinking into oblivion exactly as poor Hurstwood had. But Dreiser was too vital a "chemism" to give up. By 1907 he had become one of the best magazine editors in New York, prominent enough to reissue his scandalous novel, to wide acclaim from younger followers like Sinclair Lewis. The great irony is that the magazines Dreiser was editing for the Butterick chain were high-grade pulp aimed precisely at ladies like Mrs. Doubleday and her friends (and their maids). His particular charge was *The Delineator*, which ran special issues on feeding babies and Santa Claus associations (he won a prize for that one). Dreiser threw himself into his job, soliciting morally uplifting fiction as enthusiastically as he had tried to sabotage it with his own work. "[W]e cannot admit stories which deal with false or immoral relations, or which point a false moral, or which deal with things degrading, such as drunkenness," he wrote to a prospective contributor, adding, "I am personally opposed" to stories "which are disgusting in their realism and fidelity to life. The fine side of things—the idealistic—is the answer for us . . ." Mrs. Doubleday could not have said it better.

William Lengel, a young law student from Kansas City who worked at Butterick's as an assistant to Dreiser, read *Sister Carrie* when it was reissued and asked its author how he could have written such a powerful book when he was not yet thirty. Dreiser shrugged and said, "Genius, I suppose." Well, then, Lengel continued, how could he stomach publishing the high-toned drivel that filled Butterick's magazines? "One must live," Dreiser replied coldly—hadn't Lengel *read* the book he had just praised? Dreiser was an inch over six feet in height, weighing close to two hundred pounds, and slightly wall-eyed; the intimidating look he must have given Lengel is easy to imagine.

In fact, he loved the money, the prestige, and the power of his position—the expansive corner office, the desk as large as a billiard table, dressing for success in soft collars and flowing ties, the luncheons at Sweet's, the writers begging for his attention—and the attractive secretaries. H. L. Mencken, Dreiser's friend and most influential advocate for many years, said the champion of the downtrodden was a German peasant at heart, humorless, ignorant, sensuous, and something of a bully. Dreiser himself admitted in his diary that he was "blazing with sex and a desire for superiority." When he looked in the mirror, he saw "egotism written in every lineament, a strong presentiment of self love in every expression"—"I have a semi-Roman nose, a high forehead and an Austrian lip, with the edges of my teeth always showing. . . . People say I look cold and distant." He was also a man so obsessed with sex that he sometimes carried on three different affairs simultaneously, filling his diaries with lovingly lurid accounts of fornication ("long rounds," "heavy unions," "fierce screws").

It was Theodore Dreiser as respected novelist and powerful

businessman, with the dangerous aura of the sensual exploiter only suggested, who impressed Sinclair Lewis when they met for the first time, in 1907. Dreiser was thirty-six years old, Lewis was twenty-two. Dropping in and out of Yale, Lewis worked briefly as an assistant editor for a small travel magazine and as a freelance writer of magazine articles, including one on Dreiser called "Editors Who Write." Dreiser's presence at *The Delineator* struck the young Lewis as "surprising, for 'Sister Carrie' is not the sort of lady who is readily associated with household recipes and a children's page." Also surprising was his appearance: "He looks more like a wholesale hardware merchant than a properly hollow-cheeked realist. Mr. Dreiser wears waistcoats, real vescits, and they are well-filled!"

A few years later, in October 1910, Lewis would be hired to work at *Adventure Magazine*, a new Butterick pulp magazine whose offices were down the hall from Dreiser's. But Dreiser was no longer there. For more than a year he had been infatuated with the beautiful daughter, only seventeen when they met, of Mrs. Annie Cudlipp, an assistant editor at Butterick's. Thelma Cudlipp (the name is *not* an invention by Sinclair Lewis) was a beautiful young woman, a dark-haired art student in whom, as his biographer W. A. Swanberg writes, Dreiser saw "a freshness and beauty that he could only compare with dewy roses." He called her Honeypot, Little Blue Bird, Flower Face, Divine Fire. Thelma's watchful mother, aware of Dreiser's reputation with women, intervened with Butterick. On October 15, Dreiser was fired. His career as an editor was over.

But by now Dreiser had enough connections and prestige to survive through his writing. *Jennie Gerhardt*, his novel about a young woman who is seduced by a United States senator, was a critical and popular success in 1911. It was followed by weighty—many said leaden—tomes that sold poorly: *The Financier* in 1912, *The Titan* in 1914, and in 1915 *The "Genius,"* an autobiographical novel about the plight of the artist. *The*

"Genius" was attacked by the anti-vice crusader John Sumner, who forced Dreiser's publisher to withdraw it from circulation for seven years. In the interim Dreiser wrote a play, a sympathetic look at a child molester called *The Hand of the Potter*, and worked on his masterpiece, *An American Tragedy*.

Lewis and Dreiser met only rarely during this period—most amusingly, they sat together at Emma Goldman's Anarchists' Ball in 1910—but each was aware of the other's work. Lewis had tried unsuccessfully to persuade William Morrow at Stokes Publishers to publish *Jennie Gerhardt* before Harper had bought it. In March 1914 he sent Dreiser a copy of *Our Mr. Wrenn*—addressing the older writer respectfully as "Mr. Dreiser," he asked for a blurb that the publisher might use. It was, Lewis said, "my first attempt at a novel and it would be invaluable to me if you might comment upon it." Dreiser apparently did not respond.

By the end of 1920 Lewis needed no puffery; his career was launched on what Malcolm Cowley called its rocket-like trajectory, "up, up, up, from *Our Mr. Wrenn* (1914) through *The Job* (1917) to *Main Street* (1920); then leveling off a little but still rising through *Babbitt* (1922) to its highest point in *Arrowsmith* (1925); then sinking, not too rapidly at first, through *Elmer Gantry* (1927) and *Dodsworth* (1929); then down, down, down, in the books of his later years." Dreiser's career also peaked in 1925, with *An American Tragedy*, his only work, other than *Sister Carrie*, to receive anything like the attention that Lewis's had been given. When they next met, in Europe in 1927, Lewis was an equal contender for the Nobel Prize that Dreiser had been hoping to win for many years—as far back as when Lewis was begging him for a plug for *Our Mr. Wrenn*.

Theodore Dreiser moved to Greenwich Village in 1924 and adopted its "Latin quarter promiscuity," Mencken wrote later;

he was now "a German peasant turned Bohemian," susceptible
to "prehensile messiahs and designing females" and, especially,
to "frowsy" intellectual frauds, one of which was Soviet Communism. Like many others, Dreiser was infatuated with the
Russian efforts to create a just society in the Soviet Union. In
1927 he toured the country as an invited guest of the regime,
which understandably approved of his grim portrayals of
American capitalism and corruption; a year later his book,
loftily titled *Dreiser Looks at Russia*, appeared. It was tedious
and naïve; the tough, cynical police reporter had swallowed
whole the propaganda fed to him by the Russians. It was also
plagiarized, in part—from a book by Sinclair Lewis's wife,
Dorothy Thompson.

Mark Schorer, who came to know Dorothy Thompson while
working on his biography of Lewis, admired and liked her. She
was a "handsome and brilliant" woman, "fair and of imposing
presence," open, hearty, and "perfectly at ease with men." The
daughter of a Methodist minister from upstate New York, she
was only thirty-three when she met Lewis in 1927, but she
already had eight years behind her as a reporter in Europe—
four years in Vienna and four more in Germany, where she was
now the Berlin correspondent for the *Philadelphia Public Ledger*
and the *New York Evening Post*, as well as chief of the Central
European Service.

In September 1927, Dreiser fell ill in Berlin while en route to
Moscow. Sinclair Lewis was also there, visiting Thompson,
whom he had met and fallen in love with earlier that year. He
was working on *Dodsworth* while he waited for his divorce from
his first wife to be concluded so that he could marry Thompson.
They both looked after Dreiser, who had a respiratory infection.
Lewis found him a doctor while Thompson, whom Schorer
calls "a warmhearted young woman," helped nurse him back to
health. A few weeks later Dreiser and Thompson were both in
Moscow, enjoying, in Mencken's words, "the dizzy ride always

given to visiting American literati," while Lewis remained in Berlin to work on his novel.

Thompson and Dreiser spent a good deal of time together in Russia, both being taken as part of a group to various locales by their guides. Dreiser thought that this handsome young woman—Lingeman calls her "Junoesque"—was "making overtures" to him, and that she might be open to more than simple "flirtation." "After a supper with the American delegation she comes to my room with me," Dreiser recorded in his diary, "to discuss communism. . . . I ask her to stay but she will not—tonight."

Thompson seems to have been unstirred by Dreiser's fabled sexual magnetism, or oblivious to it—though she did complain lightly in a letter of November 8 to Lewis that Dreiser had become "quite a gay dog" and was "facetiously nudging" her a bit too often. He was "constantly making rather lumbering jokes," but she had to admit that they had had a good time the night before, "almost in hysterics with the accumulated laughter of the day. . . ."

Dreiser tried to seduce almost every woman he met, so he may have intended no particular malice against Lewis in propositioning his wife-to-be. Still, he had reproached Lewis, after recovering from his illness back in Berlin, for refusing to provide him with a publisher's quote a few years earlier for *An American Tragedy*. (How things had changed since the days of *Our Mr. Wrenn*.)

Lewis's unwillingness to comment on Dreiser's great novel, supposedly because he disliked it, has been a basic component of accounts describing their quarrel for more than half a century. The omnipresent Mencken, who knew both men well, said Dreiser was "seething with ill-concealed dislike" of Lewis because of this refusal, and every commentator on the life of either man has repeated the story. This is understandable, for it was not until recently, in the mid-1990s, that a cache of lost letters from Sinclair Lewis to various people was discovered, including one written in September 1925 to Dreiser about *An American Tragedy*. Far from disliking the novel, Lewis compared its "intricate, painstaking weaving of character and fatalism" to Hawthorne's *Scarlet Letter*, with particular reference to "Hawthorne's woods" as they related to the dismal Adirondacks through which the perhaps accidental murderer Clyde Griffiths flees to his doom. In reading this book, Lewis said, he had "witnessed genius." "Surely this will be the American book that Nobel cannot ignore." He invited Dreiser to send his comment to his publisher, presumably for use in promotion, but Dreiser apparently did not bother to do this, just as he never responded to Lewis's own gift to him of a copy of *Arrowsmith*.

Perhaps Dreiser never saw the letter, but we can reasonably assume that Lewis tried to remind him of it in that Berlin hotel room. Nothing he could say had any effect. "I smile believingly," Dreiser says in his diary, but Lewis is "noisy, ostentatious, and shallow. . . . I never could like the man."

Lewis never gave any indication, then or later, that he thought Dreiser had been pursuing Thompson, but he left off working on *Dodsworth* in late November, soon after receiving Thompson's letter, to follow her to Moscow. The Russians liked Lewis's work almost as much as they did Dreiser's for its criticism of America, but Lewis was indifferent to the great experiment of Communism. He was there to see Thompson, not to posture for the local party officials; he drove Russian interviewers crazy, answering questions like "What do you think of American movies from an artistic standpoint?" with "How long is a piece of string?" There is no record of any conversation with Dreiser about his behavior with Thompson.

A year later, back in New York and married to Lewis, Thompson was furious with Dreiser. She had just read his book about Russia, which was published in mid-November 1928, two months after her own book, *The New Russia*, had appeared.

"Really, it's too irritating," she wrote to a friend. "The old beast simply lifted paragraph after paragraph from my articles"—it was not enough for him to say, as he had, that they had both been given copies of the same boilerplate by their hosts, because much of what he had taken was "purely literary impressions" such as the following:

Thompson: "The businessmen sit moodily in the restaurant of the Grand Hotel watching the dancing and thinking themselves lucky if they have a ballerina from the opera to dance with."

Dreiser: "They [the businessmen] sit moodily in the restaurant of the Grand Hotel, drink Russian wines, watch the dancing and think themselves lucky if a ballerina from the opera dances with them."

Though the dates of publication were so close that some thought it was impossible for Dreiser to have used Thompson's book, his own had been tossed together hastily, and his secretary was on record as having said that he sent her out to "collect Dorothy Thompson's newspaper pieces to aid in the padding." These columns, which formed the bulk of Thompson's book, had of course appeared early enough to be used in Dreiser's. Thompson was willing to regard the plagiarism as accidental, the result of merely careless revision on Dreiser's part, but he was evasive and unrepentant. A newspaper account said that Dreiser "denied emphatically . . . that he had 'lifted' any material from Miss Thompson's book and, on the other hand, asserted that she, in the course of talks with him in Russia, had obtained from him material later incorporated in her articles and book." "*That* swine!" Thompson exploded. Not only had he stolen her work, he had "started a whispering campaign to the effect that I was on intimate enough terms with him that I may have gone to his room and purloined his notes!"

Lewis was as angry as his wife was with Dreiser, and there was talk of taking him to court. But the affair was not worth fighting about—Dreiser's most fervent advocates have always dismissed his book on Russia, and Thompson's was little more than a collection of forgettable columns. Lewis was busy with the forthcoming publication of *Dodsworth*, which would be his best novel after the big four he had already done. The Dreiser contretemps was forgotten—for the time being.

For all the complaints against the Nobel Prize as a political sham, an artistic hoax, and an intellectual travesty, very few writers follow George Bernard Shaw's example and turn it down. Even fewer win it without considerable expenditure of effort, directly and through their publishers, agents, and fans in the press. Dreiser was speculating about the prize as far back as 1911, when he had only published two books. In 1921 he asked Mencken to help him win the award, then worth forty thousand dollars. Mencken's share would be five thousand dollars, Dreiser said—presumably in jest. Mencken, in fact, followed up on the request: "I have an idea of a possible procedure, and shall attempt it," he wrote Dreiser a week later: "It involves working through a Dane." Nothing happened.

A few years later, in 1926, Dreiser spent the summer traveling through Scandinavia, visiting publishers in Sweden and Denmark to discuss translations of his works—Swedish publishers had an inside track to Nobel nominations and Dreiser hoped to advance his cause through his visit that summer. By the time he returned to the United States in mid-October, he had made arrangements that resulted in thirteen of his books being published in eight languages between 1927 and 1930, including eight in German and five in Swedish. In England there was a "new uniform edition" of all thirteen works. Dreiser was not a bestseller, either at home or abroad, but some influential critics respected and admired him. His chances for the prize looked good.

Sinclair Lewis had been typically naïve and enthusiastic

about his own goals, saying in 1929 that "his one hope in life was to win the Nobel prize." By June 1930 it was clear that Dreiser and Lewis were the two front-runners for the literature prize—the only year either was considered. The proceedings were, as usual, not only secret but had been expunged of any suggestion of controversy following Alfred Nobel's original stipulations that "if conflicts of opinion have arisen, they shall not be recorded in the minutes or otherwise revealed." The five-man committee did, however, release a report suggesting less than enthusiastic support for either writer. Lewis had achieved greatness only once, the report said—and then not, as one might suppose, with *Main Street*, but with *Babbitt*; Dreiser also only once, with *An American Tragedy*. Lewis won essentially because his books—eleven were in translation by 1930—were bestsellers in Sweden, while Dreiser's were abysmal failures: The Swedish translation of *An American Tragedy* sold fewer than two hundred copies a year after its initial publication.

As the Swedish scholar Rolf Lunden has explained, the Swedes, and Europeans in general, did not read Lewis or Dreiser because they loved America. Quite the contrary. Both writers were valued because they portrayed the United States as a nest of grasping, materialistic, bourgeois philistines and hypocrites, at best shallow and silly, at worst brutal and stupid. Europeans reading Lewis's "satirical caricatures . . . could laugh at what they were convinced was a true picture of the land over there. Dreiser was closer to the truth," in Lunden's opinion, "much less flamboyant, and so less popular." The Nobel Prize was given to Lewis, in a word, because he insulted his country more entertainingly than Dreiser did—as Sherwood Anderson said, "his sharp criticism of American life catered to the dislike, distrust, and envy which most Europeans feel toward the United States."

Many Americans thus had some cause to see the award as an insult by the Nobel Prize committee and by Sweden. Ordinary citizens who didn't read novels anyway, including Calvin Coolidge, thought Lewis was simply wrong and irrelevant, while the press and the literary intellectuals dismissed him as superficial. Much of the vast general audience that had responded so enthusiastically to Lewis's works in the first place had the good sense to see that he remained what he had been all along: the village crank, a romantic rebel against conformity who half loved what he attacked—though he had generated an unusual amount of hostility, even among his faithful readers, for his *Elmer Gantry*. (*Time* said Lewis had "made another large roundup of grunting, whining, roaring, mewing, driveling, snouting creatures—of fiction—which, like an infuriated swineherd, he can beat, goad, tweak, tail-twist, eye-jab, belly-thwack, spatter with sty-filth and consign to perdition.") For intellectuals, though, Lewis's real crime was that, unlike Dreiser, he didn't think the American system was rotten beyond redemption and corrupt at its core. Moreover, Lewis was said to be merely an acute observer and a clever recorder of manners; he lacked the "tragic sense" of doom that great writers have to have—and that Dreiser had so compellingly evoked in *An American Tragedy*.

Lewis got no great support from fellow writers. Although Edith Wharton sent him a generous telegram of congratulation from Paris, Lewis Mumford argued that Lewis's Nobel Prize was a "subtle disparagement" of America—he offered Robert Frost as a desirable alternative. Ernest Boyd accused Lewis of measuring literature merely "in terms of advertising and royalty checks." Even college students were getting into the act: Eugene Rostow, later a prominent member of Lyndon Johnson's administration, was then a student at Yale, where he won a literary prize for an essay that was critical of Lewis. Ernest Hemingway, Lewis's fellow Midwesterner, groused that it was all a "filthy business" and that the only merit of Lewis's victory was that the "Dreiser menace" was eliminated.

Dreiser himself feigned indifference to his loss, saying he could not imagine "the prize lessening or improving the mental standing of any serious writer." But one friend said that he was "almost suicidal," and another said Dreiser was convinced that Lewis had snagged the award through his "clever maneuvering." Lewis went out of his way to ease Dreiser's pain. In a letter to Dreiser dated November 25, 1930, shortly before he was to receive the award, and addressed "Dear Theodore," he enclosed the comments on Dreiser that he planned to make in his acceptance speech. The award had come to him in part, Lewis said in his letter, "because I am the most conspicuous of a generation of writers that followed in your path. . . . Circumstances, fortuitousness, and timing have you, like the parent of a famous child, standing in the wings while your progeny stands in the floodlight. I am merely the first in the family of American writers that has come of age in the eyes of the world—you are father to us all." As James F. Hutchisson and Stephen R. Pastore, who discovered this letter in 1997, note, this sounds almost as if Lewis is reaching out, "asking Dreiser to acknowledge him as literary son. The older man, however, continually refused to do so." Neither did he ever acknowledge Lewis's public praise for his pioneering role in American literature. He knew it was his last chance for the Nobel Prize, and he had lost it, he believed, to a lesser man.

Sinclair Lewis arrived home from Europe on March 4, 1931. Always a sought-after public speaker, in part because he was so unpredictable, his appearances following his return were livelier than ever. In Washington a scheduled talk at Constitution Hall had to be moved to a local high school when the Daughters of the American Revolution, who owned the hall, objected to his presence there. On March 19 he gave much the same talk to a large crowd at New York's Town Hall. His subject was

"American Literature Comes of Age," during the course of which, as usual, he praised the novels of Theodore Dreiser. After the lecture he went to a dinner for writers and journalists at the Metropolitan Club, where the guest of honor was the Russian novelist Boris Pilnyak.

Though most of the names are not familiar today, it was an illustrious group, including Heywood Broun, Irwin S. Cobb, Lawrence Stallings, Burton Rascoe, J. Donald Adams, and Arthur Brisbane. Theodore Dreiser, who had met Pilnyak in Russia, was of course invited. The dinner had been arranged by Ray Long, a journalist whose aide was Dreiser's former assistant, William Lengel. Long had hesitated before inviting Sinclair Lewis because Dreiser would be there, but it was impossible not to invite the winner of the Nobel Prize to a dinner for writers, and Lengel assured him there would be no trouble.

Dreiser was late—as was typical of him, he had absentmindedly gone to the wrong hotel and had to phone his wife at home to get the right address. Dinner was delayed for him; in the interim, the cocktail hour was extended and the hard-drinking writers imbibed even more than they ordinarily would. Lewis was not one to fall behind the crowd in such circumstances— Lengel observed him "eating little sausages and drinking, drinking, drinking."

Dreiser arrived at last. He walked up to Lewis and extended his hand, saying "Congratulations, Lewis." Lewis turned away from the outstretched hand with a sneer. J. Donald Adams said that during the meal that followed Lewis fondled a bottle by the neck and muttered how he'd like to break it over Dreiser's head. Nevertheless, during "the dinner everyone seemed happy," *The New York Times* reported two days later: "Wit, whimsy, and the more lowly wisecrack were passed about with the fowl and the dessert. Then, with the cigars there came the speeches. . . . The tall, lanky figure of the novelist unwound itself from the chair and rose slowly. Very calmly, and in a lack-adaisical fashion rather than challenging, he made the follow-ing address."

He was happy to welcome the Russian writer, Mr. Pilnyak, Lewis said, his bulging eyes a bright blue in his florid, ravaged face. "But I do not care to speak in the presence of a man who has stolen three thousand words from my wife's book, and before two sage critics who have lamented the action of the Nobel Prize committee in selecting me as America's representa-tive writer." He resumed his seat as the audience murmured uneasily. Dreiser reddened with obvious anger but said nothing. Neither did the two critics, presumably Heywood Broun and Arthur Brisbane, who had both strenuously objected to the selection of Lewis for the award. The humorist Irwin J. Cobb was summoned to speak next, and broke the tension with a few jokes. Dreiser then spoke, limiting his brief remarks to a defense of communism as he had seen it in Russia. Pilnyak, the Russian guest, avoided any reference to the Nobel award win-ner in his remarks, pointedly and with obvious deference refer-ring instead to "Père Dreiser."

As the meal was ending, Dreiser went over to Lewis. "Hello, how are ya?" he said, asking him to step outside with him to an adjoining anteroom. There were no witnesses to the first part of their conversation, which was later recounted by Dreiser to Lengel. "You made a statement about my taking stuff from your wife's book," Dreiser recalled saying to Lewis. "I know you're an ignoramus, but you're crazy. You don't know what you're talking about." Say it again or take it back, Dreiser demanded. Lewis said it again. "So I smacked him. And I asked him if he wanted to say it again. He said it again. So I smacked him again. And I said, 'Do you want to say it again?'"

At this point Lengel entered the room and heard Lewis say, "Theodore, you are a liar and a thief." Lengel grabbed Lewis, thinking to restrain him from attacking Dreiser, but Lewis was limp and unresisting. Lengel told Dreiser that he'd better leave. Lewis said again, "I still say you are a liar and a thief." "Do you want me to hit you again?" Dreiser demanded. "If you do, I'll turn the other cheek." Dreiser said, "Aw, Lewis, you shit!" Lengel was pushing the bigger man through the door when he turned and shouted, "I'll meet you any time, anywhere. This thing isn't settled." Lewis followed, muttering something. Dreiser said, "Lewis, why don't you peddle your papers somewhere else?"

"What happened . . . is still a matter of discussion," the *Times* report said. "One school held that both the charge and the answer were repeated for a third time, and that thereafter Mr. Dreiser backed away and began rolling up his sleeves. The other had it that some anonymous heroes stepped between and begged both to remember Mr. Long and the Metropolitan Club. At all events the two separated, both very angry, with Mr. Lewis's face about the same color as his hair." Afterward, questioned by the reporter for *The Times*, Lewis said, "Dreiser's a pretty big fellow, and must weigh pretty close to two hundred pounds. I'll bet he could have put up a good scrap if they'd let us go. Still, he's pretty old. He must be sixty. He was an established editor in New York when I was just a kid trying to get along." Dreiser, "difficult to find at all times, was eventually located [by the reporter] in his apartment at Fifty-seventh Street and Seventh Avenue. Music came through the open door, and laughter, but all he would say about the night's affair was: 'It was the proper retort to any insult.'" Later, he said that "rash and unwarranted insults were rewarded with two slaps upon the face."

Malcolm Cowley, in *Exile's Return*, his indispensable survey of Americans who went abroad and then came home, describes how frantic life was for writers in New York in 1930, as the Depression took hold. "There seemed to be more drinking than before . . . a different sort of drinking, with more desperation in the mood behind it." Psychiatrists' offices were overflowing with writers, all of whom knew each other—it looked to one like "a publisher's tea." The newspapers, always delighted to find writers behaving badly, were full of stories about authors killing themselves, destroying their marriages, and punching each other in "speakeasy brawls."

It's not surprising, then, that the fisticuffs between big Teddy Dreiser, the "heavyweight champ of American letters," and "Kid" Lewis gave the tabloids a field day. A fight promoter, Jimmy Johnston, wired the combatants, offering them a fifteen-rounder at Ebbets Field. Westbrook Pegler suggested that writers should have "ghost-fighters," just as some fighters had ghostwriters. Most of the public was rooting for Dreiser, or, more accurately, against Lewis—because, as the *Philadelphia Public Ledger* put it, he hadn't "improved his manners since the famous occasion in Stockholm, when he openly bewailed the intellectual and artistic shortcomings of his own country. . . ." Dreiser got telegrams saying, "Thank you for slapping Sinclair Lewis. You did just what many thousands of Americans would like to do. Thank you," and "Congratulations! You have stabbed the dirty dog!" One complained that he had not used his closed fist.

Dreiser could perhaps be excused for being startled and puzzled by Lewis's inconsistent behavior toward him, mixed as it was between frequently voiced admiration for his work and condemnation of him as a thief. But then, Lewis often puzzled even his admirers, and he was much too complex a character to be easily understood by either his readers or by newspaper reporters. Thomas Wolfe, who met him in London only a month before the fight with Dreiser, based the character of Lloyd McHarg in *You Can't Go Home Again* on Lewis; Wolfe's "physical portrait of Lewis is perfect and no less is the representation of his behavior," Schorer says. "His restlessness, his drinking, his compulsive informality, his generosity, his sweetness and his willfulness, his suffering, his dissatisfaction, his fits of exhaustion and sudden recovery, his imitations, his meaningless companionships—they are all here." Dorothy Thompson thought when she first met Lewis that he conveyed "a disturbing atmospheric tension such as that which precedes an electric storm" but that he was a "lonely, unhappy, helpless man! Somebody must love and take care of him!" Vincent Sheean offers a more flattering explanation for Lewis's behavior that night with Dreiser: "I knew Lewis extremely well for many years and never could see any evidence of contrivance or deliberation in his oddest behavior. On the contrary: his responses were so swift and imperative as to belong in the category of the half-conscious, the instinctive and the irresistible. If you poke a lion he will roar. . . . Red Lewis was a lion in his time—mangy and indeed half-broken from the start, but a lion just the same, pacing his narrow cage with irremediable fury and despair."

"The slap heard round the world" made the papers from Adelaide to London to Moscow, but there was no follow-up bout and the incident was soon forgotten. Dreiser, surly as ever, told a reporter a few months later that he saw no reason to be friendly with Lewis. Asked if he respected Lewis's work, Dreiser said that "*Arrowsmith* is a good story. . . . Paul de Kruif, who gave Lewis the material, first asked me to write the book, but I didn't have time." Lewis was astonished and angered by Dreiser's suggestion that *Arrowsmith*, the result of several years' worth of intense effort on his part, was no more than a Dreiser reject. But he continued to voice his admiration for Dreiser's work. In 1944 Lewis led a successful effort to get the old and ailing writer a special prize for distinguished achievement from the American Academy of Arts and Letters. On December 30, 1945, two days after Dreiser's death, he sent a condolence note to Helen Dreiser, his widow: "He was the standard by which we all could be judged. While the public only remembers our notorious disagreements, I knew his greatness and never failed to admire his innate talent. . . . He opened the door to this century and we all followed through it."

It has always been understood that Dreiser's lasting reputation would be based on *An American Tragedy*. Like all of his fiction, it was drawn from life—in this case, the 1906 trial transcripts and other materials relating to charges brought against a young man named Chester Gillette, whom Dreiser renamed Clyde Griffiths. Gillette was a poor relative of a factory owner in Cortland, New York. He had lured his pregnant lover onto a lake in the Adirondacks, intending to kill her. She died in the lake, though whether she died as a result of intention or accident was never made clear. Gillette's escape plan was ludicrously flawed; he was quickly caught, tried, convicted, and finally executed.

It was vital to Dreiser that Gillette's case was anything but unique—he had collected a dozen examples of similar crimes, all involving what Richard Lingeman calls "a kind of crime peculiar to American society, in which an ambitious young man who is involved with 'Miss Poor' falls in love with 'Miss Rich' and resorts to murder to eliminate the obstacle to his happiness." Alfred Kazin finds Dreiser often "silly" and "pedestrian," and laments his "proverbial lack of taste," but discounts these flaws as part of the "curiously unconscious masterliness" with which he "virtually devours a subject." The consequence is that *An American Tragedy* remains one of the few seven-hundred-page novels that will captivate undergraduates today.

By 1964, however, twenty years after Dreiser's death, both he and his great novel were nearly forgotten. Irving Howe, in his afterword for a new edition that year of *An American Tragedy*, thought that the old pioneer had "dropped out of the awareness of cultivated Americans." *An American Tragedy* appeared to have become the "colossal derelict on the ocean of literature" that a hostile early critic hoped it would be. Younger writers agreed with Dorothy Parker that Dreiser was a "dull, pompous, dated, and darned near ridiculous writer" whose only virtue was sincerity, which he shared with other worthies such as Zane Grey and Horatio Alger. His prose style had always been called "elephantine"; now Dreiser himself was being called a dinosaur.

The turnaround in Dreiser's literary reputation since 1964 has been dramatic, particularly when measured against that of Sinclair Lewis. Jonathan Yardley noted in 1985 how the centenary of Lewis's birth had stirred little interest outside Sauk Centre, a "sad commentary on how quickly, and how far, Lewis' reputation has declined since his death in 1951." This is understandable, Yardley says, for both Lewis and Dreiser were writing "about people, places and subjects that have now almost disappeared from American fiction. . . . about life in the world as Americans actually live it." Still, Yardley is "struck by how lively Lewis' prose remains and how penetrating his satire still seems . . . the energy of the novels is just about as impressive now as it was when they first came to the attention of a startled nation."

Lewis was indeed, as Yardley says, "a supremely perceptive student of American society who recorded what he saw with a sharp, telling pen." Why then has he faded, while the lumbering Dreiser continues to grow in stature? In large part it is because Lewis is simply too clear and efficient in saying what he wants to say and doesn't need others to explicate him. This explains why he was, for a long time, the first great writer that many high school students read on their own; no intervening priesthood of teachers or critics was needed to interpret his script. The novels do not lack for style or substance or ideas; indeed, these elements are what attract later observers as various as Tom Wolfe and Gore Vidal to them. But they do not reward the kinds of literary criticism that have dominated the scene since Lewis's death, or before it: the New Criticism that celebrated complexity of structure and images, for example, or Freudian criticism that requires complicated psyches to unravel.

Even more disabling for the many critics today who regard the United States as irredeemably racist, sexist, and imperialist, Lewis was, at heart, a sentimental idealist who believed he could help make things better. Though he mocked and criticized American life in a variety of ways, he did not hate or despise the country or its people. He thought of himself as a firebrand, but he was out to enlighten, not to destroy. Postmodernists who read (and teach) everything as a gloss on race, gender, and politics find Lewis irrelevant (or inimical) to their concerns.

Orphaned by the various critical schools, the novels of Sinclair Lewis are rarely taught, even in high school, where they would be accessible to most students. When casual or new readers do discover Lewis, usually by chance, they see that he still has an extraordinary magnetism—and that even now, a half-century after his death, his best novels are nearly as much fun to read as they ever were.

Dreiser was never fun, and his complex and messy novels cry out for critical paramedics to fix them. He also had a darkly pessimistic view of human nature, even as he turned to communism in his last years as a desperate means of compensating for it. But Sinclair Lewis, to his credit, recognized the worth of Dreiser's work, and brilliant critics like Ellen Moers, among many others, talk about it in useful ways. Dreiser consistently has far more entries in annual bibliographies of critical articles than Lewis does. It is worth noting that *Sixteen Modern American Authors*, a 1989 compendium of research done on important writers in the twentieth century, devotes a section to Dreiser while omitting Sinclair Lewis entirely. Virtually all of these articles are by teachers who, naturally enough, want to convey their ideas about Dreiser while using his novels in the classroom.

A related reason for the disappearance of Lewis surely is that

Dreiser has been much luckier in his biographers. Robert Elias, W. A. Swanberg, and Richard Lingeman have all written with insight and sympathy about a man who evokes wonder, sympathy, and scorn. Lewis, on the other hand, was given the undivided attention of one of America's most assiduous and reputable literary scholars, Mark Schorer. While that should have been a blessing, Schorer apparently came to dislike Lewis intensely as a man and as a writer (one of "our worst," he called Lewis) for reasons that are not entirely clear. In any event, Schorer's massive, essential, and destructive biography has shaped opinions of Lewis and his books for the worse since its publication in 1962. (Gore Vidal goes further, saying that though it would seem to be "impossible that a mere biographer could effectively eliminate a popular and famous novelist," Schorer, with "serene loathing" of Lewis, had done just that. When Vidal asked Schorer why he had devoted so much energy to a writer he despised, the answer was, "the money.")

Fortunately, a revised picture of Lewis is now available from Dreiser's biographer, Richard Lingeman. Written with sympathetic insight instead of disdain, Lingeman's *Sinclair Lewis: Rebel from Main Street* was published early in 2002; although it adds nothing to our understanding of the quarrel between the two writers beyond what Lingeman had already described in his earlier works about Dreiser, it should help Lewis toward the literary resurrection he deserves. At the least, Lewis should be placed side by side as a literary giant with Theodore Dreiser, the difficult man he admired so much, and from whom he got so little in return.

4

Not Always a "Pleasant Tussle"

THE DIFFICULT FRIENDSHIP OF EDMUND WILSON
AND VLADIMIR NABOKOV

One of Vladimir Nabokov's favorite stories in his later years concerned his arrival in New York on May 28, 1940, with his wife, Vera, and their six-year-old son, Dmitri. Customs inspections are not normally recalled by stateless immigrants at any time with fondness, but Nabokov—no doubt accustomed to brusque dealings in Europe—was pleasantly surprised by the patience and good humor of the "two large Customs men" and the "diminutive Negro porter" when he could not find the key for his large steamer trunk. A locksmith arrived shortly, after the Russian had "stood bantering" with the officials, and "opened the padlock with one blow of his iron bar." On the top level of the trunk lay two pairs of boxing gloves that Nabokov had used to teach Dmitri how to box. The Customs officials donned the gloves and started sparring energetically with each other, while a third official admired the small sample of the butterfly collection that Nabokov had managed to bring with him and even suggested a name for one species. When Nabokov asked his wife where she thought they might get a newspaper, one of the Customs men said "Oh, I'll get one for you," and rushed off to find them a *New York Times*. Safely out of Customs, upon arriving at a cousin's apartment in a taxi that reminded Nabokov of a shiny yellow scarab, he was dismayed to see that the bill was "nine, o, oh God, ninety, ninety dollars"—misreading the 90 cents on the meter—but resign-edly offered the cabbie a hundred-dollar bill in payment. Nabokov said later that "the simplest thing would have been to give us $10 change and call it a day," but the cabbie just laughed and said that if he had enough change for a hundred dollars, he "wouldn't be sitting here driving a car."

For the next twenty years, until he returned to Europe, Vladimir Nabokov would delight in the easy good humor and informality of Americans, even though he would be best remembered by most of them for his brilliant satire of their cul-ture in his quirky road-buddy novel, *Lolita*, concerning the adventures of the pedophilic Humbert Humbert and his nymphet, Dolores Haze. A man of immense charm, flexible and adaptive both by nature and by circumstance, Nabokov had himself been a rootless exile for most of his life. Born in 1899, the indulged scion of a wealthy St. Petersburg aristocrat, he and his family had been driven from their homeland after the Revo-lution with a fraction of their fortune—just enough to let the family settle in Berlin while he earned a degree in French and Russian at Cambridge. He rejoined the family in 1922, in time to suffer the shock of his father's accidental, and absurdly unjust, assassination at the hands of a fanatical Czarist who was aiming for a visiting Russian Communist. Nabokov continued to live in Berlin, eking out a living by tutoring wealthy Ger-mans in English and tennis while writing half a dozen novels in Russian. Moving to Paris in 1937 as the Nazis made Berlin intolerable for him and his Jewish wife, then escaping to Amer-ica barely ahead of the German occupation of France, he was a part of the hegira of European artists and intellectuals who would find refuge here from Hitler, including Thomas Mann, Bertolt Brecht, Marc Chagall, and Albert Einstein.

Unlike his famous compatriots, Nabokov arrived as a middle-aged nonentity, so far as Americans were concerned, with hardly more to his name than the hundred dollars he almost gave the cabbie. His brilliant early novels, especially *The Gift*, had so far been published only in Russian, and were known only to the expatriate Russian community in New York. Though he had already done groundbreaking scientific research into butterflies, lepidoptery being his passionate avocation, his true calling was literature. With no advantages other than mastery of what he called his three "maternal languages"—Russian, French, and English—Nabokov was compelled to cast around for college teaching jobs and reviewing stipends, neither easy to come by even for Americans at the tail end of the Great Depression.

Nabokov and his wife, admired then and for the rest of her long life for her beauty and intelligence, had arrived in New York at a time when almost all writers and intellectuals were temperamentally sympathetic to the social experiment known as the Soviet Union and anxious to meet Russians. Disinclined themselves to stay within the Russian expatriate community, the Nabokovs quickly became popular party guests. Edward Weeks, then editor of the *Atlantic Monthly*, would later recall in an interview how the slender, athletic Russian would fill a room with his presence: "He would come in in a shabby tweed coat, trousers bulging at the knee, but be quite the most distinguished man in the room, with his perfectly beautiful hazel eyes, his fine brown hair, the *élan,* the spark. . . . He just had to walk into the room and the girls looked around—the clothes didn't make any difference. He had a way of carrying himself, a *joie* in his eyes, a zest."

Of the many writers, teachers, and critics whom Nabokov would meet in New York, the dominant figure was the short, pudgy, and combative Edmund Wilson. Now forty-five and at the midpoint of his long career, Wilson had been the book reviewer for *The New Republic*, as he later would be for *The New Yorker*, but he was regarded as a literary journalist rather than merely a book reviewer, as a "man of letters" in the honored tradition of Samuel Johnson and Matthew Arnold. Wilson always tried to keep his distance from the academy that supported most of his contemporaries such as Lionel Trilling and Mark Van Doren—he hated teaching and was not good at it—but he had already written two books that would become classroom staples in literature and history. *Axel's Castle*, published in 1931, was a brilliant and defining introduction to James Joyce, Proust, and T. S. Eliot as Modernists—or Symbolists, the word he chose because "Modernism" had not yet been coined; and *To the Finland Station* (1940) explained Lenin's contribution to the Russian Revolution, perhaps the most important political event of the century. Even Wilson's antagonists (such as Kenneth Burke, who twitted Wilson for just "giving you the news about books") recognized his great and generally good influence.

Two things particularly distinguished Wilson's writing about literature. The first was that he was interested in almost everything; the second was that what he wrote was accessible to every reader, from Oxford don to subway straphanger. Simply scanning the titles of his collection of essays and reviews from the 1920s and 1930s, *The Shores of Light*, reveals an unparalleled breadth of interests and an engagement with the issues of his time and with those of the past: "Sophocles, Babbitt and Freud," "Gertrude Stein Old and Young," "Woodrow Wilson at Princeton," "Pope and Tennyson," "Houdini," and even a two-part essay on "Burlesque Shows" that includes the enticing "Peaches—A Humdinger." Pick a paragraph at random from a Wilson essay and you will see that he never wrote a dull sentence:

Most Americans of the type of [John] Dos Passos and [T. S.] Eliot—that is, sensitive and widely read literary people—have [an] agreeable fantasy in which they can allow their minds to take refuge from the perplexities and oppressions about them. In the case of H. L. Mencken, it is a sort of German university town, where people drink a great deal of beer and devour a great many books, and where they respect the local nobility—if only the Germany of the Empire had not been destroyed by the war.

On a far less familiar figure than Mencken, the long-forgotten French poet Corbière, he is no less interesting:

> He made a pose of his unsociability and of what he considered his physical ugliness, at the same time that he undoubtedly suffered over them. Melancholy, with a feverishly active mind, full of groanings and vulgar jokes, he used to amuse himself by going about in convict's clothes and by firing guns and revolvers out the window in protest against the singing of the village choir; and on one occasion, on a visit to Rome, he appeared in the streets in evening dress, with a mitre on his head and two eyes painted on his forehead, leading a pig decorated with ribbons.

It was Wilson's ability to make a story out of a review, to provide a narrative even within a paragraph, that gave his writing such vitality—that, and his conviction that writers had to be understood in terms of their times and of their personal lives, as well as by what they wrote. He recognized the dangerous arrogance that reviewers and critics could be guilty of—making and breaking reputations—and reminded his readers (and perhaps himself) of this danger:

> The reviewer, like other kinds of writers, has his ego; and, since he is continually occupied with other people's books, it is somewhat peculiarly difficult for this ego to assert itself. One of the best ways in which a reviewer can give himself a vicarious sense of creation is by encouraging

and presenting new writers who have previously been unknown, but when a writer is already known, the reviewer may procure the sensation of power by making the gesture of putting him down. This psychology must always be reckoned with. In the literary world in the last few years, one has seen a number of writers cried up at the time when they were still obscure, by the more discerning critics, and then afterwards disparaged by them.

An example of Wilson's ability to define and encourage new writers is seen in his early comments on Ernest Hemingway's 1926 novel, *The Sun Also Rises*; other reviewers had dismissed Hemingway's stories and this novel as merely "sordid little catastrophes," and even today many students often react negatively to the "lost generation" of drunks and louts that they feel Hemingway imposes on them. Wilson agrees that the world described in the novel is cruel and treacherous, but adds,

> The whole interest of *The Sun Also Rises* lies in the attempts of the hero and the heroine to disengage themselves from this world, or rather to arrive at some method of living in it in such a way as to satisfy some code of their own. The real story is that of their attempts to do this— attempts by which, in such a world, they are always bound to lose out in everything except honor.

Throughout his career Wilson would encourage other writers—most famously, his Princeton classmate F. Scott Fitzgerald and Hemingway, but scores of lesser-known authors as well. The notion that "recognition of his contemporaries was not Wilson's strong suit," as an early Nabokov biographer claimed, could not be more wrong, at least in his early and mid-career years. But it is true that he rather deliberately cultivated a reputation as a grouch. He had never been physically impressive; at thirty he was described by a friend as "a short [five feet six inches], sandy-haired, youngish man . . . already inclining to stoutness and baldness, with pale, blinking eyes and a high, strained-tenor voice, his profile as regular as a plump Roman emperor's but his expression like an absent-minded cantankerous professor's." By 1940, married to the beautiful and difficult young journalist Mary McCarthy, who was then only twenty-eight, he had thickened into middle-aged rotundity. Their marriage was a stormy one, including flagrant infidelity on her part and occasional physical violence on his, according to McCarthy (denied by him), and she got her revenge years later, in 1952, skewering Wilson as the Irish intellectual journalist Henry Mulcahy in *The Groves of Academe*. There was enough of Wilson in McCarthy's caricature for his friends and enemies to recognize him—a "fat, freckled fellow" with a pear-shaped body and slouching posture, a "soft-bellied, lisping man with a tense, mushroom-white face, rimless bifocals, and graying thin red hair," addicted to "candy bars, frosted cupcakes, nuts and pickles, second helpings of mashed potatoes . . . defiantly conscious of a porous complexion, bad teeth, and occasional morning halitosis."

No man is a hero to his valet—or to his ex-spouse. Though the real Wilson could be disagreeable or forbidding, as Alfred Kazin recalled—"With his round bald head and that hoarse, heavily breathing voice coming out of the red face of an overfed fox-hunting squire, Wilson looked apoplectic, stiff, out of breath"—he was nonetheless impressive for his "great bald dome, the lack of small talk, the grumpy concentration on every topic he came to." Out of place among the bohemians who flocked to Cape Cod, his home, Wilson invariably wore formal attire in public, including a hat, white shirt, and necktie even on the beach. At home, in the comfort of his old converted farmhouse, he reminded one visitor of an idle lounger in a Russian novel, with his "light gray pajamas and a salmon bathrobe," buried deep within his library, like the minotaur in his cave, Mary McCarthy said. Many people who never met Wilson would know him only through the "Edmund Wilson regrets" printed card that he devised to fend off a score of bothersome demands on his time, including publicity blurbs, responses to questionnaires, personal photographs, or "opinions on literature or other subjects."

Often—though not always—this grumpiness was merely for show, and even the card is amusing in its hyperbole. Wilson was a talented amateur magician and puppeteer who enjoyed entertaining his own children and others' with magic and Punch and Judy shows—he joked that he identified with Punch and his "big belly, a stick, a temperament of extreme truculence and a tendency to unscrupulous philandering." He loved practical jokes, once duping his third wife with a telegram supposedly from her son announcing that he had just gotten engaged to marry a "very rich, old and frog-like friend of the family." He almost landed in jail for painting a beard on his passport photo. For all his apparent gruffness, as his biographer Jeffrey Meyers says, Wilson "loved tricks, jokes, satires, backward rhymes (livid-devil), nonsense verse, limericks, anagrams, palindromes, clerihews and cartoons: the verbal toy as an embellishment of life."

He could be tenderhearted as well. His old house in Wellfleet, on Cape Cod, was frequently overrun by rodents toward which he showed uncommon solicitude, once rescuing a mouse, swimming for its life in the toilet, by daintily picking it up by the tail and carrying it outside. When his maid screamed about rats in the kitchen, Wilson reluctantly consented to poison them but refused to kill the babies. In a Christmas-card poem, he sympathizes with the rats even as he ruefully surveys his books "with glued backs eaten off with their titles/By rats when keen hunger was eating their vitals."

More than any other American writer, Wilson was fascinated by foreign languages and literatures. "I have always been greedy for words," he once said. "I always find a pleasure almost sensual in attacking a new language, especially if it has a strange alphabet whose barrier I can penetrate." For Americans who may have shared his interest in foreign writers but lacked his knowledge of other tongues, Wilson served as a sensitive guide, as even this casual remark in a letter to Nabokov concerning Flaubert will indicate. He had been reading and comparing passages from early and later revisions of *Madame Bovary*, Wilson said, and had been struck by the way in which Flaubert "at a given point turned on the music and magic" and made a mundane text great. Wilson could "turn on the music and magic" in his own writing about many subjects, but never more effectively than when he talked about the Russians. Alexander Pushkin, the nineteenth-century Romantic poet, had long been one of Wilson's favorites, and as a consequence of his visit to the Soviet Union he had acquired enough Russian to comment in 1938, two years before meeting Nabokov, on the difficulties involved in translating Pushkin's epic narrative poem *Eugene Onegin*. The poem was

> difficult for the same reason that Dante is difficult: because it says so much in so few words, so clearly and yet so concisely, and the words themselves and their place in the line have become so much more important than in the case of more facile or rhetorical writers. . . . Furthermore, the Russian language, which is more highly inflected and able to dispense with pronouns and prepositions in many cases where we have to use them and which does without the article altogether . . . renders the problem of translating him closer to translating a highly articulated Latin

poet like Horace than any modern poet we know. . . . It would require a translator himself a poet of the first order to reproduce Pushkin's peculiar combination of intensity, compression and perfect ease. . . .

Eugene Onegin was a poem that, like Pushkin's life itself, centered around a deadly duel between two former friends. The friendship that began in 1940 between Edmund Wilson, influential critic and enthusiast for all things Russian, and Vladimir Nabokov, aspiring but penniless immigrant, would grow out of the American's desire to help the Russian gain a foothold in the New World. It would end three decades later when the Russian, now more famous as the author of *Lolita* than Wilson himself, saw his former mentor attack Nabokov's own translation of *Eugene Onegin* as inept.

But for now, at least, the two men would form a close bond. In part, the bond was intellectual. Each recognized the extraordinary abilities of the other and both delighted in their mutual approbation. Jeffrey Meyers notes that Wilson knew almost everybody in the international world of letters, including Ernest Hemingway, F. Scott Fitzgerald, and William Faulkner in the United States, and asserts that only four of the distinguished people Wilson knew over the course of his lifetime "matched his intellect, achievement, and international stature." These were W. H. Auden, Isaiah Berlin, André Malraux, and Vladimir Nabokov.

To a considerable degree their friendship was the attraction of opposites. Harry Levin, a professor of English at Harvard, and his Russian-born wife, Elena, often entertained the Wilsons and the Nabokovs at their home in Cambridge, and Elena later remembered how different Wilson and Nabokov were. Nabokov was lean then, taut and intense; Wilson chubby, with a high-pitched voice. "Volodya [was] subtle, reclusive, familial; Edmund blunt, commonsensical"—but prone to collapsing "after three drinks 'like a bag of potatoes,' in Volodya's words." Others would note their similarities, especially in their assertive strides—Wilson walking "briskly through New York crowds thoroughly wrapped in his own thoughts and looking straight ahead," Nabokov "famous for his almost ethereal flying gait," his eyes fixed on some distant point.

The emotional aspect of their friendship, amounting even to joy, was also significant for Mary McCarthy: The two men "had an absolute ball together. Edmund was always in a state of *joy* when Vladimir appeared; he *loved* him." Even Wilson's young son, Reuel, joined in the fun, mistaking Nabokov's Russian nickname "Volodya" as "gardenia," as a consequence of which Wilson affectionately proclaimed Nabokov "the gardenia in the buttonhole of Russian literature." But fond as Wilson may have been of the Russian, Nabokov wrote to a mutual friend that the relationship lacked the kind of emotional "lyrical plaint" found in Russian friendships, as was generally the case among Anglo-Saxons, he had found: "I love a violin in personal relationships, but in this case there is no way one can let out a heartfelt sigh or casually unburden a soft fresh bit of oneself. Still, there's a good deal else to make up for it."

As it happened, Wilson and Nabokov met only infrequently over the years, both being busy with their work and their lives apart from each other. Their friendship and their conversation would be mainly epistolary, perhaps a personal loss for them but a gain for the reader who never knew them. The immediacy, charm, and vigor of their correspondence, collected and published by Simon Karlinsky in 1972, survive the destruction of the troubled friendship even as their letters explain it.

The most intense period of their correspondence was from 1940 through 1952, though the exchanges would continue into the sixties. Soon addressing each other as "Bunny"—Wilson's implausible childhood nickname—and "Volodya," they wrote about many things common to most of us: about money worries, about their children, about their health, and other mundanities. But mostly they wrote about literature, language, and politics, Wilson's three obsessions, of which only the first two were shared by Nabokov. And they wrote, rather reluctantly on Wilson's part and teasingly on Nabokov's, about each other's works.

Wilson's perspective on literature was much wider and more generous than that of Nabokov, who, like Ernest Hemingway, saw most other writers as competitors. They agreed in their enthusiasm for a few writers and works, such as Pushkin and Laurence Sterne's *Tristram Shandy*, and they shared a few mutual distastes, such as *Tom Jones*, whose author, Henry Fielding, was to Wilson tediously full of the "solid English qualities in their more uninteresting form: commonsense, good humor, heartiness and honest manliness." And eventually Wilson would persuade Nabokov to share something of his enthusiasm for Charles Dickens ("I am extraordinarily good on Dickens in *The Wound and the Bow*—I think you ought to read my essay"). But even when Nabokov agrees that *Bleak House* was indeed worth his time and assigns it to his class at Cornell, the essential difference in perspective between the two men is clear: Nabokov drops "all sociological and historical implications" in favor of tracking "fascinating thematic lines (the 'fog theme,' the 'bird theme,' etc.) and the three main props of the structure—the crime-mystery theme (the weakest), the child-misery theme and the lawsuit-chancery theme (the best). I think I had more fun than my class."

Consistently more interested than Nabokov in exactly those elements of literature—its "sociological and historical" as well as psychological implications—Wilson presses Nabokov to share his enthusiasm for Henry James, William Faulkner, and André Malraux, among others, all of whom Nabokov scorns. On James, Nabokov writes, "I have read (or rather re-read) *What Maisie Knew*. It is terrible. Perhaps there is some other

Henry James and I am continuously hitting upon the wrong one?" Later, he has just read a collection of The Master's short stories—"miserable stuff, a complete fake. . . ." Somebody "ought to debunk that pale porpoise and his plush vulgarities. . . ." As for William Faulkner, much praised for his insights into the South at the time and widely regarded in Europe today as America's greatest writer, Nabokov says, "It is incredible that you should take him so seriously . . . as to condone his artistic mediocrity." *Light in August*, which Wilson had recommended highly, was "one of the tritest and most tedious examples of a trite and tedious genre," full of "white trash [and] velvety Negroes," all of which "might be necessary in a social sense but it is not literature . . . Maybe you are pulling my leg when you advise me to read him, or impotent Henry James, or the Rev. [T. S.] Eliot."

But it is Wilson's enthusiasm for André Malraux, whose *Man's Fate* Wilson had praised upon its publication in 1933, that most excited Nabokov's scorn. Malraux, a hero of the French Resistance during World War II, had written a number of novels whose protagonists were the forebears of Jean-Paul Sartre's existentially engaged men, aware of the precarious nature of existence but willing to challenge and meet their fates. *Man's Fate*, which dramatized the battle between the heroic Communists and Chiang Kai-shek's corrupt Nationalists for control of China in the 1930s, particularly outraged Nabokov as tendentious propaganda: "I am at a loss to understand your liking Malraux's books (or are you just kidding me? or is literary taste so subjective a matter that two persons of discrimination can be at odds in such a simple case as this?)"

Wilson's enthusiasm for social justice had led him, like many American writers, to regard the Russian Revolution of 1917 much as Wordsworth and his fellow Romantics had the French Revolution of 1789: "Bliss was it in that dawn to be alive." The equivalent Terror that resulted in Russia under Stalin, and the transparently cynical nonaggression pact between Hitler and Stalin in 1939, would eventually disgust and repel most of the Soviet Union's American sympathizers, including Wilson— who was never as starry-eyed as other writers, most notably John Dos Passos, Malcolm Cowley, and Lillian Hellman, were about the glories of the Communist state. But Wilson retained much of his enthusiasm for Lenin, in large part because Lenin seemed to be a humane and civilized man who loved literature. In his 1938 book, *The Triple Thinkers*, Wilson noted that Lenin had been "fond of fiction, poetry and the theater, and by no means doctrinaire in his tastes," and that he had "tremendous admiration for Tolstoy's genius." Wilson allowed these flattering remarks to stay in his 1948 reissue of *The Triple Thinkers*, even as the regime that Lenin had fathered was reaching its most atrocious extremes of repression under Stalin.

Nabokov, whose father had been murdered and whose home and nationality had been lost to him more or less through Lenin, was remarkably temperate in his letters to Wilson on Russian politics and history. "Your concept of pre-Soviet Russia, of her history and social development[,] came to you through a pro-Soviet prism," he wrote, explaining that there was much greater intellectual and artistic freedom under the Czars "despite the inept and barbarous character of their rule" than in the Soviet system that replaced them. As for Lenin's literary acumen, which presumably makes him a more admirable man in Wilson's eyes, his remarks on Tolstoy were simply "childish." Could Wilson "really believe," Nabokov asked plaintively, "that in the first few years of the Soviet regime it was laying (with blood-stained hands) the (blood-soaked papier-mâché) foundation for a new humanity?"

Nabokov himself tackled the subject of totalitarianism in his 1947 novel, *Bend Sinister*, which "rather disappointed" Wilson: "You aren't good at this kind of subject, which involves questions of politics and social change, because you are totally uninterested in these matters and have never taken the trouble to understand them." Nabokov replied—one can almost hear him sighing—"In historical and political matters you are partisan of a certain interpretation which you regard as absolute. This means that we will have many a pleasant tussle and that neither will ever yield a *thumb* (inch) of *terrain* (ground)."

Didactic by nature, unequaled as an instructor in his writing, Edmund Wilson took on temporary university teaching assignments only when he was desperate for money and earned a continuing reputation as a tedious bore who read his lectures, head buried in his text, indifferent to his audience of students. Vladimir Nabokov, hostile to the very idea of instruction in literature and convinced that teaching was generally a waste of time for himself and for his students, was a wonderful teacher whose course in European authors at Cornell would achieve the status of legend. In his early years of teaching elementary Russian at Wellesley, during the war, he was regarded as a romantic European intellectual, gaunt, cerebral, trench-coated, but with a winsome, joking manner. By the time he was hired to teach Russian at Cornell in 1948, he had become as heavy as Wilson as a result of giving up smoking, and his weight, combined with his absolute certainty and his jocular manner, gave him a commanding classroom presence. In 1950 he reluctantly accepted an assignment to teach the European Fiction class, grudging the time that it would take from his own writing, and turned it within two years into one of the university's most popular courses. The students dubbed the course "Dirty Lit" because of *Anna Karenina* and *Madame Bovary*; the syllabus eventually included Dickens, Kafka, and James Joyce—the latter one of the few writers Nabokov ever acknowledged as a master.

Every lecture was a performance, with even the apparently parenthetical remarks carefully scripted, right down to reminders in his notes to "look at the clock." The class—the audience—was apprised of its role and its duties at the first meeting with "affable severity": "The seats are numbered. I would like you to choose your seat and stick to it. This is because I would like to link up your faces with your names. All satisfied with their seats? Okay. No talking, no smoking, no knitting, no newspaper reading, no sleeping, and for God's sake take notes." As he did in his letters to Wilson, he dismissed all those—students and colleagues alike—who depended on approaching literature in terms of " 'trends,' and 'schools,' and 'myths,' and 'symbols,' and 'social comment,' and something unspeakably spooky called 'climate of thought.' " He said that the writer "may be considered as a storyteller, as a teacher, as an enchanter. A major writer combines" all three, "but it is the enchanter in him that predominates and makes him a major writer." He insisted that all great novels were "great fairy tales" and that the primary obligation of students was to read closely and to remember—to "fondle"—every word, every detail, of everything they read. Consider, for example, a trivial passage from Dickens in which a messenger who, upon being paid, "receives his twopence with anything but transport, tosses the money into the air, catches it over-handed, and retires." The essence of the enchantment that makes Dickens eternal is in "this gesture, this one gesture, with its epithet 'over-handed'—a trifle—but the man is alive forever in a good reader's mind."

Equally vivid in the memories of many students were Nabokov's enthusiastic readings of dramatic passages from the texts he was teaching, and even pantomimes of significant moments in the lives of their creators. One student recalled how Nabokov would relive the agonies of Gogol at his death: "How the hack doctors alternately bled him and purged him and plunged him into icy baths . . . Gogol so frail that his spine could be felt through his stomach, the six white bloodletting leeches clinging to his nose . . . Sinking behind the lectern . . . Nabokov for several moments *was* Gogol, shuddering and shivering, his hands held down by a husky attendant. . . . Then, after a pause, Nabokov would say, dispassionately . . . 'Although the scene is unpleasant and has a human appeal which I deplore, it is necessary to dwell upon it a little longer in order to bring out the curiously physical side of Gogol's genius.' "

In his first years of teaching, at Wellesley, Nabokov, less sure of himself, had ingratiated himself with his students. They remembered him as having awakened "in all of us the wonderful sensual possibilities of poetry and literature," as being "a marvelous man. Kind, thoughtful, gentle, . . . charming . . . a perfect gentleman. He was what the word 'gentleman' meant." After *Lolita*, with the advantage of hindsight, another woman recalled Nabokov as having an erotic "effect like adrenaline . . . How much one *wanted* him!" By the time he was teaching at Cornell, however, despite the lively Dirty Lit class, Nabokov was growing more distant from all but the very best students and increasingly frustrated at the demands on his time when he should have been working on his own writing. He was "sick of teaching, sick of teaching, sick of teaching," he complained in a letter to Wilson in early 1952. His only hope for escape from the drudgery of grading papers and preparing lectures lay in the long novel that he was currently researching. He intended to call it *Lolita*.

In June 1948, Wilson had sent Nabokov a work uncovered by the English sex researcher Havelock Ellis that Wilson described as a "Russian sex masterpiece." Written in French by an anonymous Ukrainian, it describes a sexual predator's guilty but titillating sexual adventures with a series of young girls, all of them sexually precocious and enticingly cooperative. Nabokov later noted that the story made our present-day "innocence" seem "almost monstrous." Four years later, Nabokov was immersed in newspaper and magazine accounts of sex crimes in America, including one involving a middle-aged man who kidnapped a fifteen-year-old girl from New Jersey and kept her for nearly two years as his "cross-country slave," until she was found in a Southern California motel. As his biographer Brian Boyd summarizes Nabokov's meticulous research, he "consulted a history of the Colt revolver, gun catalogues, an article on barbiturates, a book on Italian comedy. He took song titles from jukeboxes, and phrases from teen magazines, women's magazines, home decorating guides, billboards, motel guest notices, [and] Girl Scout manuals," and he eavesdropped on teen talk: " 'She's quite a kid' . . . 'It's a riot' . . . 'I have *zillions* of them' . . . 'She was loads of fun.' " Driving across the country on summer vacations, he collected butterflies, anecdotes, and motel names—Wonderland Motor Courts, Maple Shade Cottage, Bright Angel Lodge—that would surface later in *Lolita*. And he read widely in the professional journals, taking careful notes on index cards, on such subjects as "Attitudes and Interests of Premenarchal and Postmenarchal Girls" and "Sexual Maturation and the Physical Growth of Girls Age Six to Nineteen."

The novel that would result from Nabokov's research continues today to shock and repel, as well as to fascinate, readers who have had half a century to get used to more graphic depictions of sex in all its various forms. Not surprisingly, *Lolita* had trouble finding an American publisher; its publication in Paris in 1955 under the Olympia Press imprint of the notorious Maurice Girodias—the self-proclaimed "pornologist"—only confirmed American impressions that it was just another dirty book. But by the time it finally was released here by G. P. Putnam, at least some members of the literary establishment had pronounced *Lolita* a work of genius, confirming Nabokov's assertion that it was both serious and comic.

Nabokov always said that he was indifferent to the opinions of critics, even Edmund Wilson's, but he had written to his friend soliciting his reaction in 1954. Although he could see how his story might "strike readers as pornographic," Nabokov considered "this novel to be my best thing in English and though the theme and situation are decidedly sensuous, it is pure and its fun riotous. I would love you to glance at it some time." Elsewhere, he said he meant the book as a tragedy, a love story—Humbert Humbert realizes too late that he has loved Lolita from the beginning, not simply lusted after her as a pedophile, but by the end of their affair she is a slattern without beauty or charm: "The tragedy of the book is that having started the affair from purely selfish motives, he falls in love with her when she is beyond loving."

Edmund Wilson had had his own brush with the law some years earlier when one of his rare excursions into fiction, *Memoirs of Hecate County*, was judged obscene and ultimately pulled from publication. Nabokov teased him about the cold-blooded and clinical descriptions of sex that had gotten Wilson into trouble; they struck the Russian as "remarkably chaste," inasmuch as the "copulation-mates" of the story's randy protagonist mount such "formidable defenses" that he as a reader can get "no kick from the hero's love-making. I should have as soon tried to open a sardine can with my penis." Given their reputations as ladies' men, as well as Wilson's own interests in pornography, Nabokov could be excused for having thought his daring work would be warmly received by his old friend. But Wilson told Nabokov that he "like[d] it less than anything else of yours that I have read." It was simply "nasty." "Nasty subjects may make fine books; but I don't feel you have got away with this. It isn't merely that the characters and the situation are repulsive in themselves, but that, presented on this scale, they seem quite unreal." He found the "various goings-on and the climax at the end become too absurd to be horrible or tragic, yet remain too unpleasant to be funny."

According to one account, Wilson at some point "told

Nabokov that he understood what his purpose had been: to write a modern *Fanny Hill* that would enjoy runaway sales because of its sexual theme." The novel is no *Fanny Hill*—even those who detest it usually admit that its satire, at least, is worthy of Swift or Molière—but there is no question that *Lolita* was a big success, even a blockbuster, for its time. First earnings were $250,000, plus $150,000 for movie rights, and the author received $40,000 to write the screenplay (none of which was used) for the 1962 Stanley Kubrick movie starring James Mason, Peter Sellers, and Sue Lyon. More than 300,000 copies had been sold by 1959 (the number would reach fourteen million by the mid-eighties.)

Some of Nabokov's admirers have argued that Wilson was jealous of his friend's financial success and sought to punish him for it by denying the novel's virtues: "It seems quite likely," writes one, "that an ulcerous trace of Wilson's spite toward Nabokov became noticeable by the mid-forties, worsened over the years, and turned especially acute after *Lolita* . . . because he thought that Nabokov had succeeded commercially where he [himself] had failed." But this kind of pettiness was not among Wilson's flaws; he was, the English critic V. S. Pritchett said, "the least envious, the most generous of men." The author of a recent biography of Vera Nabokov, Stacy Schiff, suggests that Wilson's enthusiasm for Boris Pasternak's *Dr. Zhivago* was a more likely cause of the growing distance between the two men. Nabokov regarded his countryman's celebrated novel as "a sorry thing, clumsy and melodramatic," and was even driven to complain that the wait-list at the local Ithaca library was longer for Pasternak's book than it was for *Lolita*. Wilson mischievously sent Nabokov a rubber-band-powered butterfly, with opposing wings labeled "Lolita" and "Zhivago," but he was not joking when he praised *Dr. Zhivago* in *The New Yorker* as "one of the great events in man's literary and social history"—which

Schiff sees as an example of "how to unravel a friendship in twenty words or less."

During the decade of the fifties, Edmund Wilson moved from one literary triumph to another. His groundbreaking study *The Scrolls from the Dead Sea* in 1955 was followed by the splendid collection of essays, *A Piece of My Mind: Reflections at Sixty* in 1956 (which caused the present writer, then a young soldier in Korea, to become an English major). His sympathies for the Indians of New York State who had been displaced and abused by officials who wanted their land for reservoirs for New York City resulted in 1960 in *Apologies to the Iroquois*. He was involved for several years preparing his pioneering study of Civil War literature, *Patriotic Gore*, published in 1962. It was an astounding series of works, hardly matched in its scope and achievement in American literary history.

Unfortunately, Wilson had neglected to file any federal income tax returns for a decade, from 1946 through 1955—out of sloth, indifference, or principle, or a combination of all of these. In his 1963 tract, *The Cold War and the Income Tax*, Meyers explains, he "cleverly transformed a flagrant case of tax evasion into an effective political protest," but the fines, penalties, and payments due to the IRS kept him poor—relative to his extraordinary status and achievement in the world of letters—almost to the end of his life. His old friend, Harry Levin, had secured a place for Wilson at Harvard for the 1959–1960 academic year, but Wilson still hated teaching and admitted that he was a "downright failure" at it, and it was obvious to at least one of his students that the only reason he was there was "to earn money to pay off the IRS."

In the meantime, Vladimir Nabokov in 1960 was a rich man, able at last to give up the teaching that he liked as little as Wilson (but did so much better) and retire in style to Montreux, on

Lake Geneva in Switzerland. If there is any justice in the charge that Wilson was jealous of Nabokov's financial success, it probably derives more from his frustration with the IRS than from envy of Nabokov's windfall; except as a necessity, Wilson was virtually indifferent to money. He did, however, care immensely about words and how they were used, and a few years later he thought his old friend had badly misrepresented the writer often referred to as the Russian Shakespeare, Alexander Pushkin. He said so, in his usual direct manner, in a long essay-review of Nabokov's translation of *Eugene Onegin* in the July 15, 1965, issue of *The New York Review of Books*.

Nabokov had always considered himself as an artist first, rather than a scholar or a critic. But he was a meticulous observer, researcher, and recorder of detail, as he had shown in his butterfly research as well as in his own novels and in his teaching. There could be no better response to the charge that he was a frivolous esthete and quasi-pornographer than the years he devoted to seeing that Pushkin's impetuous Romantic hero, inspired by Byron's *Don Juan*, was brought to an English-speaking body of readers. Wilson's own recognition of how difficult it was to translate Russian adequately into English, as well as his own labors in translation, should presumably have elicited a sympathetic response to Nabokov's excited news in early 1958: "I have just completely completed my *Eugene Onegin*: 2500 pages of commentaries, and a literal translation of the text."

That it did not, then or later, was owing in part to Wilson's uneasiness with Nabokov's method of translation. Surprisingly, the man most often compared to James Joyce as a magician with language—or, in his own words, an enchanter—had completely subsumed his own gift in the service of another writer's work: "I have sacrificed to completeness of meaning," Nabokov wrote in his introduction, "every formal element including the iambic rhythm, wherever its retention hindered fidelity. To my ideal of literalism I sacrificed everything (elegance, euphony, good taste, modern usage, and even grammar) that the dainty mimic prizes higher than truth. Pushkin has likened translators to horses changed at the posthouses of civilization. The greatest reward I can think of is that students may use my work as a pony." As for his detailed notes—stretching over three volumes, far out-weighing the narrative poem itself, which is the length of a novella—Nabokov said the information and interpretation he provided was essential.

To prove his point, Nabokov offered these versions of a stanza from the poem, concerning the illness of the hero's uncle and his satiric reaction to it.

First is the "lexical" example, which simply represents the words in their Russian order and could be done by "a machine" (today, a computer) and "an intelligent bilingualist":

> *My uncle [is] of most honest rules [:]*
> *when not in jest [he] has been taken ill,*
> *he to respect him has forced [one],*
> *and better invent could not.*

Nabokov offers this possible paraphrase:

> *My uncle, in the best tradition,*
> *By falling dangerously sick*
> *Won universal recognition*
> *And could devise no better trick.*

Here is an alternative competing translation by Babette Deutsch:

> *My Uncle always was respected;*
> *But his grave illness, I confess,*
> *Is more than could have been expected:*
> *A stroke of genius, nothing less:*

And here is Nabokov's way, the literal translation that he feels is essential:

> *My uncle has most honest principles:*
> *when he was taken gravely ill,*
> *he forced one to respect him*
> *and nothing better could invent.*

None of these translations seems particularly exciting, but Nabokov's note at least explains what the original intent was: Pushkin alludes here to a line from a Russian fable, "The Ass and the Boor," a satire on foolish literalism: "The donkey had most honest principles. . . ." Commanded to "patrol the vegetable garden, he did not touch a cabbage leaf; indeed he galloped about so vigilantly that he ruined the whole place, for which he was cudgeled by its owner: asininity should not accept grave tasks, but he errs, too, who gives an ass a watchman's job." This much is useful. The nice little Aesopian moral at the end lets us see how the original passage is indeed cleverly satirical. But Nabokov's note is three times as long as this excerpt from it and shifts the reader's attention away from his translation to his own cleverness in finding and explicating the solution he has found.

Such at least seems to have been the thinking behind Wilson's review of Nabokov's work as "something of a disappointment." Although Wilson was, he said, "a personal friend of Mr. Nabokov—for whom he feels a warm affection sometimes chilled by exasperation," he did "not propose to mask" his problems with the work under review. The problems had to do with Nabokov's theory and practice of translation, his overbearing and oppressive editorial scholarship, and his misreading of human motives and actions.

Concerning the first point, Wilson had long argued with Nabokov over the Russian's insistence that he had developed a system of metrics that would allow him to represent Russian poetry in an equivalent English form. Wilson correctly said this was impossible, a judgment confirmed by several "Slavists" or Russian-language experts who were even harder than Wilson on Nabokov's translation. As for Nabokov's odd scrounging for archaic English words that he thought would approximate Pushkin's, the result for Wilson was disastrous. Nabokov's "infelicities" included *"rememorating, producement, curvate, habitude, rummers, familistic, gloam, dit, shippon,* and *scrab*. All these can be found in the *OED* [*Oxford English Dictionary*], but they are all entirely dictionary words, usually labeled 'dialect,' 'archaic,' or 'obsolete'"—the use of so many "rare and unfamiliar English words" was "entirely inappropriate" "in view of [Nabokov's] declared intention to stick so close to the text that his version may be used as a trot." The three volumes of notes and editorial apparatus on which Nabokov had spend years are dismissed in a few lines.

Most serious among Nabokov's deficiencies was what Wilson regarded as Nabokov's misreading of the central action of the poem: the duel between the hero and his friend Lensky, after a falling-out over a woman. Wilson believed, as he had written in 1938, that Onegin reveals himself as a cold-blooded killer; he destroys "in the most cowardly fashion a man whose friend he had believed himself to be and whom he had thought he did not want to kill. . . . Evgeny has been jealous of him, because Lensky has been able to feel for Olga an all-absorbing emotion, whereas Evgeny, loved so passionately by Tatyana, has been unable to feel anything at all." Nabokov, for his part, emphasizes the code of honor in his note for this scene: Lensky simply had to challenge his friend who had insulted him by dallying with his fiancée; "far from being a temperamental extravaganza, [it] is the only logical course an honorable man could have taken."

If this had been all that Wilson said, Nabokov would have felt aggrieved but not insulted. It was Wilson's wounding tone as he referred to Nabokov's dismissal of earlier translations that seems intended to harm rather than merely point with regret:

> Since Mr. Nabokov is in the habit of introducing a job of this kind which he undertakes by an announcement that he is unique and incomparable and that everybody else who has attempted it is an oaf and an ignoramus, incompetent as a linguist and a scholar, usually with the implication that he is also a low-class person and a ridiculous personality, Nabokov ought not to complain if the reviewer, though trying not to imitate his bad literary manners, does not hesitate to underline his weaknesses.

And more:

> One knows the perversity of [Nabokov's] tricks to startle or stick pins in the reader, and one suspects that his perversity here has been exercised in curbing his brilliance. That—with his sado-masochistic Dostoevskian tendencies so acutely noted by Sartre—he seeks to torture both the reader and himself by flattening Pushkin out and denying to his own powers the scope of their full play. Aside from this desire both to suffer and make suffer—so important an element in his fiction—the only characteristic Nabokov trait that one recognizes is the addiction to rare and unfamiliar words.

The malicious gibe of Wilson the practical joker is important here. Nabokov's violent dislike for both Dostoyevsky and Sartre had been a running joke between them for the past twenty-five years. Jeffrey Meyers suggests, perhaps a bit too ingeniously, that Wilson may have "inadvertently revealed his own 'malignant cold blood' and unconscious wish to 'kill' their friendship," in the same way as "Nabokov's understanding of Lensky and lack of sympathy for Onegin reflected his instinctive urge to defend his artistic honor (almost extinct in modern Russia) and retaliate against his old friend." But it is true that Nabokov himself later said Pushkin thought self-regard or *"amour propre"* was sometimes more powerful than friendship. . . ."

Nabokov's first reply to Wilson's review a month later, in the August 26 *New York Review of Books*, was relatively mild, mostly confined to pointing out inaccuracies concerning language: "I suggest that Mr. Wilson's didactic purpose is defeated" by his errors and by his "strange tone," a mixture of "pompous aplomb and peevish ignorance" that was not "conducive to a sensible discussion of Pushkin's language and mine." Wilson, in the same issue, admitted that his article sounded "more damaging" than he had intended but then ludicrously compounded his error by trying to show that Nabokov had confused regional variations of Russian pronunciation.

There the matter might have rested. But during the ensuing months Nabokov, always "touchy as a samurai," in Brian Boyd's apt phrase, became increasingly irritated, then finally incensed, at what he considered a personal insult and betrayal. For one thing, Wilson and his wife, Elena, had visited the Nabokovs in January 1964, in Montreux—it would be their last meeting—and he had said nothing about his negative opinion of Nabokov's *Onegin*. Also galling was the widespread support for Wilson from writers who knew no Russian, such as Robert Lowell, who said he didn't really feel qualified to judge but "common sense and intuition tell us that Edmund Wilson must be nine-tenths unanswerable and right in his criticism of Nabokov." But what most outraged Nabokov was what a sympathizer called Wilson's "almost unbelievable *hubris* of reading Nabokov several petulant little lessons about Russian grammar and vocabulary, himself blundering all the while."

The Russian's final salvo appeared in the February 1966 issue of the English magazine *Encounter* as "Reply to My Critics." "A number of earnest simpletons" having written to congratulate Wilson for taking him to task, Nabokov feels compelled as a proper "sportsman" to defend himself from his old friend's "blunt jabs and incompetent blame." He reciprocates Wilson's "warm affection" as well as the "exasperation" that Wilson feels for him and says that he has always been "grateful" that Wilson refrained from reviewing his novels "while constantly saying flattering things about me in the so-called literary circles where I seldom revolve." The pleasantries concluded, Nabokov then remembers with amusement Wilson's attempt, while Nabokov was visiting him in Talcotville, in upstate New York, to "read *Evgeniy Onegin* aloud, . . . garbling every second word, and turning Pushkin's iambic line into a kind of spastic anapest with a lot of jaw-twisting haws and rather endearing little barks that utterly jumbled the rhythm and soon had us both in stitches."

Wilson's qualifications to comment on Russian are those of a "commonsensical, artless, average reader with a natural vocabulary of, say six hundred basic words." (Privately, Nabokov said Wilson's command of the language was "primitive, and his knowledge of Russian literature gappy and grotesque.") Nabokov goes on to dispute at endless length the words and translations that Wilson had cited in his review, occasionally drawing blood with darts at Wilson's own etymologies: "The most sophisticated suggestion, however, volunteered by Mr. Wilson, concerns the evolution of the adjective *krasnyy*, which means both red and beautiful." Wilson had wondered, "may this not be influenced 'by the custom in Old Russia, described in Hakluyt's *Voyages*, of the peasant women's painting large red spots on their cheeks in order to beautify themselves?' This is a preposterous gloss," Nabokov gleefully notes, "somehow reminding one of Freud's explaining a patient's passion for young women by the fact that the poor fellow in his self-abusing boyhood used to admire Mt. Jungfrau from the window of a water closet.")

The true source of the quarrel lay beyond quibbling over words or motives or, as Nabokov said elsewhere, his disappointment that a "dear friend" had become "transformed into an envious ass." It had to do with the very purpose of literature itself, and what readers were to do with what they read. Wilson had complained that Nabokov's "most serious failure is one of interpretation," with reference both to the text of *Onegin* and to the extended commentaries. "Had he read my commentary with more attention," Nabokov says,

> he would have seen that I do not believe in *any* kind of "interpretation" so that his or my "interpretation" can be neither a failure nor a success. In other words, I do not believe in the old-fashioned, naïve, and musty method of human-interest criticism championed by Mr. Wilson that consists of removing the characters from an author's imaginary world to the imaginary, but generally far less plausible, world of the critic, who then proceeds to examine these displaced characters as if they were "real people."

Satisfied, finally, that he has demonstrated how Wilson's disparaging review of his book was full of "quibbles and blunders," Nabokov stalks majestically off the stage: "and that is the last look I shall ever take at the dismal scene."

Perhaps the most interesting thing about this long friendship is that Edmund Wilson, the great critic, and Vladimir Nabokov, the great novelist, each had relatively little use for or insight into the other's work. Wilson is generally regarded as correct in his judgment of Nabokov's deficiencies as a translator and editor, but his Freudian explanation of the essence of Nabokov's fiction seems simplistic, even callow. Wilson had argued in *The Wound and the Bow* that artistic creativity springs from trauma. In his last book, *Upstate*, he said that the secret source of Nabokov's art lay in the fact that "everybody is always being humiliated," just as Nabokov himself, exiled from his homeland, had been humiliated. The fact is that Wilson and Nabokov were opposites in temperament—a rooster and a cuckoo in John Updike's amusing formulation, or a bulldog and a butterfly, in Jeffrey Meyers's—and that what Wilson liked in Nabokov was his strength and integrity, not his writing:

> And yet he is in many ways an admirable *person* [italics added], a terrific worker, unwavering in his devotion to his family, with a rigor in his devotion to his art. . . . The miseries, horrors and handicaps that he has had to confront in his exile would have degraded or broken many, but these have been overcome by his fortitude and his talent.

The very quality that aided Nabokov in his survival—the extraordinary self-confidence that Wilson notes—grew in his later years to overweening vanity. Earlier, he had dismissed Dostoyevsky and Mann as incompetents and unworthy competitors. Now he denied Wilson's status as an equal, a status that he had eagerly accepted earlier in their relationship. "We were never competitors. In what, good gracious?" Not on their common ground of Russian language and literature, he knew; and not as writers either—the creative work of art was for Nabokov worth more than any critical work, no matter how good that work might be. And, as Nabokov saw it, Wilson had not only failed to write fiction of any lasting value but had failed in his critical evaluation of Nabokov's fiction as well as of his scholarly work on Pushkin.

Nabokov had good reason to resent Wilson's attack on him as a kind of betrayal—as an old friend, Wilson could have simply remained silent about his dislike of the Pushkin translation. But in March 1971, toward the end of Wilson's life, Nabokov tried to retune the violin of their friendship with a warm "Dear Bunny" letter. Earlier, in 1967, he wrote in his diary that he had had an "odd dream" about his old friend: "somebody on the stairs behind me takes me by the elbows. E. W. Jocular reconciliation." Now, having heard that Wilson was ill, he wrote that he no longer held a "grudge for your incomprehensible incomprehension of Pushkin's and Nabokov's *Onegin*." Wilson responded in kind to "Dear Volodya" that he was "very glad" to get his letter. He had been thinking about Nabokov, he wrote, in the course of jotting down some impressions in his forthcoming book, *Upstate*. He hoped that what he had to say there would not "again impair our personal relations (it shouldn't)."

Of course, it did—or it would have, had Wilson not died in 1972—because Nabokov regarded Wilson's final comments as misguided. But by 1974, only three years before his own death, Nabokov's indignation had subsided sufficiently for him to recall the best rather than the worst of his long association with Edmund Wilson. He wrote to Wilson's widow as she was preparing her husband's letters for publication. With an emotional openness and intensity rare in him, Nabokov summed up the friendship that he and Wilson had shared—and also the cost to him of losing it: "I need not tell you what agony it was rereading the exchanges belonging to the early radiant era of our correspondence."

5

The Battle of the "Two Cultures"

C. P. Snow and F. R. Leavis

What we have here, said the avuncular old gentleman one fine spring day in 1959 to a group of English undergraduates, is an unfortunate situation: Our writers and our scientists are not talking to each other, because they are separated by "a gulf of mutual apprehension—sometimes (particularly among the young) hostility and dislike, but most of all lack of understanding. They have a curious distorted image of each other."

Thus begins C. P. Snow's famous 1959 Rede lecture at Cambridge University, "The Two Cultures and the Scientific Revolution," perhaps the most provocative talk of its kind of the postwar era. Yet Snow's ideas were remarkable chiefly for their juxtaposition and their clarity, not for their novelty or any unusual eloquence of expression. What gave them their lasting public prominence was the extraordinarily vitriolic personal attack on Snow by his onetime Cambridge colleague F. R. Leavis: Snow was not the national sage that he aspired to be, said Leavis, but, in effect, the village idiot. The flood of articles and books that ensued after Leavis's assault continues until today, ensuring that neither Snow's ideas nor Leavis's intemperance will be soon forgotten.

Poor, ambitious, and hardworking, Charles Percy Snow enrolled at Christ's College, Cambridge, in the autumn of 1928. As a Ph.D. student in physical chemistry, he worked under the famed physicist Ernest Rutherford at the Cavendish Laboratory. Snow's work in infrared spectroscopy was good enough to win him election, still just twenty-five years old, as a Fellow of Christ's College in 1930. He could have remained a sheltered and secure researcher in his established niche. But Snow was intellectually adventurous, curious to cast a wider net. He was both daring and somewhat careless in his research when he branched out into other areas. He claimed in 1932 that he had produced vitamin A in his laboratory. After a burst of publicity reminiscent of the claims in the 1990s for controlling nuclear fusion, Snow had to admit that his research had been fatally flawed. The resulting bad press and professional scorn "put Charles off scientific research irrevocably," his brother noted later.

Ever resilient and adaptable, Snow diverted himself from this early disaster by writing a detective story in 1932, *Death Under Sail*, and a novel about a young scientist in 1934, titled *The Search*. In 1935, encouraged by his good reviews, he began work on the first of eleven novels that would become famous as the *Strangers and Brothers* series, published between 1940 and 1970. Taken as a group, they provide an insider's picture of British political and social life in the twentieth century that is often compared to Anthony Trollope's *Palliser* series; while they lack his Victorian predecessor's urbane wit and style, the best of Snow's novels, *The Masters* (1951) and *Corridors of Power* (1964), are very good indeed. Even a commentator not otherwise very sympathetic to Snow, Geoffrey Heptonstall, praised *The Masters* in 1994 as "one of the great novels of university life ... beautifully-written, sensitive to human needs and alert to human failings."

In the United States, respected critics including Jerome Thale, Frederick Karl, and Robert Gorham Davis wrote admiringly and at length about Snow's works. Alfred Kazin echoed their praise for the intelligence of Snow's novels—and for their "melancholy," a rather surprising quality in a man accused of being a technocratic Pollyanna, a proper Victorian in his belief that progress in science would make a better world. Popular enough to make the bestseller lists of their time, the *Strangers and Brothers* novels were more demanding than most bestsellers; for Kazin, at least, they were "the products of a man who has had to think long and hard . . . ; one of the real pleasures in reading Snow is actually the way in which he draws the reader into this gentle activity of reason."

The public tends to admire both scientists and writers without paying much attention to them outside their areas of expertise. Snow was different. He was a practical man of affairs during and after World War II as well as a scientist and a writer. Initially charged with recruiting scientists for the war effort, he then recommended their assignments, an enormously complex set of duties requiring judgment, tact, and organizational competence. He remained in government as an important adviser on technology until 1960, when the continuing success of his books and plays allowed him to devote all of his time to writing and speaking. Knighted in 1957, he returned briefly to government service as Harold Wilson's Minister of Science in the 1964 Labour government and was awarded a life peerage in the same year.

By 1959 Snow was reaping the rewards of a busy and productive life—or three lives—as scientist, novelist, and administrator. He was a household name in Great Britain. Indifferent to such creature comforts as food and clothing, he was spectacularly shabby—in the affectionate words of an American admirer, John Halperin, "no matter what he wore, Lord Snow looked as if he'd been left for dead by a bunch of thugs." Tall, wide, and soft, bald as a Buddha, Snow peered benevolently from behind thick spectacles upon a public that found him a comforting repository of wisdom. Especially in his later years, Snow was a popular public speaker and a fixture on the BBC's *Third Programme* series of chats about science, technology, and culture. Plays drawn from his books were a staple of the London theater, and he and his wife, the novelist Pamela Hansford Johnson, were sought-after dinner guests and engaging hosts—as Dr. Johnson would say, they were "clubbable."

A reading of Snow's famous Cambridge lecture, along with his other published comments, shows why he was so popular. He had an unusual ability to talk clearly about complicated matters, cloaking intense, frequently biting conviction and harsh words with droll and placid diffidence. Concerning "the two cultures," Snow suggested that he wouldn't trouble anyone with his opinions except that the things he wanted to talk about were important and nobody else seemed willing to take them on. His "only credentials" for offering his thoughts on the matter, he said disarmingly, lay in the fact that "by chance" he was both a scientist and a writer—"[a]nyone with similar experience would have seen much the same things and I think made very much the same comments about them."

The two cultures, he said, were two groups of people with approximately the same intelligence and ability—scientists and what Snow called "literary intellectuals." He wanted to see each group reach out more to the other, in the interests of social progress and comity. More in sorrow than in pique—Snow never appeared angry—he told the story that would become the single most quoted part of his talk:

> A good many times I have been present at gatherings of people who, by the standards of the traditional culture, are thought highly educated and who have with considerable gusto been expressing their incredulity at the illiteracy of scientists. Once or twice I have been provoked and have asked the company how many of them could describe the

Second Law of Thermodynamics. The response was cold:
it was also negative. Yet I was asking something which is
about the scientific equivalent of: *Have you read a work of
Shakespeare's?*

Leaving aside the merits of the analogy, which seems
strained, it is already clear that Snow saw the nonscientists as
mainly responsible for the gap between the two cultures.
Although he was himself a prominent novelist, he had little use
for the large subset of pessimists and naysayers who, as he saw
it, controlled the literary agenda and set the tone for literary discussion in England, and to a lesser extent in America. It was this
group that he attacked, both in his talk and elsewhere— the one
that appropriated the term "intellectuals" "while no one was
looking," as opposed to scientists, who were also intellectuals
but never referred to themselves as such.

The "archetypal figure" of this literary group was T. S. Eliot.
A generation older than Snow, who was born in 1905, Eliot was
the high priest of the Modernism that Snow despised for what
he considered its antisocial bleakness and its negative force.
Snow pointedly contrasted the famous lines from Eliot's "The
Hollow Men,""*This is the way the world ends/Not with a bang but
a whimper,*" with that of his old mentor Ernest Rutherford, who
had exclaimed, "This is the heroic age of science! This is the
Elizabethan Age!"

Ostensibly quoting a puzzled scientist friend, Snow also criticized certain writers as criminally irresponsible in terms of
recent history and politics: "Yeats, Pound, Wyndham Lewis,
nine out of ten of those who have dominated literary sensibility
in our time—weren't they not only politically silly, but politically wicked? Didn't the influence of all they represent bring
Auschwitz that much nearer?" And then there was D. H.
Lawrence, one of the darlings of the twentieth century, who, as

Snow noted elsewhere, thought a good flogging was "a natural form of coition, interchange," between a ship's captain and a wayward crew member, that it helped to maintain "the vital, quivering circuit of master and man."

When they weren't felonious or brutal, the literary intellectuals were ignorant and culturally elitist, a point that Snow elaborated in his follow-up comment on his lecture. It offended Snow, whose father was a clerk in a shoe factory and whose grandfather was a day laborer, that his opponents sentimentalized the past—and that they had inflated notions of their own worth. "Ask any of them what they would have been two hundred years earlier, and they will say 'squire' or 'cleric.'" In fact, most of us would have been peasants, Snow said, and our lives as miserable as those described in the "dry but appalling language of statistics" drawn from medieval French life. The forces of "nostalgia, myth, and plain snobbery" were what stirred these "natural Luddites"—including "[John] Ruskin and William Morris and Thoreau and Emerson and Lawrence, [who] tried various kinds of fancies that were not in effect more than screams of horror."

A few years earlier, in a 1956 essay, Snow had dismissed the "literary culture" as an irritating irrelevance; it was "behaving like a state whose power is rapidly declining—standing on its precarious dignity, spending far too much energy on Alexandrian intricacies, occasionally letting fly in fits of aggressive pique quite beyond its means, too much on the defensive to show any generous imagination to the forces which must inevitably reshape it." But now, in 1959, he saw its advocates as much more dangerous, responsible for a gross misunderstanding of the industrial and agricultural revolutions that have transformed the world, mostly for the better. Far from being a curse, with its Blakean "dark satanic mills," "[i]ndustrialization is the only hope of the poor." The rich had an obligation to help the poor: In order for Western civilization to survive, the entire world must be advanced to its level. It was "technically possible to carry out the scientific revolution in India, Africa, South-east Asia, Latin America, the Middle East, within fifty years," Snow argued. There was "no excuse for western man not to know this. And not to know that this is the one way out through the three menaces which stand in our way—H-bomb war, over-population, the gap between the rich and the poor. This is one of those situations where the worst crime is innocence." Among the guilty were those who perpetuated the innocence, the "literary intellectuals."

Snow obviously wanted to provoke an intellectual debate. He could not have known that he had just declared war.

The counterattack would, however, be some time in coming; the academic mills grind slowly, and the commanding general, Frank Raymond Leavis, was a busy man. He was born in 1895 in the city of Cambridge, never leaving it except during World War I. Broad-shouldered, athletic, and competitive by nature, he would have made a perfect soldier, but he declared himself a conscientious objector. At the age of nineteen, he volunteered to join the Friends' ambulance unit and served as an ambulance train orderly for twenty-one months. His biographer, Ian MacKillop, notes that it is "part of the Leavis legend that he was 'in the trenches' or 'gassed'" and that the trauma of his war experiences helps to explain his acidity as a critic, but it is just as likely that his lengthy exposure to suffering enlarged his sympathies for those who were the victims of misfortune, as Walt Whitman's similar experience during the Civil War did his. What is certain is that Leavis was unable to speak for a month after returning home, and that he frequently stammered when his speech did return.

Leavis joined the faculty at Cambridge University as a lowly lecturer in 1919. A vivid, intense teacher, he won over students who were excited by his advocacy of "moderns" such as Eliot, James Joyce, and Lawrence, all regarded by his superiors as mere living authors—contemporaries—and thus not worthy of study. He was also notorious for his dismissal of writers he disliked ("If a talented monkey could write novels, these are what you would get," he said of one) or who, like T. S. Eliot in later years, had disappointed him, though for different reasons than Snow's ("Tom. Petering out like that! How many poems has he written since *The Four Quartets*?!"). His student "acolytes" adopted not only his enthusiasms but the "F. R. Leavis look" ("Cheap open-neck shirt, three buttons undone, collar wide open, baggy trousers with a horrible belt"), as well as his contempt for anyone who lacked his total commitment to the study of literature—which Leavis thought included most of his tenured and influential colleagues, as he let them know.

Not surprisingly, his fellow professors saw to it that Leavis's contract was not renewed in 1932, only to have him bounce back that year with his first book, *New Bearings in English Poetry*. He won grudging reinstatement. Embittered and increasingly isolated from his colleagues even as his celebrity as a teacher and writer grew, Leavis became notorious as an academic street fighter—Noel Annan recalled how he "cultivated to perfection the sneer, which he used like an oyster-knife, inserting it into the shell of his victim, exposing him with a quick turn of the wrist, and finally flipping him over and inviting his audience to disparage him as tainted inedible." By the mid-sixties Leavis had become famous enough to be parodied by Frederick Crews in *The Pooh Perplex* as "Simon Lacerous," the "implacable foe of sentimentality, flabby aestheticism, and inflated reputations" of "the entire English University system. Of his fellow Fellows he has said: 'They can all go to hell. Of course, some should go before others. One has a responsibility to make discriminations.'"

But Leavis was far more than just another grouchy don. In 1932 he founded the quarterly literary journal he called *Scrutiny* (or *Thumbscrew* to Crews) with his wife, Q. D. "Queenie" Leavis, who shared his labors as well as his paranoia (she said they were both "allotted the status of pariahs, which socially and academically lasted our lifetime . . . far from suffering from persecution mania, [we] suffered very damaging slander and discrimination"). Leavis's sense of persecution, his self-righteous egomania, and his intensity of moral purpose shine through his later appraisal of the journal and its influence on the literary world: "surviving the hostility of the institutional academic powers"—meaning the university that paid his salary—*Scrutiny* became

> the clear triumphant justification to the world of Cambridge as a human centre. In Cambridge it was the vitalizing force that gave the English School its reputation and influence, and its readers in the world at large, small as the subscribing public was, formed an incomparably influential community. . . . It established a new critical idiom and a new conception of the nature of critical thought.

The hyperbole is typical—*Scrutiny* (that is, Frank Raymond Leavis) the "triumphant justification" for *Cambridge*? Still, it is true that by the mid-fifties, Leavis and his journal had achieved such prominence in literary studies that his best book, *The Great Tradition* (1948), was one of a handful of titles that every graduate student in literature, in England or abroad, knew by heart. His essays on George Eliot, Joseph Conrad, and Lawrence in particular conferred a kind of literary sainthood on those writers. The common thread for all the writers Leavis admired, whether novelists or poets such as William Blake and Wordsworth, and above all Gerard Manley Hopkins, was their creation of literature as a positive moral force within society, particularly in the ways it exemplified the virtues associated with preindustrial rural life and exposed, as he saw it, the hollow and degrading materialism that the Industrial Revolution had unleashed.

Not content with mere right thinking, Leavis insisted, following in the tradition of Matthew Arnold, that there were necessary standards of judgment for literary art. He thought that few works were worth reading at all, in particular bourgeois novels about the middle class such as John Galsworthy's *The Forsyte Saga* or popular works glorifying science and progress such as those by H. G. Wells. These he dismissed as beneath contempt (or, as Crews's Simon Lacerous says about *Winnie-the-Pooh*, "another book to cross off your list"), along with their advocates and the public that thought they were of value. Leavis's admirers, like George Steiner, praised his "superbly exact" intelligence and his "absolute conviction that criticism is a central, life-giving pursuit. . . ." The usually genial J. B. Priestley, on the other hand, called Leavis "a sort of Calvinist theologian of contemporary culture" who "makes one feel that he hates books and authors, that his astonishing severity does not come from exceptional fastidiousness but is the result of some strange neurosis, as if he had been frightened by a librarian in early childhood."

One reason for Leavis's delay in answering Snow's charge may have been that it had already been made much earlier, and there was no reason to believe that it would have the resonance that it did now. In 1880 the scientist and professor T. H. Huxley (grandfather of Aldous Huxley) proposed that classical education in the arts and literature should give way to scientific education. Matthew Arnold tried to finesse the issue by claiming that all great science came under the rubric of what he called literature—"the best that has been thought and said." But in fact Arnold wanted to distinguish between the training that a scientific and technical curriculum provided and the education that literature, especially classical literature, offered. The first satisfied our mind and our bank account, and was desirable; the second gratified our soul, and was essential.

Huxley came from modest circumstances and taught at a vocational college. Compared with Arnold, the privileged son of the headmaster at Rugby, professor at Oxford, respected poet and influential critic, Huxley was an outsider—but he represented the world that was to come, Arnold the world that had been. Despite their opposition of institutional status, class, and ideas, the two men respected each other greatly, and their interchange was remarkably friendly and civil.

More recently, Henry James and H. G. Wells had quarreled over the nature of literary art in a way that even more clearly anticipated the Snow-Leavis dispute. The author of *The Portrait of a Lady* (1881) and *The Turn of the Screw* (1898) was revered by many as the most sensitive of novelists; moreover, as a critic he had given the English novel a sense of coherent theory, raising it above the level of mere picaresque adventure or social documentary to the highest degree of literary art. James was generous in his encouragement of younger writers as various as Stephen Crane and Edith Wharton, even as his own work declined in popularity owing to its increasing complexity—or opacity.

James had liked the younger H. G. Wells (1866–1946), whose vivid use of science in such novels as *The Time Machine* (1895), *The Island of Dr. Moreau* (1896), and *The Invisible Man* (1897), had made him famous, but he regretted Wells's increasing hyperactivity as he matured and his indifference to style—his ceaseless churning out of novels, popular histories of the world, and drumbeating paeans to technology was ruining him, James said. Wells needed to develop a sense of literary art to match his social enthusiasms and scientific abilities.

Wells ultimately came to feel that James and his exalted view of literature were irrelevant obstacles to social and cultural progress, and that the Master was patronizing him. In 1915 he parodied the sick old man (James would die in 1916) mercilessly for his refusal, as Wells saw it, to engage real life. A James novel, Wells said, was "like a church lit, but without a congregation to distract you, and with every light and line focused on the high altar, and on the altar, very reverently placed, intensely there, is a dead kitten, an eggshell, a bit of string. . . ." James resembled a whale "retrieving pebbles," or a hippopotamus intent on "picking up a pea which has got into a corner of its den." He was, sad to say, irrelevant.

James was deeply hurt by this ungrateful attack, which echoed the then-popular line on his later work; Wells apologized fulsomely, though he remained convinced that he was right, just as he thought T. H. Huxley had been right in his debates with Matthew Arnold. A better man and a better writer than this incident suggests, Wells continued to be admired by many of his contemporaries and successors, among them C. P. Snow, but within the academy he was dismissed as a writer too inconsequential even to bother to attack on literary grounds. If Wells was discussed at all, it was, in the words of a typical journal review in 1932, as "a case, a type, a portent" of the technocrat for whom "the efficiency of the machinery becomes the ultimate value," as opposed to an "expanding and richer human life." Another attack in the same journal, on Max Eastman, scorned him as a typical mindless Yankee for believing "with implicit faith that [science] will settle all our problems for us. In short, he lives still in the age of H. G. Wells." The author of both of these attacks on Wells was F. R. Leavis, in the first number of his new journal, *Scrutiny*.

In a 1934 *Cambridge Review* essay, Snow's essay "H. G. Wells and Ourselves" responded indirectly to Leavis's remarks. He wrote that too many critics wallowed in nostalgia for simpler times, busily persuading undergraduates that "Gerard Manley Hopkins was the only justification for the nineteenth century" (an insider's gibe at Leavis, Hopkins's champion). Naturally they would dismiss Wells. But for the twenty-nine-year-old Snow the aging visionary was a man healthily engaged with his own time—the age of science, the twentieth century. He was "the least nostalgic of great writers" and a positive counterweight to prevailing literary attitudes: "If art be all gestures of futility, despair, and homesick escape, then Wells is less of an artist than anyone who ever wrote."

The issue between Snow and Leavis, then, went back many years—conceptually, well before their own time and, more personally, early into the beginning of their respective careers as men of influence and prestige. Snow would later say that he had of course occasionally met Leavis at Cambridge in the thirties and that their relations had been "civil," but no more. They did not meet again once Snow had moved into the administrative arms of government. By 1959, the year of Snow's address at Cambridge, each man knew and disliked the other's work, personality, attitudes, and most of all his ability to persuade others to agree with him. Leavis was influential in his narrow sphere, while Snow, particularly in the several years after the Rede lecture, was lionized by the general public and courted by important people.

The reason for the unusually enthusiastic response to Snow's talk was its context—the Cold War had gotten colder and more dangerous in the late fifties and early sixties. The Russian launch of *Sputnik* in 1957 and the resulting crash program to rejuvenate American (and British) science instruction, both components of the increasingly sophisticated standoff between East and West, meant that science and technology were self-evidently essential; everything else came second to survival. Snow walked the corridors of international power. President John F. Kennedy called "The Two Cultures" "one of the most provocative discussions that I have ever read of this intellectual dilemma which at the same time is of profound consequence to our public policy." Praise and prominence can be dangerous: D. Graham Burnett, a historian of science, said in a 1999 essay on "the two cultures" debate that it is easy to see "how Snow's cocktail of education, economics, technology, and moral duty could have become a cultural incendiary."

It was F. R. Leavis who lit the match. By 1962 he had had his fill of hearing, mostly in the popular press, that Snow had "beautifully exposed the basic crisis of our existence," that "The Two Cultures" was "brilliant," "profoundly important," "easily the most important statement on English education" in a hundred years, "shrewd," "sane," and "not likely to be controverted." He offered his own lecture at Richmond College, Cambridge, in February of that year, as a corrective, calling it "Two Cultures? The Significance of Lord Snow." It was less a lecture than a howl of rage. "Gentle reader," advises an anonymous marginal note in a Columbia University library copy of Leavis's essay uncovered by Burnett, "you are approaching the most virulent, petty, feculent string of ad hominems ever produced by internecine British snobbery. Forewarned!"

The essence of Leavis's argument is contained within his title, especially in its question mark. He does not accept Snow's definitions of the scientific and literary cultures, finding them at once too general and too exclusive to make sense—as others had already noted, and as Snow later agreed, there is a large intermediate group of social scientists, and specifically historians of science, who are eager students of both "cultures." And what is the "significance" of Lord (with implied scornful quotation marks around "Lord," one senses) Snow? He is "insignificant," a cipher, a mere "nullity." Does he speak across the cultural divide with the authority of a published novelist? Well, Leavis begins to acknowledge, then catches himself: "Snow is, of course, a—no, I can't say that; he isn't . . . as a novelist he doesn't exist. He can't be said to know what a novel is." His novels are "composed for him by an electronic brain called Charlie."

Does Snow speak then as a scientist? He says so, but there's no evidence of "qualities that one might set to the credit of a scientific training. . . ." On the contrary, Snow lacks "the advantage of an intellectual discipline of any kind." He is "portentously ignorant" of everything, particularly history and literature, and "utterly without a glimmer of what creative literature is, or why it matters." Hardly the "genius" that he clearly thinks himself, he is "intellectually as undistinguished as it is possible to be." The poor fellow's attempts to think through, much less define, the problem he has set forth are "pathetic and comic." He is simply stupid: "a mind to be argued with—that is not there."

But let this not be construed as a personal attack, Leavis says. The true "significance" of Snow rests not in his personal failings. Surely Snow is a satisfied man, "being a sage, a familiar of the Corridors of Power, a member of the Athenaeum, a great figure in the Sunday papers, a great novelist. . . ." Leavis offers his strictures not on Snow the person but on Snow as a symbol, an omen, a "portent" in his "crass Wellsianism" of a world characterized by "blindness, unconsciousness, and automatism"—a precise echo of his 1932 comments on H. G. Wells.

Does Snow deserve some credit for proposing that the poor of the world be brought up to the level of the West—to the "vision of our imminent tomorrow in today's America"? Hardly, because all that science and technology have resulted in there is a "high standard of living and . . . life-impoverish-ment—the human emptiness; emptiness and boredom craving alcohol—of one kind or another. Who will assert that the average member of a modern society is more fully human, or more alive, than a Bushman, an Indian peasant, or a member of one of those poignantly surviving primitive peoples, with their marvelous art and skills and vital intelligence?"

The reaction to Leavis's talk was both amused and outraged. Undergraduates, always keen to see dignity affronted, promptly posted "weather reports" on campus bulletin boards: "Snow Falls Heavily," "Snow Turns to Slush." A few writers, then and later, looked in their metaphor closets and found "a hawk pouncing on an overweight mouse," a judo demonstration (Leavis, "on the eve of retirement, threw Sir Charles Snow over his shoulder several times and then jumped on him"), a nuclear strike, an eruption of the San Andreas Fault, and epic warfare (". . . no two stones of Snow's argument are left standing: each and every pebble is pulverized; the fields are salted; and the entire population is sold into slavery"). Although Geoffrey Heptonstall would later argue that Leavis's attack "was mild by Cambridge standards" because it "didn't involve the sort of physical abuse of which Wittgenstein was capable," some of Snow's friends thought at the time that it was "actionable," and that he should sue Leavis for defamation after the lecture appeared in *The Spectator*. Snow declined to do so, preferring to remain dignified and aloof: He took comfort in citing Schiller's aphorism, *"Mit der Dummheit kämpfen Götter selbst vergebens"* ("The gods themselves contend in vain with stupidity").

Snow did not lack for defenders. A torrent of criticism charged Leavis with a gross violation of the laws of civilized discourse. Consistent with *Scrutiny*'s "tradition of all-out personal destruction," he was "ill-mannered, self-centered, and adolescent," his arguments reeking of "insincerity, incapacity and envy" and "reptilian venom," amounting to "a demonstration of ill-mannered, self-centered and destructive behaviour" and "an insult to the audience and to Snow himself."

In the United States, which Leavis had condemned as the personification of the techno-culture he thought Snow wanted, *The New Republic* reviewer, Hilary Corke, saw Leavis in the grip of "pure hysteria": There was "not the slightest reason why the thought of the good Snow should bring blood-flecked froth to the mouth." She quoted Leavis's words, suggesting that he had little right to criticize anyone for "vulgarity of style," when his own writing was incomprehensible:

> Though I spoke of the "literary world" as "metropolitan," I wasn't forgetting that, most significantly, an essential element in it (and I don't mean my "literary" to be taken in a narrow sense—I am thinking of what, borrowing a license from Snow, I will call the whole publicity-created culture) belongs to the universities.

How, Corke wondered, could anyone who wrote like this be a "serious pretender to critical overlordship"? The old boy was obviously suffering from "persecution mania," the result of his long and barely acknowledged "passionate wooing" of Cambridge, "which denied him a Fellowship for years, until he was forty-five, while advancing Snow with hardly a second thought." For all his fame as a critic, Leavis never became a Professor. Who was to blame? Not his "angry self-aggrandizement and rasping contempt" for his colleagues but "[t]he Establishment, of course—and that is precisely the bogey that the unlucky Sir Charles" represented to F. R. Leavis.

C. P. Snow died in 1980, two years after F. R. Leavis, full of honors and accomplishments. He was said to have combined the gifts of Benjamin Disraeli as a popular novelist "intimately involved with the actual exercise of power" and of Wells for his knowledge of science. His rise from poverty to fame was interesting as a study in success: "The route [Snow's] career took was not especially devious, but on the other hand it was longer and steeper than such ascents are likely to be again, now that society is no longer surprised to discover brains among the poor."

Snow had observed that one of the chief differences between the accomplishments of scientists and artists is that no scientist "need ever read an original [scientific] work of the past," even of such giants as Ernest Rutherford, one of "the greatest of experimental physicists"; their "substance has all been infused" into what is now known because "science is cumulative, and embodies its past." Literature, on the other hand, might change, but unlike science it does not progress: Shakespeare and Tolstoy's works must be read anew by each generation. The modern reader, or the one a hundred years from now, will not understand the "Shakespearian experience better than Shakespeare." But the typical teenage physics student will "know more physics than Newton."

Snow would not have been surprised, then, that his comparatively negligible contributions to the world of science would be forgotten. He would be more unhappy to learn that, two decades after his death, his *Strangers and Brothers* novels are out of print and virtually unknown to English teachers today, let alone to students. Their high evaluations by critics in the sixties now seem excessive. *The Masters* and *Corridors of Power* remain interesting, but most of Snow's titles are justifiably tucked away in the "seldom used" sections of libraries—competent and solid, no mean accomplishments, but dated and of interest primarily to the literary historian.

Sad to say, Snow would also recognize the casual disparagement of his accomplishments by some of today's writers as typical of the kind of abuse that he suffered while he was alive—along with the adulation he enjoyed.

Not that all of the recent observations make sense: One holds that Snow was "thoughtful without being clever" (Leavis would have said the opposite). A second calls him "a fool"—although also a sage. And a third, the most tendentious, claims that he "distinguished himself not so much by attempting to work in both the arts and sciences, as by achieving nothing in either of them" other than "writing numerous unspeakable novels" and mangling his vitamin A experiment.

Why should Snow, who did a great deal more than any of his critics are likely to, arouse such scorn? In part, because he was far too cavalier in asserting that writers past and present were thoughtless in their opposition to the effects of the Industrial Revolution. Granted, one of the typical critical works of the twentieth century, Leo Marx's study of how nineteenth-century American writers reacted to technology, is called *The Machine in the Garden* and thus seems to imply that the century was in the grip of the nostalgia that Snow despises. But Emerson, whom Snow includes in his list of sentimental Luddites, was not only a nature poet but also an apostle of optimism and progress. One of his disciple Walt Whitman's greatest poems is the ode "To a Locomotive in Winter" ("Type of the modern! emblem of motion and power! pulse of the continent!").

Leavis was clearly right in noting Snow's limited perspective on these and other writers. That said, there is no question that many writers since the Romantic period have scorned and derided middle-class or "bourgeois" culture, or that the twentieth century is generally regarded as the age of anxiety, alienation, and angst, of the underground man, the antihero, the rebel with or without a cause. Even apparently comforting and accessible writers such as Robert Frost are revealed to have their "dark" side, and virtually no important twentieth-century writers share the optimistic belief in progress of some of their nineteenth-century predecessors. So Snow's characterization of modern literature as morbid and pessimistic is not wrong—it's just that the jury is still out on whether or not the pessimism is justified.

Snow's notions concerning politics also seem odd. He had suggested that scientists were frequently liberal, even "on the left," free from "paternalism" and "racial feeling," glowing with "social hope." Their opposite numbers harbored political attitudes that "would have been thought slightly reactionary in the court of the early Plantagenets" and spent their time ruminating about a mythical Eden of pre-industrial rustic grace, before the machine got into the garden. Interestingly, Leavis collected his attack on Snow in a volume he called *Nor Shall My Sword*, whose evocation of divine justice—or retribution— comes not from the Old Testament but from William Blake, the Romantic poet who railed against England's rising industry. Blake's poetic introduction to his "Milton" reflects Leavis's state of mind:

> I will not cease from Mental Fight,
> Nor will my Sword sleep in my hand,
> Till we have built Jerusalem
> In England's green and pleasant Land.

But Leavis and most of the literary community were hardly "reactionary" in their politics, and the moral or immoral beliefs of scientists were irrelevant to their calling. Consider the case of Germany, noted for its excellence in both literature and in science. Even as Thomas Mann and Bertolt Brecht led the moral opposition to the Third Reich and were forced to flee to America, enough scientists and engineers remained in Germany to help Hitler design and build the Nazi gas chambers and the Tiger tanks and V-2 rockets and Messerschmitts that powered his nearly perfect war machine.

Even in more normal times and places than Nazi Germany, Snow's notion that the "literary intellectuals" had greater influence than scientists in Western society is unpersuasive. As an English journalist, Jonathan Rees, has noted, today's "stereotypical leftist intellectual is not an optimistic scientific researcher, but a demoralised teacher of cultural studies; and today's typical scientist is not a cheeky outsider but a powerful mandarin, cosseted by great corporations and courted by rich universities." The most attractive part of Snow's argument in his Rede address, the appeal to end world hunger and injustice, and its corollary reprimand of the literary establishment for ignoring its social responsibilities, also has its problems. For one thing, it seems tacked on, a way of shielding himself from criticism—who could possibly be opposed? For another, as violent protests against World Trade Organization policies that echo Snow's ideas indicate, solutions for problems in what used to be called the Third World prompt violent condemnation as often as approval.

The final, and largest, problem with Snow's talk lies in its concept of culture. Leavis, for all his bad manners, was correct in seeing that Snow's ideas were oversimplified. Stepan Collini explains in his 1993 edition of *The Two Cultures* that Snow was

> not a systematic thinker nor, in some ways, a particularly exact writer. His preferred ground was that of the Big Idea: he seized it, turned it in a somewhat unconventional direction, illustrated it with a few facts and anecdotes taken from widely different domains, and reiterated it in accessible forceful prose. As he became more famous, the idea tended to get bigger, the facts fewer, and the prose

more forceful. He aimed, above all, to attract attention to
what he had to say.

Snow himself later admitted that he had left out that large
middle group of people who did not belong to either of his
groups. That middle group is even larger and more influential
today. Some of the most interesting recent nonfiction bestsellers,
obviously not limited in their appeal to either scientists or literary types, are those by Stephen Jay Gould, Richard Dawkins,
Stephen Hawking, and Edward O. Wilson. The separation of
the two cultures, insofar as humanists respecting the significance of science and technology is concerned, is a nonissue.
(*Comprehension* of the science and technology by people other
than experts in such essentials as personal computers is another
thing entirely!)

Snow even undercut his own argument for the optimistic
and progressive nature of science, as a number of his critics
have noted, by making the second law of thermodynamics his
key point of reference. The idea of the second law is much
more complex than Snow's cocktail-party analogy with
Shakespeare suggests; roughly, it holds that "no isolated process is possible in which heat is absorbed from a reservoir at a
single temperature and converted completely into mechanical
work." (*Random House Dictionary of the English Language*,
1966 ed.) This sounds innocuous, but glosses on the definition
suggest that it means the universe is ruled by entropy and
randomness. The second law has been taken as a metaphor of
dissolution, adapted by writers such as Thomas Pynchon,
with amusing grimness, in *Gravity's Rainbow*, even as it
is denounced by Christian fundamentalists, who see it as
another pernicious theory, like evolution, undermining bibli-
cal teachings.

But the most telling weakness of the Two Cultures argument is suggested by the fundamentalists' complaint: We live in the age of multiculturalism. There are not one or two cultures, but dozens of them, all competing for attention if not supremacy, each with its own demands. The melting-pot metaphor for assimilation of different peoples in the United States is gone, replaced by a"tapestry," a "mosaic," a "salad." The very idea of a national culture is suspect, here and abroad: "English-only" initiatives in the United States and recent efforts in Germany to define a *Leitkultur*, or basis for German culture, are condemned as cultural fascism. Snow can hardly be blamed for not anticipating this state of affairs, but he did much to make the discussion of separate "cultures" respectable.

F. R. Leavis, whose concept of culture turned around the great tradition of critical inquiry found in literature, would also be unhappy with today's cultural fragmentation, for two reasons. The first is that his kind of criticism, a close examination of the text in the context of social and political history, assumes that there is indeed one national culture per country or people, and that literature is its linchpin—that there is a "canon" of great works that deserve study, that critics exist to study it, and that nothing is more important to take seriously. Today the idea of the canon has been replaced by considerations of "race, creed, and gender" and, in Ian MacKillop's words, the "very name Leavis has become a synonym for 'Over and Done With.' He has become a legend of political incorrectness." The consequence is that F. R. Leavis is almost as unknown to English majors today as C. P. Snow.

The second reason why Leavis would be unhappy is that the standards of judgment on which he insisted have been obliterated, along with the canon, by the politics of race, creed, and gender, abetted by studies in popular culture. If he thought Snow's contributions to literature were mediocre, what would he say about two-volume biographies of Elvis and academic papers on signifiers in Madonna? Roger Kimball, the managing editor of *The New Criterion*, sees the late twentieth century's cultural landscape as a wasteland cluttered with "the debris of a civilization seemingly bent on cultural suicide." Its chief characteristics are "the triumph of pop culture in nearly every sphere of artistic endeavor, the glorification of mindless sensationalism, the attack on the very idea of permanent cultural achievement. . . ."

This is not a cheering vision, though it shows that Leavis's critical spirit has survived his passing. It also points up the final irony of Leavis's quarrel with Snow. He attacked Snow for suggesting that the scientific community was the best means of correcting the cultural fragmentation and absence of purpose found in modern society, but he agreed that his country, and the world, suffered from these problems. He failed to see that an alliance between his camp and Snow's would provide the best means of defense against the real dangers that were to come, the suicidal chaos and fragmentation of modern culture.

But why the fury of his dismissal of Snow? In part, it may have derived from his intellectual distaste for Snow's sloppy criticism. Another reason might be that he was afraid Snow was being too generous in saying that the two cultures were equal in influence, even granting the literary culture a degree of predominance. Snow may have been employing the debater's tactic of assigning his opponent more strength than he really possessed. In fact, Snow's middle-class, bourgeois, technocratic culture had already supplanted whatever was left of the literary culture; the process described by T. H. Huxley a century earlier was complete. Snow's call for a rapprochement between the cultures was pointless, if not a sham: The future clearly belonged to the technocrats. Meanwhile, even at Cambridge, the defining elements of Leavis's high literary culture—the canon, the individual text, the disinterested critical observer making judgments about what was good and what was bad—were on the verge of being "over and done with." Leavis's attack was not so much a cry of rage against Snow as an expression of anguish at the recognition that the Great Tradition, and F. R. Leavis, had become irrelevant.

6

"Now *There's* a Play"

LILLIAN HELLMAN AND MARY McCARTHY

The face that she had once hated was famous by the mid-seventies, variously compared to that of George Washington, the prow of a sailing clipper, and the statues on Easter Island. And the reputation that went with the weathered, austere countenance in the Blackglama mink ad, "What Becomes a Legend Most?" was equally dignified and grand. Lillian Hellman had indeed become an American legend, the best-known woman of American letters of her time, an icon in an age of iconoclasm, a craggy outpost of integrity and courage.

She had been a celebrity for decades. Born in 1905 to a wealthy Jewish family in New Orleans, she earned early notoriety in 1934 with her scandalous play about a malicious school-girl, *The Children's Hour*; she kept her hold on Broadway audiences with a series of well-crafted melodramas that turned around race, sexual intrigue, and politics, including *The Little Foxes* (1939) and *Watch on the Rhine* (1941), until the tepid critical reception of *Toys in the Attic* (1960) turned her from drama to writing her memoirs—bestsellers in their turn.

She had much to write about. There was her long love affair with Dashiell Hammett, the author of *The Maltese Falcon* and the creator of Sam Spade, to this day the archetype of the tough private eye. Hammett was eleven years her senior; they met in 1930 and lived together, never marrying, until his death in 1961.

The last thing Hammett published, in 1934, was a mystery called *The Thin Man*, about a flippant society couple named Nick and Nora Charles, who spice their frivolous lives with adventures in detection. Lillian Hellman was the model for Nora, the sexy, wisecracking, hard-drinking wife of the suave, hard-drinking, wisecracking Nick, represented in several films by William Powell and Myrna Loy.

In real life, Hammett himself, hatchet-faced, emaciated, alcoholic, and morose from terminal writer's block, was the temperamental opposite of his carefree Nick Charles. Hellman was similarly unlike the blithe and frivolous (and beautiful) Nora. She had been politically *engagé*—to use the word then in vogue—from her college years at New York University. Like Hammett, who joined the Communist Party, she was sympathetic to what she regarded as the brave Russian struggle against the twin evils of capitalism and fascism. She had visited the Soviet Union in 1937 and had come away impressed. That same year she worked with John Dos Passos, Ernest Hemingway, and Archibald MacLeish to produce a documentary film sympathetic to the Spanish Loyalists, who were enthusiastically egged on by the Communists in their doomed fight against General Franco.

Hellman went well beyond mere sympathy for the victims of fascism when she involved herself later that year with the underground opposition to the Nazis. Responding to a letter from an old childhood friend whom she called "Julia," now a medical student in Vienna, she took a train from Paris to Berlin. After a series of mysterious messages and meetings in cafés and railway stations with various intermediaries, she collected $50,000 from the anti-Nazi underground for delivery to Julia, to be used for bribes to spring Jews from prison before they were killed. Hellman's harrowing experiences and the touching story of her friendship with the brave Julia, who would soon be martyred by the Nazis, were described with becoming modesty in the second volume of her memoirs, *Pentimento*, published in 1973. That account provided the basis for the acclaimed 1977 film, *Julia*, in which Jane Fonda plays the character of Lillian Hellman, with Vanessa Redgrave as Julia.

But perhaps Hellman's finest hour came in 1952, when she was summoned to testify before the House Committee on Un-American Activities (HUAC). A series of spectacular cases of Soviet espionage in the United States had resulted in executions (the Rosenbergs), in prison sentences (Alger Hiss), and in the vilification of prominent men as "Communist dupes" (General and Secretary of State George C. Marshall) by Senator Joseph McCarthy. Now the committee members wanted to determine how seriously Communist ideology had infiltrated and affected the nation's colleges, its arts, and its entertainment media, including Hollywood. They were prompted in part by the already proven pattern of Soviet espionage and also by the still-vivid success—and unspeakable consequences—of Nazi indoctrination of millions of Germans. Was there a conspiracy among artists, entertainers, and intellectuals, led from Moscow, to undermine the country, to subvert its laws, to turn it into an ally of Stalin's murderous tyranny? Empowered to call witnesses to answer questions about what they knew about Communist influences in their spheres of activity, HUAC learned enough to confirm conservatives' fears that Communist ideology was believed by many people. But only the most extreme conservatives thought that there was any concerted or coordinated treason on the part of enough Americans to threaten the country.

Many witnesses were asked if they themselves had been Communists, if they had friends or associates who were or had been Communists, and if they or their friends had been involved in activities that were harmful to the United States. To be sure, the government itself had praised Stalin as a noble ally during the war, and in the thirties even the saintly Will Rogers had a good word to say, in the middle of our great Depression, about the Soviet Union—"Those rascals in Russia have got mighty good ideas. Just think of everybody in a country going to work." The consequence was that, in certain circles, it was virtually impossible to find anyone who had come to intellectual maturity in the thirties who had not at least made the acquaintance of a Communist.

Compelled either to "name names," to perjure themselves if they denied knowledge, to risk contempt citations if they refused to answer specific questions, or to suffer from presumed guilt if they cited the Fifth Amendment against self-incrimination, hundreds of men and women participated in a national morality play that ran for several years. What was more important, one's friends or one's country? What were the demands of honor, duty, loyalty—of self-respect? The passions aroused by decisions made then continue today, as evidenced by the refusal of many at the Academy Awards in 1999 to applaud the Oscar awarded to Elia Kazan, the director who cooperated in 1952 with HUAC. Arthur Miller took the opposite tack and was sentenced to prison for refusing to cooperate, though he never served any time in jail. His 1953 play, *The Crucible*, ostensibly about the witchhunts in seventeenth-century Salem, is a thinly disguised allegory of persecution, second today in popularity among his works only to *Death of a Salesman*.

Lillian Hellman was called to testify in 1952. She had worked in Hollywood and written the screenplay for a movie called *North Star*, a sympathetic portrayal of the Soviet Union; she had lived with Dashiell Hammett, a Communist Party member now in jail for refusing to testify; she had supported the Communists who opposed Franco in Spain. Of course she knew people who were Communists, though she said she had never been one herself. She wrote a letter to the committee two days before her appearance in which she offered to answer any questions concerning herself. She was concerned, she wrote, that by so doing she would waive her right to take the Fifth

Amendment, as she intended to do if asked to name others. She said that she did "not like subversion or disloyalty in any form" but that "to hurt innocent people whom I knew many years ago in order to save myself" would be "inhuman and indecent and dishonorable." She refused, in the most memorable phrase of her letter, "to cut my conscience to fit this year's fashions."

The committee declined to acknowledge her letter, but its questioning of Hellman on the morning of May 21, perhaps as a consequence of it, was perfunctory. As she retells the events of that day in *Scoundrel Time*—no other accounts of similar detail are available—the most dramatic moment of her appearance came as a result of the stir caused in the press gallery after her attorney passed out copies of her letter to the committee. Nervous, sweating, almost sick to her stomach with apprehension, she was distracted by one of the voices in the press gallery, louder and more insistent than the others, presumably as he read the letter. Then the voice interrupted the questioning to announce, clearly enough for all to hear, "Thank God somebody finally had the guts to do it." Years later, Hellman still thought that "that unknown voice made the words that helped save me." She was excused by lunchtime and neither charged with misbehavior nor called back for further testimony.

Hellman's principled defiance of the HUAC bullies, as represented in *Scoundrel Time*, came to form the granite pediment of her legend. "The letter," as it came to be known, was later used by Eric Bentley as the climax to his play about the McCarthy era, *Are You Now or Have You Ever Been*, read over a period of weeks by a series of prominent actresses, including Colleen Dewhurst, Liza Minnelli, Tammy Grimes, and Peggy Cass. Jules Feiffer saw her as beyond simple heroism: "I don't believe it was ever a matter of choice with her to play it safe or not play it safe, to defy the Un-American Activities Committee or to cave in. Others saw her as courageous at these times in her life. I don't think she ever saw it that way. She honestly knew of no other way to behave." John Hersey admired her as a personification of "rage" against injustice of all kinds. William Styron, then and until the end of her life, "simply was in awe of this woman," who was "a mother, a sister and a friend and in a strange way a lover of us all."

Good-humored equanimity was never prominent among Hellman's virtues, and her famous temper did not improve as her fame grew and her health declined. By early 1980, in her seventy-fifth year, she was nearly blind from glaucoma, restricted to bed and a wheelchair, and tortured by chronic bronchitis and emphysema, the result in part of years of chain-smoking unfiltered Camel cigarettes. "Goddamn old age," she griped to a friend. "Everything that's wrong with you crystallizes. Goddamn my eyes and my pacemaker and goddamn my arteries."

Unable to read, she tuned in to the Dick Cavett show on the evening of January 26 to watch a program on American authors. His guest was Mary McCarthy, the literary critic and novelist. Seven years younger than Hellman, and like her a fixture of the New York literary scene since the thirties, McCarthy had crossed paths and swords with her only a few times over the years.

As her biographer, Carol Gelderman, explains, McCarthy had become known and feared for scathing criticism early in her career, blasting her fellow critics for mutual back-scratching and laziness, attacking Tennessee Williams's *Streetcar Named Desire* for "reek[ing] of literary ambition as the apartment reeks of cheap perfume," sneering at *The Iceman Cometh* and at Eugene O'Neill for being "probably the only man in the world who is still laughing at the Iceman joke or pondering its implications." But she had seldom commented on Hellman's plays during her years as a drama critic (1937–1962), regarding them as tedious and contrived and not worth the bother. In 1944 she had complained about Hellman's romanticized Hollywood war movie *North Star* (without mentioning her by name), in which "the Soviet Union appears as an idyllic hamlet with farmhouses and furniture in a style that might be labeled Russian Provincial and put in a window by Sloane." And in 1956 McCarthy criticized Hellman's libretto for the musical version of *Candide* as "bowdlerized" and un-candid: "Miss Hellman and her collaborators have elected to play it safe. Anything in the original that could give offense to anyone—Jews, Arabs, or Holy Church—has been removed." Beyond these and a few other rather mild comments and a short story based in part on an encounter with Hellman, the famous critic had said almost nothing about the famous playwright.

For her part, Hellman had professed contempt in a 1964 interview when prodded with a McCarthy comment that her plays depended on "a certain 'lubricity,' of an overfacility in answering complex questions." McCarthy, Hellman said dismissively, was merely "a lady magazine writer" and not one of the "few people" whose opinions she respected. If she thought McCarthy was right about her work, she would quit.

It was not really much of a record of mutual antagonism, given the combative reputations of both women. Indeed, their careers were virtually over, and whatever they thought of each other could be considered as living history rather than current events. Hellman in particular was nearly out of the picture, revered but ill and less than five years from her death. McCarthy was still physically active, with the self-assurance of a beautiful woman who had aged gracefully, and she was a frequent guest on talk shows like Cavett's and at literary affairs. She still had, even in her late sixties, a dangerous charm. In her youth she had been known for her famous smile—Dwight MacDonald joked that it was "rather sharkish. When most pretty girls smile at you, you feel terrific. When Mary smiles at you, you look to see if your fly is open"—and Randall Jarrell said "torn animals were removed from that smile." McCarthy herself, as vain as she was beautiful, had considered herself "a princess among trolls" as a young woman and delighted in her later reputation as, in Norman Mailer's mock-epic list of epithets, "our First Lady of Letters . . . our saint, our umpire, our literary arbiter, our broadsword, our Barrymore (Ethel), our Dame (dowager), our mistress (Head), our Joan of Arc."

In her broadsword mode, McCarthy was prone to flip comments that often got her into hot water, such as her joke in 1944 that she felt a bit sorry for Hitler because the poor guy only wanted to be loved. Her "compulsion to say what she thinks—even when it is damaging to herself—has gotten her into trouble again and again," Gelderman notes, including McCarthy's own rueful admission, "I do not seem to live and learn." She could be counted on to say something startling about well-known writers like Alfred Kazin (she found a new book by him slippery and unreliable, "permeated with a special kind of oil he produces"). But she was now generally regarded as not so much a critical gadfly (or, less charitably, "a celebrated bitch") as a "grand old lady . . . amusing but not really mean-spirited, somewhat above it all."

The interview that Hellman watched in January had been taped months earlier, on October 18, 1979, at WNET, the public television station in New York. Dick Cavett, boyish and ingenuous, tickled McCarthy's old antagonism toward the Kennedys. Eileen Simpson, a friend of McCarthy's who was watching, heard McCarthy say, as she had said before, that she thought the Kennedys in general were Catholic but not Christian. McCarthy laughed at her own joke, Simpson said, stopped herself to "make sure there [was] nothing libelous here," and was reassured by Cavett, who said "no, no problem about libel, and she relaxed. . . ."

Could she, Cavett asked, name some contemporary writers who were "overrated and we could do without ... ?" Surprisingly, McCarthy replied with a generous dismissal of the question: "I don't think we have those anymore." There were, of course, plenty of books filled with gratuitous sex and violence that had no claim to being literature, but most of what she was familiar with had at least some merit. Cavett persisted: "We don't have the overpraised writer anymore?"

"At least I'm not aware of it," she replied. "The only one I can think of is a holdover like Lillian Hellman, who I think is tremendously overrated, a bad writer, and a dishonest writer, but she really belongs to the past."

"What is dishonest about [Hellman]?"

"Everything. I said once in some interview that every word she writes is a lie, including 'and' and 'the.'"

The studio audience laughed at the *bon mot,* and the interview turned to other writers.

An ocean away, giving a series of lectures in England, Mary McCarthy had forgotten the interview she had given months before. On February 16 Herbert Mitgang, a *New York Times* reporter, wrote that he had telephoned McCarthy at her hotel in London to ask her reaction to the suit that Hellman had brought against her for libel, along with Dick Cavett and WNET. She said the suit was news to her: On what grounds? Mitgang read the charges on the phone: McCarthy's statement was "false, made with ill-will, with malice, with knowledge of its falsity," and intended to injure Hellman "personally and professionally." McCarthy laughed. How much was she being sued for? Two and a quarter million dollars, including $1,750,000 for pain and anguish and $500,000 for punitive damages. Mitgang wrote that Miss McCarthy, who lived comfortably with her husband James West, a diplomat, but who was not wealthy, laughed even more loudly, and "made no effort to modify what she said about Miss Hellman during the interview."

McCarthy's sangfroid seemed reasonable. She was a professional critic who had offered an opinion about another professional writer. Exaggeration even to the point of hyperbole was one of the tools of the literary trade. Libel was notoriously hard to prove in American courts, requiring clear evidence of "malice" as well as knowledge that the statement made was untrue. Public figures, in particular, were expected to live with the discomfort of negative publicity as well as positive encomiums.

Then, too, she often lacked a proper appreciation for the damage she did. Years earlier, when she had been married to Edmund Wilson, she had caricatured him in a short story that he read without comment in manuscript form. When it appeared in *The New Yorker*, Wilson was outraged. She said, "But I showed it to you before." And he said, "But you've improved it!" Alfred Kazin, understandably churlish about McCarthy's wit, said she had a "wholly destructive" ability "to spot the hidden weakness or inconsistency in any literary effort and person. To this weakness she instinctively leaped with cries of pleasure—surprised that her victim, as he lay torn and bleeding, did not applaud her perspicacity."

For readers whose necks were not being held to the knife, McCarthy came across as, in Larissa MacFarquhar's words, a "delightfully vicious and lighthearted 18th-century satirist who has, through some dreadful mixup at the heavenly registrar, found herself raised in a religious Roman Catholic household and writing in a world preoccupied with Stalin, the Holocaust and the Vietnam War." She was temperamentally close to another acerbic Irish writer, Jonathan Swift; both found the world inhabited mostly by only two classes of people, fools and knaves. Like Swift, McCarthy thought the knaves of the world were constantly seducing the fools and that the serious questions of debate were political rather than literary. She thought hypocrisy was the great enabler of sin. And she was certain that Lillian Hellman, who had "long been known as a moral force, almost an institution of conscience for the rest of us," in John Hersey's estimation, had used her talent to defend the indefensible and to lie about herself and about others. She had always thought so, and now that the battle had been joined, McCarthy responded with her customary vigor. The war would last for more than four years.

Initially, it must have appeared to Hellman that she had little to lose and much to gain in terms of making life miserable for her traducer. She had plenty of money for lawyers, unlike McCarthy, and in any case her attorney, Ephraim London, an old friend, volunteered his services. If Hellman ever did need money, according to McCarthy in a later interview, she had been offered an "offense fund" of up to half a million dollars by "one of her tycoon friends who had said to her, 'Let's have some fun with this thing.'"

Hellman's initial purpose seems to have been to force McCarthy to offer a public apology. McCarthy was willing to admit privately to a friend that she would have kept her peace if she had been aware of the state of Hellman's health—"You can't believe that I would attack a blind, dying old lady"—but it was impossible for her to apologize, as "that would be lying." Hellman pressed on with the suit, clearly intent on bankrupting McCarthy. She very nearly succeeded, but at an enormous and unanticipated cost to herself. As Hellman's sympathetic biographer, William Wright, notes, "By suing McCarthy, Hellman forced one of the country's sharpest and most energetic minds to pore through the entire Hellman *oeuvre* in search of lies."

McCarthy was still in London when Hellman's lawyers asked her to cite every instance of their client's alleged dishonesty. Her files were all at her house in Paris, McCarthy responded, but she could remember five specific instances of "intellectual dishonesty." Two of these would form the heart of McCarthy's argument. The first was that Hellman misrepresented her active and devoted allegiance to Stalin's regime even in its most murderous phase, maintaining her sympathy with Communist repression well into the fifties. The second was that "Julia" was simply unbelievable, for a variety of reasons. These were the rocks on which Hellman's reputation rested; if they were revealed as sand, the legend would crumble.

McCarthy's authority for the first objection—and the most important, to her—came from personal knowledge of Hellman's involvement with the pro-Stalin faction of Communist sympathizers in the United States, dating back to 1937. The notorious Moscow Trials, kangaroo-court proceedings designed by Stalin to eliminate all possible competitors for power, were in full swing. Leon Trotsky, revered by many in Russia and abroad as a more humane leader than most of his associates, had been accused by Stalin of inspiring a counterrevolutionary plot to kill him, expelled from the party in 1930, and forced to flee for his life to Mexico, where, in 1940, he was ultimately assassinated. In 1939 Stalin and Hitler signed their notorious (and short-lived) nonaggression pact; because Stalin subsequently became our ally against the Germans in World War II, it was government policy for a time not to speak ill of the Soviet regime.

But even before the war, the intellectual left in the United States split along the lines represented by McCarthy and Hellman (anti-Stalin liberals and pro-Stalin "antifascists"), and the personal enmities that grew out of this divide were intense. In 1949 the Cultural and Scientific Conference for World Peace, the last big push by American Stalinists to regain respectability here, included not only Hellman and her lover, Dashiell Hammett, but also Aaron Copland and Leonard Bernstein and such eminent scholars of American studies as F. O. Matthiessen— indicating, if one is to assume that these men were neither fools nor knaves, that the distinction between the right and the wrong sides of the question were by no means as obvious then as they are today.

These warring factions seldom met in social situations—party lists were carefully vetted—but the two women did have an unpleasant encounter in 1948 at a dinner at the home of the president of Sarah Lawrence College. McCarthy later recalled in a letter to her lawyer how she had entered a room where Hellman was telling a group of wide-eyed students how John Dos Passos had "turned against" the Spanish Loyalists, linking him in effect with the Fascist and Nazi supporters of General Franco. McCarthy said that Hellman at first ignored her, perhaps mistaking her for "a student, because I looked quite young then, or for a younger faculty person of no importance." Unable to "hear those lies so smoothly applied . . . , as if they were coming out of a dispenser tube," McCarthy said Hellman was mistaken, that Dos Passos had rightly objected to the Communists' cold-blooded murder of former allies who they thought might undercut them. Hellman's "fury and surprise . . . at being caught red-handed in a brain-washing job" was evident from the way the "many bracelets, gold and silver," on her arms "began to tremble." (Hellman repudiated this account entirely.)

What particularly irritated McCarthy was what she considered the self-righteous quality of Hellman's and Malcolm Cowley's (among others) distortion of words as well as facts. They preferred, for example, the term "antifascism" to "Stalinism" and called themselves "premature antifascists." By this they meant to aim a mocking irony at their detractors, implying that they were deluded by Hitler and Mussolini far longer than those who had sided with Stalin had been. Thus, even if Stalin had not lived up to their hopes, they had been right to see that he would help destroy the greater evil of Hitler. While the subtleties of such posturing now seem as precious as Swift's battle between the big-enders and the little-enders (of eggs, that is), reputations were won and lost in the fifties according to how one reacted to the depredations of both communism and the HUAC. As Irving Howe, the editor of *Dissent*, memorably if rudely commented on Hellman's suit against McCarthy, "It's not just two old ladies engaged in a cat fight. The question involved—of one's attitude toward communism—is probably the central political-cultural-intellectual problem of the 20th century."

It was certainly no laughing matter to McCarthy. She had objected to Hellman's account of her adventures in *Scoundrel Time* when the book was published, but only in a letter: "I mean you'd read this god-damned *Scoundrel Time*, and you'd think she went to *jail* almost!" Now McCarthy was prepared to go to court to convey her disgust: "To me the woman is false through and through," she wrote to her personal attorney, Benjamin O'Sullivan. "It's not just the fresh varnish she pours on her seamy old Stalinism."

Ephraim London, Hellman's lawyer, deposed McCarthy on August 12, 1981. (Cavett and WNET had been dropped from the suit.) Inasmuch as McCarthy was obviously in error if taken literally—as it was certainly not true that every word Hellman wrote was a lie—her planned defense rested in part on claiming that her statement was "rhetorical hyperbole." Questioned about this by London, McCarthy said, "I don't mean *literally* nothing when I say 'nothing in her writings rings true.' . . . I mean the general tone of unconvincingness and falseness."

Q: And that was your intent in making the statement?
A: To point to this trait in her work.
Q: The trait in the work, or your opinion of the trait in her work?
A: It is the same. When I give it as my opinion, I am point-

ing to this trait in her work, that is, to what I see as this trait in her work.

This remained her position as the case dragged along for two more years. Finally, in June 1983, McCarthy asked the Superior Court of New York to dismiss Hellman's suit on the purely legal grounds of the First Amendment privilege of freedom of speech and the associated freedom to criticize a public figure. In May 1984, Judge Harold Baer, Jr., denied McCarthy's motion to dismiss. The judge held that "to call someone dishonest, to say to a national television audience that every word she writes is a lie, seems to fall on the actionable side of the line—outside what has come to be known as 'the marketplace of ideas.'" Baer also accepted Hellman's argument that she was not a public figure, on the ground that "simple notoriety" was not enough; a public figure had to be involved in a "public issue, question or controversy."

The decision was a strange one, from a judge who had a history of controversial decisions (a few years later Baer would be threatened with impeachment for ruling that a black drug dealer was entitled to run when approached by the police for questioning, simply because of his race). McCarthy had already said the same thing about Hellman, including the *and* and *the* part, several years earlier, in a Paris interview. Was it simply the fact of numbers that made her statement actionable now—millions of television viewers as opposed to a few hundred readers of an obscure foreign periodical? How could Lillian Hellman, whose accounts of controversies in *Scoundrel Time* and *Pentimento* had brought her continuing fame and fortune, be considered other than "involved" in the continuing controversy that Irving Howe thought was "the central political-cultural-intellectual problem of the 20th century"?

Knowing that despite logic and common sense she might

lose her appeal, and be forced to prove in court that Hellman had lied, McCarthy had spent the previous four years gathering material—and allies. From the first days of the filing of the suit, writers had been taking sides in print, with vigorous letters to the editors of a variety of journals. McCarthy's defenders included Norman Podhoretz, Diana Trilling, Susan Sontag, and Irving Howe. (Trilling herself was involved in a bitter separate dispute with Hellman that would lead her to consider filing suit against her.) Hellman was supported by John Hersey, Malcolm Cowley, and Richard Poirier.

Norman Mailer, who knew both women and who was no slouch at literary squabbling, published an "Appeal to Lillian Hellman and Mary McCarthy" in *The New York Times* (May 11, 1980) that many found condescending if not silly. McCarthy had sinned by hitting an opponent who was down, Mailer said. Hellman, famed civil libertarian, had sinned by suing. They should call it a draw and quit fighting. Besides, Mailer said, all writers, including Henry James and Norman Mailer, are "dishonest" in that their works are the results of invention. McCarthy was entitled to "detest" Hellman's work but not to "issue the one accusation against which no writer can defend himself or herself"—dishonesty.

George Plimpton applauded Mailer for lecturing these "cranky women." Richard Poirier rebuked him for his "maudlin appeals" to "make nice," to which Mailer responded, "It makes me want to be wealthy enough to sue you." And Mary McCarthy no doubt remembered the sage words of Philip Rahv, editor of the *Partisan Review* in the thirties and her former lover, concerning the participants in literary disputes: "They're supposedly arguing about something, but they're really saying, 'I disagree with you. Therefore there's only one thing left for me to do and that's kill you.'"

As it turned out, Hellman had many enemies whose bite was deadly and who had already gone on record, or who would soon do so (without being sued). Alfred Kazin, no friend of McCarthy's, said Hellman's *Scoundrel Time* was "historically a fraud, artistically a put-up job and emotionally packed with meanness." Sidney Hook, the eminent philosopher, charged in "The Scoundrel in the Looking Glass" that she was "an eager but unaccomplished liar" and that her books were "a compound of falsity and deliberate obfuscation." Hook summarized the evils committed under Stalin—among them the Moscow purges, Trotsky's murder, the invasion of Poland and the murder of the Polish officer corps in the Katyn forest, the subjugation of the Baltic states, the invasion of Finland, and the suppression of the Hungarian revolution—and said Hellman's readers would never guess from reading her account that she "was once one of the most vigorous public defenders of those 'sins' which even Khrushchev did not hesitate to call crimes." Hilton Kramer, writing after Hellman's death, said it was now clear that she was a "shameless liar," that *Scoundrel Time* was "one of the most poisonous and dishonest treatments ever written by an American author," and that "the 'memoirs' that brought her wealth, fame, and honors of every sort are now shown to have been a fraud."

Hellman's defenders countered that she herself had frequently said that she was a playwright and a memoirist, not a historian, and that the question of "truth" and "memory" was a fascinating puzzle that she could not begin to solve: "I always wonder if I'm telling the truth"; "Very tricky business, the business of oneself, plus memory, plus what you think you can do plus what has moved you, sometime without your knowing it"; "Everybody's memory is tricky and mine's a little trickier than most, I guess."

Some of the evidence adduced by Kazin, Hook, and Kramer is either partisan assertion rather than proof, or simple dislike of Hellman's personality. But she did seem to have created some incidents out of whole cloth. The awestruck voice shouting from the press gallery at the famous HUAC encounter, "Thank God somebody finally had the guts to do it!" was not heard by anyone else that day, including her attorney, Joseph Rauh, who was present. As for her courageous insistence on telling the truth to the committee about herself, we know now that that in the original draft of her letter to HUAC, Hellman said she had been a Communist Party member from 1938 to 1940, the years of the notorious Hitler-Stalin pact, though she claimed in *Scoundrel Time* and to the committee that she had not been— clearly a lie, though not one that McCarthy could have known about since the draft was not discovered until 1988.

Political controversies are so common and so complex that most of us, despairing of ever getting at the truth, cleave to the disputant we like the most. If Hellman's problems with distinguishing truth from invention had been limited to quarrels between old lefties, her reputation probably would have suffered little damage. But in 1983, a year before Hellman's death, a book appeared that would make her last months extremely uncomfortable. Called *Code Name Mary*, it was an autobiographical account by a retired physician, Muriel Gardiner, of her adventures with the Austrian resistance when she was a medical student in Vienna in the mid-thirties. The details in her account, all verifiable through Austrian records and through witnesses like the Socialist leader Joseph Buttinger, who had later married her, were very like those in Hellman's "Julia," the most compelling part of *Pentimento*. Gardiner had written to Hellman in 1978; she was curious about the resemblance to her own life in "Julia" and was puzzled why she had not heard, at least, of another young American woman doing work for the Austrian resistance when she was there.

The two women had never met, though they were both clients of the well-known Austrian-born lawyer—and raconteur—Karl Schwabacher, who, as Carol Brightman puts it in her biography of McCarthy, "may well have entertained his

New York friends with tales of Gardiner's . . . clandestine work during a period when Hellman's imagination was afire with the antifascist cause." Hellman did not respond to Gardiner's letter. In August 1983, she denied in a letter to Stephen Spender that she had ever heard from Gardiner (Spender had had a brief affair with Gardiner in Vienna, and was still friendly with her). Spender, for his part, said that Hellman had indeed heard from Gardiner, and that she had called Gardiner after receiving her letter. Hellman wanted to come to visit her, with "a charming young man who happened to be her lawyer." Gardiner said that was fine, and that she would also invite a "charming young man who was *her* lawyer." No meeting took place.

A year later, in June 1984—a month after Judge Baer's ruling that the case would go to trial, meaning that McCarthy would have to prove that Hellman had deliberately lied—Samuel McCracken published " 'Julia' and Other Fictions by Lillian Hellman," in *Commentary*. He exhaustively documented inconsistencies and probable falsehoods in "Julia" and concluded that Hellman's self-image of a "ruthlessly honest writer" was not only undeserved, but that her memoirs constituted a "contaminating effect on our knowledge of our time."

Hellman's lawyer feared that the "Julia" controversy would wreck his client's chances of prevailing in court and urged her to reveal the identity of her heroine if it was not Muriel Gardiner. Her friends, fearing for her health, pressed her to drop the suit. Deathly ill and unquestionably distressed, Hellman remained silent for perhaps the first time in her long and contentious life. She died on June 30, 1984, of a heart attack. Her lawyers withdrew the suit later that summer. Her files on "Julia" at the University of Texas in Austin, where Hellman left her papers, remain closed to researchers. Until we learn otherwise, it seems likely that Carol Brightman is right in saying there is "little doubt that Lillian Hellman had helped herself to large portions of [Gardiner's] life."

As it was with Hellman, this would be Mary McCarthy's last battle—she died at seventy-seven of lung cancer in New York City
on October 25, 1989—but she never doubted that she was in the
right. She had, indeed, been "disappointed" when Hellman died,
because she was still "disgusted by the amount of lying that didn't
stop after my remarks" on the Cavett show and there was "no
satisfaction in having an enemy die—you have to beat them."

McCarthy's own reputation has not suffered as a result of the
dispute: Michiko Kakutani's appraisal for *The New York Times* a
few years before her death is still appropriate in noting that her
nineteen books

> chronicle the follies and preoccupations of McCarthy's
> own liberal intellectual set, but they also open out onto
> broader issues: sexual freedom in the 1930s; radicalism in
> the 40s and 50s; Vietnam and the social upheavals of the
> 60's; Watergate and terrorism in the 70s. Whatever the
> subject, the voice has always been consistent. The point of
> view is always moral (at times, moralistic); the angle of
> vision, feminine; the tone, logical and cool.

One of her admirers believes she ranks among the finest
American novelists of her period, but most readers find her
characters, even in the bestselling novel *The Group* (1963),
unsympathetic and often brittle stereotypes. Her late-blooming
interest in art led to two well-received books in the 1960s, *The
Stones of Florence* and *Venice Observed*. Her intelligence and her
engagement with key issues of the time, expressed in her graceful, pithy style, led to her inclusion in texts devoted to the New
Journalism of Tom Wolfe, Norman Mailer, and Truman
Capote; her book on the participants in Watergate, *The Mask of
State: Watergate Portraits* (1974), is still interesting, but her books

on Vietnam, written as a stern opponent of American involvement, seemed even then like little more than shrill polemics.

Many of her books remain in print, and a collection of her reviews, *Mary McCarthy's Theatre Chronicles, 1937–1962*, was released in 2000. In general, it is only her shorter pieces, such as "Settling the Colonel's Hash," that survive today with any freshness, along with sections of her memoirs. Undeniably a fascinating woman, capable of inspiring three full-length biographies within fifteen years, she has come to be more interesting than her books. The thumbnail appraisal of her in Larissa MacFarquhar's review of the most recent McCarthy biography is acerbic (in the manner of its subject) but probably accurate enough: She will be remembered as a "viperously clever but minor writer, much admired, much detested."

Lillian Hellman's reputation as an icon of integrity was indeed damaged by the dispute with McCarthy. Her fame never rested on the quality of her prose, which is pedestrian compared to McCarthy's. Her plays pale beside those of her contemporaries such as Arthur Miller and Tennessee Williams and, later, Edward Albee. It's the memoirs that she continues to be remembered for, less for the truths they were originally seen to tell than for the continuing questions they suggest about the nature of autobiography and about "truth" itself.

Hellman's admirers, including three able biographers, do not dispute the essential truth of McCarthy's charges, and none echoes Hersey's claim that Hellman was the conscience of the age. They make a good case that for all her flaws, Hellman was an important writer for her time and an unusually strong and courageous woman.

But some defenders have taken a different tack, one that relies on Orwellian doublespeak masquerading as sophisticated literary criticism. Marsha Norman simply denies that the truth matters, as she said in *The New York Times* (August 27, 1984): "I am not interested in the degree to which she [Hellman] told the

literal truth. The literal truth is, for writers, only half the story."
An elaboration on this moral relativism is provided by Jeanne
Braham, who says Hellman had an "ironic" recognition that
truth is elusive—she achieved a "psychological veracity rather
than historical accuracy": "Because she is quick to admit uncer-
tainty about certain facts and is possessed of less than total recall
of some circumstances," her autobiographical accounts convey
"the feel of candor and refreshing humility." Hellman's "portraits, 'fictional' (or dramatic) as they may be, catch the essence
of the times in ways documentary might not." Once "we understand the function of (selective) memory and (representational)
metaphor, we are aware of a constructed reality, one that we
and the author are making 'real.'"

Truth is impossible to determine, then; it requires, along
with the words *real* and *fictional*, ironic quotation marks around
it and complicated parenthetical modification by the adjectives
selective and *representational*. Hellman is praised because she
conveys "the *feel* of candor." If ordinary readers are taken in by
the "feel of candor" and disappointed to learn that "Julia" was
not really Lillian Hellman's own story, it's because they don't
know how to read sensitively. They lack the proper literary
training, as Timothy Dow Adams helpfully explains. Hellman's
"major adverse critics have been political analysts, writing with
a historian's approach, rather than literary critics well versed in
contemporary autobiographical theory. . . ." (These "major
adverse critics" included writers thought to be sophisticated in
their day—Kazin, Hook, McCarthy—but they had the bad
luck to die before the invention of "contemporary autobiographical theory.") These folk misread Hellman's tone, her
"ironic, tongue-in-cheek style," the fact that she "often pretends
to be pretending," her use of "calculated understatement."
Katherine Lederer agrees: "Any final judgment must include a
perception of Hellman as ironist, with a way of seeing, and see-

ing again," in her "ironic vision of the fools met in the forest—and the fools these fools meet."

Pretends to be pretending? Fools in the forest? Who is fooling whom? Mary McCarthy would howl in rage over these observations. A master of irony, she would never have used it to excuse falsehood. To a degree, of course, McCarthy succeeded in discrediting her antagonist as a moral force, and others took up the battle against Hellman, for their own reasons: Diana Trilling attacked her as a "monster," and Muriel Gardiner was on the verge of suing her when Hellman died.

Nevertheless—and appropriately—Hellman continues to have a life of sorts through the theater. Zoe Caldwell portrayed her in a one-woman play in 1992; a play by Peter Feibleman, *Cakewalk*, about his friendship and affair with Hellman, appeared in 1996; and a PBS program, *Lilly and Dash*, was shown in 1999. She was a theatrical presence all her life, never more so than at its conclusion. As William Wright said in a reminiscence in 1996, "What a fitting end to this amazing career: in her upper 70's, crippled, blind, wasted to 80 pounds—yet slugging it out in a national arena with three other over-70-year-olds. Now *there's* a play. . . ."

7

Les Enfants Terribles

TRUMAN CAPOTE AND GORE VIDAL

"Fortune is a woman," said Machiavelli, "and likes the young and audacious." In the months following the end of the World War II there were brigades of hungry and ambitious young veterans seeking literary fortune, men with energy, talent, and stories to tell. Norman Mailer was working on *The Naked and the Dead*, James Jones on *From Here to Eternity*, Thomas Heggen on *Mr. Roberts*, Irwin Shaw on *The Young Lions*. The old lions were dead or past their best work: F. Scott Fitzgerald had died of drink at the beginning of the war, William Faulkner had peaked with *The Sound and the Fury*, and Ernest Hemingway now spent most of his time writing adventure and travel nonfiction for magazines.

In this postwar world of tough guys Gore Vidal seemed to fit right in. Tall and slender, Byronically handsome, well connected socially and politically through a family that included Senator Thomas P. Gore, he was only twenty-one years old when his first novel, *Williwaw*, was published in early 1946. It was bleak, cynical, and spare, reminiscent of Stephen Crane and Theodore Dreiser in its remorseless naturalism, and it would sell only moderately. But Vidal was being boomed in New York, even before he had been discharged from the army, as a young writer with a future. He had more than talent, he had a presence: He was "luminous and manly," Anaïs Nin confided, rather hopefully, to her diary in November 1945, "clear and bright . . . active, alert, poised," with "cool eyes and sensual mouth." And "he talks."

Good talk was as important to Nin as sex. The promiscuous wife of a long-suffering banker, she had been Henry Miller's mistress in Paris during the thirties. When the war broke out and she and her husband moved to Greenwich Village, she continued her fruitless efforts to publish her own work even as she recorded her affairs and her ambitions in the diary that would later make her famous. In the French tradition, and after the fashion of Gertrude Stein, she offered the writers of her time a salon to which she invited new potential conquests and admirers like Vidal and the new playwright with the odd name, Tennessee Williams.

One day in December 1945, as she was entertaining Vidal in her apartment, the doorbell rang. Answering it, she "saw a small, slender young man, with hair over his eyes, extending the softest and most boneless hand I had ever held, like a baby's nestling in mine." It was Truman Capote. Nin introduced him to Vidal. "Well," Capote said to Vidal, his voice as high-pitched as a canary's, "how does it feel to be an enfant terrible?" The faux French accent sounded like *awn-font turrEEbul*, but, as Capote's biographer Gerald Clarke would note, his issuing of a challenge was unmistakable: "However he pronounced it, he was aware what it meant and that there could be but one enfant terrible at a time. Even as he shook that little hand, Vidal knew the same, and from the beginning theirs was more a rivalry, a bloodthirsty match of wits, than an alliance of affection."

A year older than Vidal, Capote had a slight edge in their competition, not so much by age as by having been turned down for the draft for being, in his words, "obviously neurotic"—that is, homosexual. While Vidal spent the war years serving on army transports in the Aleutians, Capote worked as a copyboy at *The New Yorker*, giving him a head start in their competition.

Only a few inches over five feet in height, Capote was, Clarke
writes, "unnaturally pretty, with wide, arresting blue eyes and
blond bangs." His voice was so high, it was said, that only a dog
could hear it, and he affected long Borzoni scarves that trailed
in his wake as he delivered his manuscripts, stopping the great
Harold Ross in his tracks the first time he saw him: "For God's
sake! What's that?"

Capote was anticipating the Andy Warhol world of camp
art, of the outrageous personality as performance, by at least fifteen years. His sexual persona would guarantee him a degree of
attention and a passport into the jet set as its bard and court
jester. His admirers, literary and personal, saw in him potential
for greater things, one of them quoting an Andrew Marvell
poem, fortuitously titled "The Picture of Little T.C. in a
Prospect of Flowers," to make the point: "Who can foretell for
what high cause/This darling of the gods was born?" In these
early years, Capote had few detractors; later they would grow in
number and would regard him as at best a wasted talent, at
worst a suicidal parody of the romantic artist destroyed by his
own excesses.

For the moment, Capote and Vidal had much in common
besides good looks, talent, and ambition. They were socially
adept, Capote for his charm and his flattery and his *New Yorker*
network, and Vidal by virtue of his wit and his family connections—through his grandfather, he had been exposed to life and
politics in Washington from his infancy, and a complicated
skein of divorces and sequential remarriages would link him
intimately with the Kennedy clan. (Hugh Auchincloss, the second husband of Vidal's mother, would divorce her in 1935 and
later marry Jacqueline Bouvier's mother—Vidal and Jacqueline
Kennedy Onassis thus had in common a stepfather, whom they
both despised.)

As writers, Capote and Vidal shared a stringently professional work ethic and a distaste for French theorists, for

"schoolteachers" like John Barth who got paid by their universities whether their books were readable or not, and for the Beats—especially Jack Kerouac and *On the Road*: "None of these people have anything interesting to say, and none of them can write, not even Mr. Kerouac," Capote said, concluding with his famous *bon mot*: what Kerouac does "isn't writing at all—it's typing."

This was also a period in our literary and social history when Malcolm Cowley could write that "the homosexual of talent, if he achieves a literary success, does so in spite of handicaps that aren't imposed on other writers." Capote and Vidal were recognizably part of a gay literary scene, a loosely knit international group that included Tennessee Williams, Paul Bowles, Christopher Isherwood, W. H. Auden, and Noël Coward. They shared the distinction of having written early novels with overtly homosexual themes and protagonists: Vidal's *The City and the Pillar* and Capote's *Other Voices, Other Rooms* were both on bestseller lists briefly in 1948 before being shouldered aside by *The Naked and the Dead*, *The Young Lions* and James Gould Cozzens's *Guard of Honor*.

Vidal's novel was dismissed by the *Chicago Tribune* as "disgusting," but Thomas Mann, to whom he sent a copy in Los Angeles, where the exiled Olympian was living, thanked him for his "noble entertainment." Leslie Fiedler in *The Hudson Review* thought it was an ambitious but heavy-handed failure. Anaïs Nin, still naively infatuated with Vidal as a possible bedmate, compared his fiction (but only in her diary) unfavorably to Capote's: "Actions, no feeling," she said of Vidal, versus Capote's "power to dream, his subtlety of style, his imagination. Above all, his sensitivity."

Capote's critical and commercial success with *Other Voices* was comparatively much greater than Vidal's with *City*, in part because his lyric voice was more appealing. But much of his success was owed to his *in*sensitivity—at least to public disapproval. Calder Willingham wrote to Vidal that Capote was "busy all the time at the job of getting ahead. . . . Also, he uses his homosexuality in this; he uses it as comedy, and plays the role of the effeminate buffoon, thus making people laugh at him. It gets attention." It didn't hurt Capote, then, when a friend called *Other Voices, Other Rooms* a "fairy Huckleberry Finn." The novel became even better known by virtue of Richard Avedon's suggestive full-jacket photograph of the young author, supine on a couch, with carmined lips and a come-hither gaze that seems to invite the viewer to ravish him.

Capote's gift for self-promotion had already propelled him into early fame. In 1946 Cyril Connolly described the "feverish and incessant" hunt for new young writers; "their names, like a new issue on the market, are constantly on the lips of those in the know. 'Get Capote'—at this minute the words are resounding on many a sixtieth floor." Later that same year *Life* magazine, in a four-page spread called "Young U.S. Writers: A Refreshing Group of Newcomers on the Literary Scene Is Ready to Tackle Almost Anything," featured Capote in a huge photograph, elegantly reclining in a simulation of an antebellum Southern parlor; Gore Vidal, who wrote "poetry and Hemingwayesque fiction," got a tiny head shot near the end of the article. (The other featured writers, all now relatively obscure, were Thomas Heggen, Jean Stafford, Calder Willingham, and Elizabeth Fenwick.)

Capote and Vidal were members of a hugely ambitious and self-promoting group. Norman Mailer would later write a book called *Advertisements for Myself*, in which he slammed most of his contemporaries, and Vidal noted to John Aldridge that "the atmosphere is heavy with competitiveness. Someone might one day remark in print that American writers are the most highly competitive and mutually antagonistic in the world." This was certainly true of Vidal. He and Capote remained cordial for a time: "Truman is everywhere, giddy and mad and not working but rather charming I think . . . ," Vidal wrote a friend in 1948. But he dismissed Capote's fiction as a "peculiar interior decorator's way . . . of constructing a Saks Fifth Avenue window and calling it a novel." Later that year their break became open, at a party in Tennessee Williams's apartment. "They began to criticize each other's work," Williams recalled. "Gore told Truman he got all of his plots out of Carson McCullers and Eudora Welty. Truman said: 'Well, maybe you get all of yours from the *Daily News.*' And so the fight was on. They never got over it." Writing to Carson McCullers, Williams seemed to be shaking his head in wonder at Vidal's ambition and envy: "He's infected with that awful competitive spirit and seems to be continually haunted over the success or achievements of other writers, such as Truman Capote. He is positively obsessed with poor little Truman Capote. . . . You would think they were running neck-and-neck for some fabulous gold prize."

In fact, the two were not neck and neck in the first few years of their acquaintance; or if they were, it was because Capote had already lapped Vidal in terms of critical approbation and was passing him again. For all the apparently insubstantial iridescence of his public personality, Capote was a writer of rare gifts and unusual self-discipline in applying them—"as calculating as an accountant checking receipts," in Clarke's apt phrase, in his endless revisions, and as tenacious as a pit bull in his reportage, as he would later demonstrate with *In Cold Blood*. Mark Schorer's 1963 edition of Capote's early work is ample proof that he had more than a wonderful style; he had a sharp, intuitive intelligence, a bizarre if not twisted imagination that turned around what he called "carnival freaks" and monsters—wounded, isolated souls—and a droll wit that leavened his morbidity. In the 1944 story that launched his career in New York, "Miriam," a little girl, perhaps a changeling, takes possession of a middle-aged widow in New York. In "The Headless Hawk" a lonely young man watches city buses moving "like green-bellied fish" through the city streets, and recalls how he had always been drawn as a child to the maimed, that "there was always a little something wrong, broken" in those he loved. Even in the slighter stories like "A Diamond Guitar," Capote's elegiac voice rings true and sweet: To be alive, the old prisoner in that story realizes, is to know what has been irretrievably lost—"brown rivers where the fish run, and sunlight on a lady's hair." His best story, "Breakfast at Tiffany's," appeared in 1958 in a collection by that name that also included the touching 1946 tribute to his aunt, "A Christmas Memory."

In retrospect, considering his decline after the success of *In Cold Blood*, it seems that Capote would have been better off sticking to fiction. But he had always had, in addition to his gifts as a writer of poetic fiction, a talent for insinuating himself into the confidence of new friends and acquaintances. A two-part series for *The New Yorker* in 1956 called "The Muses Are Heard" reveals Capote's tangible sense of place—vivid, lively, real, not a dream landscape at all, as it often is in his fiction; the ability to put himself in the scene without the story being about him; and a hardheaded, often cynical tone, in contrast to the earlier stories, that often offended those it described as much as it entertained his readers.

"The Muses Are Heard" is a good example of literary journalism—writing that can be read with profit and pleasure long after the events described are forgotten. Capote accompanied a road-show production of *Porgy and Bess* to Leningrad in 1955, a tense time in the Cold War (a year before the Hungarians would take to the streets of Budapest, six years before the Berlin Wall went up). The Soviet Union is now long gone, but Capote's "Muses" lives on, mostly because of its comic characterizations. Some of these rely, it is true, on the reader's remembering that Leonard Lyons, also on the train that took the troupe from Berlin to Leningrad, was a gossip columnist of more than usual shallowness. But we don't need to know anything about the producer, Robert Breen, to appreciate this wonderful sketch, and to see the type in the individual: "He has an actor's trained voice, 'placed' in a register so very deep that it makes for automatic pomposity, and as he speaks his manicured hands move with his words, not in an excitable, Latin style, but in a gracefully slow ritualistic manner, rather as though he were saying Mass."

Nor was Capote always as indifferent to ideas as Vidal and others charged. His analysis of *Porgy and Bess* in the context of Soviet Communism is a marvel of shrewd insight: The musical, "when slipped under the dialectical microscope, proves a test tube brimming with the kind of bacteria to which the present Russian regime is most allergic." It is "extremely erotic, a serious cause for dismay in a nation with laws so prim, persons can be arrested for kissing in public. It is God-fearing," stressing the need for faith and the "comforts to be derived from religious belief"; it is "uncritically accepting of superstition"; and "it also sings out loud that people can be happy with plenty of nothin', an unwelcome message indeed" in Soviet Russia.

Capote's success was due in part to his method, which was to become the questionable heart of the so-called New Journalism. He didn't take notes when he talked to people, relying on his memory to write down later what they said; he shifted chronologies and changed settings; he invented scenes, conflated several characters into one, and fabricated dialogue. Less sophisticated folks, like some of the actors in the Breen troupe and those in Kansas whom he interviewed for *In Cold Blood*, were often surprised to see what they had said to Capote in their delightful conversations with him. So was Marlon Brando, presumably more hip to the wiles of interviewers: What he thought was an off-the-record chat (no notes, no tape recorder) concerning *Sayonara* made him look like a brainless blowhard, mostly through deadpan quotations from Brando and from hapless friends like the comedian Wally Cox, who "probably knows him best," and who "declares him to be 'a creative philosopher, a very deep thinker ... a real liberating force for his friends.' " (At least Brando had enough wit to realize he had been ambushed by Capote when he read the profile, shouting to his producer, Joshua Logan, "I'll kill him!")

This was one side of Truman Capote—that of "the artful charmer, prone to the gossamer and the exquisite." The other side, "darker and stronger, [was] the discoverer of death." Thus did Conrad Knickerbocker, reviewing *In Cold Blood* for *The New York Times Book Review* in January 1966, set the dominant tone for reaction to Capote's new book: It was nothing less than "a masterpiece, agonizing, terrible, possessed, proof that the times, so surfeited with disasters, are still capable of tragedy." The story had begun with a brief notice in *The Times* on November 16, 1959, datelined Holcomb, Kansas: "A wealthy wheat farmer, his wife and their two young children were found shot to death today in their home. They had been killed by shotgun blasts at close range after being bound and gagged." At his request, Capote was assigned by *The New Yorker* to write a story about the murders, and was in Kansas in December when the two young killers were caught. For the next six years he stayed with the story of the murders and the ensuing trial, conviction, appeals, and executions, coming to know the young men, Dick Hickock and Perry Smith, and to sympathize with them, even as he reprobated their monstrous acts. On April 14, 1965, Capote watched them both hanged.

The book was an astonishing tour de force. Like the Greek tragedies to which it was often compared, the beginning and end of the story—the murders, the hangings—were already well known. What held its readers' attention was not the suspense of a whodunit, but the process of what Capote portrayed as the inevitable collision between "desperate, savage, violent America" and "sane, safe, insular[,] even smug America—people who have every chance against people who have none." Given virtually unhindered access to the killers, as well as to the FBI investigators and local law officials, and to townspeople and neighbors of the Clutter family, Capote created an unforgettable American story. As the decades that followed generated other terrible stories—those of Lee Harvey Oswald, Sirhan Sirhan, Charles Manson, and Jeffrey Dahmer, among too many—Capote's account of the Clutter murders came to seem darkly prophetic.

Never modest, Capote claimed that he had invented and mastered a new genre, which he called the "nonfiction novel." Journalism was limited by its nature, he said, to moving "along on a horizontal plane, telling a story, while fiction—good fiction—moves vertically, taking you deeper and deeper into character and events. By treating a real event with fictional techniques (something that cannot be done by a journalist until he *learns* how to write good fiction), it's possible to make this kind of synthesis." Later he would argue that Norman Mailer and Tom Wolfe owed him their gratitude for forging the way of the New Journalism, though in fact writers as various as Plutarch, Thomas Carlyle, Lytton Strachey and, more recently, John Hersey, Alan Moorehead, Walter Lord, Shelby Foote, and Ernest Hemingway had used fictional techniques to render reality to equal or greater effect. It was Capote's self-marketing genius, not his method of writing, that was novel.

This does not diminish the compelling force of his narrative, even today. But the debate that ensued over labels and methods obscured a more troubling hole at the heart of *In Cold Blood*. The wounded and isolated souls of the early stories, from "Miriam" through "Breakfast at Tiffany's" Holly

Golightly, are all outsiders and outcasts who reject conventional morality and are "examples of another kind of virtue," in the words of the novelist and critic George Garrett, the virtue of what Holly calls honesty: "Be anything but a coward, a pretender, an emotional crook, a whore: I'd rather have cancer than a dishonest heart." In Capote's fiction, Garrett says, people "who manage to prosper or get along in the duplicitous world of practical matters" are deceitful hypocrites who "make real mischief and cause real trouble. In the end, thanks to a kind of whimsical Providence or poetic justice, they get what is coming to them."

Consciously or not, Capote imposed what Garrett calls his "inversion of conventional, middle-class values" on the situation he found in western Kansas. By any normal measure, the Clutters were innocent victims, and Hickock and Smith were cruel and sadistic killers who got what was coming to them. Yet the Clutters were the privileged—"safe, sane, insular[,] even smug," in Capote's telling phrase. They were probably like the doltish farmers Capote tried to interview, who watched television while they talked to him: "They would go on looking straight at the TV screen . . . If the television wasn't on, if the light wasn't flickering, they began to get the shakes." Though Capote was sickened by the brutality of the murders, there is no indication that the fate of the Clutters moved him on an emotional level. Hickock and especially Smith, however, were the real-life versions of the "carnival freaks" and monsters of Capote's fiction; they were the true victims in Capote's narrative. He would never recover, he said, from the experience of watching their execution, even as their story made him almost as rich and famous as he had hoped to be.

Gore Vidal, comparing himself much later to Capote (and ignoring the achievement of *In Cold Blood*), said that his own interests lay in writing "about the fifth century B.C. and comparative religion and Confucius and the Buddha and Zoroaster and Socrates, and, of course, American history." He didn't care about marriage or "suburban adultery" or about "the awakening of the young homosexual in the South and whether or not to wear crepe de chine before sundown. . . . Once, Capote said to me, 'Thank heavens, Gore, we're not intellectuals.' I said, 'Speak for your fucking self!' 'Intellectual' was the worst word in his vocabulary."

Yet Vidal's first real triumphs were as a popular entertainer in the unintellectual new medium of television. After several more unsuccessful novels, he found a profitable niche in what is now thought of as the Golden Age of television, the early and mid-fifties, when programs like *Omnibus, Philco Television Playhouse,* and the *Goodyear Playhouse* were popular. He wrote dozens of television plays and adaptations of novels and stories by William Faulkner ("Barn Burning"), Henry James (*The Turn of the Screw*), and Stephen Crane ("The Blue Hotel"). In 1956 his own television play, *Visit to a Small Planet,* was a well-received satire on the nuclear stalemate between America and the USSR. As the interplanetary visitor to Earth sagely observes, this is a world that can only do one thing well—wage war. Vidal's confection was the forerunner of hit shows as various as *My Favorite Martian, Mork and Mindy,* and the movie *The Mouse That Roared.* Adapted for Broadway in 1957, *Visit* was a huge hit, exceeded only by his 1960 play about a presidential campaign, *The Best Man.*

As the successful Broadway revival of *The Best Man* in 2000 indicated, Vidal had an incisive and durable sense of the comic drama inherent in American politics. By 1960 he had himself been bitten deeply enough by political ambition to run for Congress as a Democrat in New York's heavily Republican twenty-ninth district, which included Vidal's home in Dutchess County. He had the blessing of the area's most illustrious resident, Eleanor Roosevelt, then living in Hyde Park near FDR's family home, and the endorsement of his shirttail relative, the glamorous Democratic presidential nominee Jack Kennedy. His talent for entertaining television talk-show audiences with witty aperçus had made him a favorite of David Susskind, Dave Garroway, and Jack Paar, and thus well known to a broader audience than most playwrights and novelists.

Even his vanity was amusing, at least to friends like Richard Rovere, the political correspondent for *The New Yorker*, and his wife, Eleanor, who were Vidal's neighbors. He "couldn't pass a mirror without straightening his hair or combing it," Eleanor Rovere said. "But he was redeemingly self-conscious and ironic about his own vanity and was very, very funny about it." He was so obviously and extravagantly gifted, as his biographer Fred Kaplan describes Vidal at this period in his life, that he seemed almost to be a potentially tragic figure:

> He had the blessing (and the occasional disadvantage) of seeming dazzlingly handsome, and often glamorous, an Apollonian figure to some, to others too attractive not to be suspected of something. Of what? Of being too talented. Of being too handsome. Of being too well born and at ease. Of being too ambitious. Of being a collection of qualities that had to have some character flaw at their hidden (or not too hidden) center, perhaps arrogance, or vanity, or some punishable vice.

For all his gifts—or more likely because of them—Vidal never came close to beating his colorless Republican opponent in 1960, but his career as a writer and as a public figure soon flowered. His novel about the Roman empire, *Julian*, was a bestseller in 1964; *Washington, D.C.* appeared in 1967, the first of a series of historical novels about the United States that would include *Burr* (1973), *Lincoln* (1984), *1876* (1976), *Empire* (1987), and *The Golden Age* (2000). *Myra Breckinridge*, his notorious novel about a transsexual Hollywood movie star, was published in 1968. With these works and particularly with his long essay-reviews for *The New York Review of Books*, beginning with the first year of that journal's existence in 1963, Vidal achieved the distinction of being "an intellectual" that he so clearly desired, in contrast to Truman Capote.

By the early winter of 1965, when Capote visited Rome, where Vidal was then living part of the time, they were both successful enough to be able to spend what Vidal termed "a pleasant drunken evening recalling who had said what about whom." Vidal was inclined to feel almost generous about his erstwhile rival: "For the first time in twenty years I suspect that he is intelligent." But he was worried by Capote's friendliness: "What can he be up to?" There was "a profound silliness at every level" in Capote's work, he said; "he is mindless in the purest sense; but an animal shrewdness has made him succeed in the jungle, like those silly lizards which can take on any shade and so avoid becoming dinner."

Capote, for his part, later said that he "rather liked Gore," though he didn't think he was much of a writer. "He was amusing, bright, and always very vinegary, and we had a lot of things in common." Of those things they had in common, perhaps the most important certainly in Capote's mind, were their various connections to the Kennedy clan, and especially to Jacqueline Bouvier Kennedy. Their differing perspectives on the Kennedys would lead to the final, bitter estrangement of the two writers.

Vidal's own association with the Kennedys came through family and political alliances. He had been close enough to Jackie before she was married, in 1953, to become her confidant and advisor—and to consider her a coldly ambitious and calculating woman. He knew Jack Kennedy well enough to like and admire him as a charming and wily opportunist, though he never claimed to be a close friend. But he despised Robert Kennedy thoroughly. In 1963 he wrote an essay for *Esquire* called "The Best Man in 1968," in which he attacked the president's brother as unqualified to be president. From that point on, Vidal was persona non grata at the Kennedy White House. Admirers of Robert Kennedy, while admitting some of his flaws, dispute Vidal's negative assessment of him. But right or wrong, Vidal had jettisoned the most powerful of political connections, with all of the favors of patronage and favors that such connections can confer, for no apparent reason other than asserting his beliefs about national politics and character.

Capote seems never to have harbored a political thought of any kind, other than a late-blooming opposition to capital punishment after watching the denouement of the events of *In Cold Blood*; his associations with the Kennedys were purely social. His biographer accepts Capote's account of their friendship as going back to the mid-fifties, when Capote "used to have dinner with her and Jack when they had this awful old apartment on Park Avenue. . . . But mostly Jack was out-of-town, and she and I would have dinner or go to the theater by ourselves. We used to sit talking until four or five o'clock in the morning." Vidal, however, says that Jackie called him in the summer of 1960 to say that she had just met Capote for the first time at a party and given him a ride home. "I asked her, 'Did he rivet everybody's attention with the most terrible, scandalous gossip about everybody not present?' " She said, yes, he did, and that he turned to her in the taxi as they drove away and "gave a great Pagliacci sigh and said, 'Well, you heard me singing for my supper.' "

Whatever the date of Capote's first meeting with Jacqueline Kennedy, he shared with Vidal the position of being estranged from her by the mid-sixties, the result not of declaring political principle but of talking indiscreetly about her to mutual friends—of too much singing for his supper. By the mid-seventies, Capote's indiscretions would make him a social pariah. He had always known that this might happen, even predicting it in a 1944 story, "Shut a Final Door." In that story, a character called Walter is cut off by an old friend for his malicious gossip about her; she can't "afford" him anymore, though she is sympathetic: " 'It's very compulsive, your malice, and you aren't too much to blame. . . . ' " Walter is puzzled—"Well, sure, he'd gossiped about her, but it wasn't as though he'd meant it." Besides, "what was the use of having friends if you couldn't discuss them objectively?"

In an *Esquire* story in November 1975 that he called "La Côte Basque, 1965," Capote vividly caricatured a glittering cast of old, rich, and soon-to-be-former friends, including Gloria Vanderbilt, Bill and Babe Paley, and Lee Radziwill, Jacqueline Kennedy's sister, all of whom had in some way offended him. Almost all of his friends except, apparently, Radziwill, found after this betrayal that they could no longer "afford" Capote. Unable to write, ostracized by the society he had glorified, increasingly prone to abuse alcohol and cocaine, Capote was now a fat and sodden wreck. The glorious youth so full of promise after the war had degenerated into a prematurely old man. He was a windbag to boot, spinning out rambling and dangerously unguarded interviews to anybody who asked for one, even to *Playgirl*, a new magazine with literary pretensions like Hugh Hefner's with *Playboy*.

It was in that *Playgirl* interview that Capote made perhaps his greatest misstep. Gore Vidal, he confided to the interviewer, had been thrown out of the White House years before, in 1961, for being drunk and obnoxious. "It was the only time he had ever been invited to the White House and he got drunk."

Annnnnnd . . . he insulted Jackie's mother, whom he had never met before in his *life*! But he'd never even met the woman. And she just went into something like total shock. And Bobby [Kennedy] and Arthur Schlesinger, I believe it was, and one of the guards just picked Gore up and carried him to the door and threw him out into Pennsylvania Avenue. That's when he began to write all those cruel pieces about the Kennedys.

Gore Vidal said repeatedly that there were no witnesses to what had happened at the White House that November evening in 1961. As he remembered it, he had been

squatting down beside Jackie in the north curve of the Blue Room. She was in an armless chaise. As I rose, for support, I needed her knee or shoulder. I picked shoulder. As I did, Bobby came up behind her and took my hand off—she sees nothing. I then went over (and there are *no* witnesses to any of this either) and said to Bobby, "Don't ever do that again." "What do you mean, buddy boy? You're nobody," something like that. I said, "Never say that; writers have so many words, we usually have the last one." Not bad for my state of rage, which escalated very quickly to "Fuck you!" "Fuck you too!" and that was the end of it. Recently I showed Hillary Clinton the spot where it took place. . . . Should there be a plaque?

The hint of ironic self-deprecation in this account by Vidal lends it credibility, though the reference to Mrs. Clinton shows that he has retained his access to the corridors of power while his antagonist is long dead—which makes the self-reflexive ironic pose a bit easier. Only a few years before Capote's remark, Vidal had condescendingly joked, "It is inhumane to attack Capote. You are attacking an elf." But Vidal is not temperamentally a patient or long-suffering man. He had been punched a couple of times by Norman Mailer for book reviews of his novels that Mailer disliked, and sued by William Buckley for implying that Buckley was a Nazi. (In 1968, during the Democratic convention in Chicago, the two men got into a heated quarrel on ABC television about unruly students and police brutality in Chicago; Buckley, the master of persiflage and rodomontade, could only splutter that Vidal was a "queer.") But now Capote's relatively harmless little tale of events at the White House seems to have been the last straw for Vidal—even though the anecdote had been circulated earlier by George Plimpton without prompting a suit for libel. In any event, he was considerably less detached at the time than his later account suggests: "I'm looking forward to getting that little toad!" he said, filing suit late in 1975 in a New York state court, demanding a million dollars plus an apology.

There was also that old Kennedy contretemps to nag at Vidal. The 1963 *Esquire* article might or might not have been written without the prompting of the earlier spat with Bobby at the White House; but Vidal always prided himself on being a political philosopher, if not a kingmaker. He may have reasoned that if readers believed Capote's account, they might think that Vidal's later disparagement of Robert Kennedy was based on personal pique and not on principle.

Vidal's detestation of RFK seems indeed to have derived from personal taste as well as from differences of class, religion, and political philosophy. He saw Bobby as insensitive and boorish: When his wife, Ethel, asked a visiting philosopher a question about God, Bobby cut her off with a short "Can it, Ethel" that made him sound (to later readers) more like Archie Bunker than his revered older brother. Politically, Vidal saw nothing but zealotry in the way RFK had run the Department of Justice as attorney general. Jack Kennedy was by temperament "perfectly suited to the Presidency," Vidal wrote. "His brother is not. He would be a dangerously authoritarian-minded President." But the true virulence of Vidal's animus against RFK was not revealed until the publication of his memoir, *Palimpsest*, in 1995. There, twenty-seven years after Kennedy's death, Vidal manages to impugn Kennedy's class, religion, and manhood in one vicious swipe that outdoes anything Capote ever wrote: "Between Bobby's primitive religion and his family's ardent struggle ever upward from Irish bog, he was more than usually skewed, not least by his own homosexual impulses [sic!], which, [Rudolf] Nureyev once told me, were very much in the air on at least one occasion, when they were together."

As might be anticipated from two such masters of vitriol and harborers of resentment, Vidal's suit and Capote's reactions were compelling drama for those who knew them and for the media, and the stuff of both high and low comedy. Initially their friends refused to take it seriously, as suggested by George Plimpton's parody: ". . . Arthur Schlesinger, Jr., had thrown Gore Vidal out of the White House onto Pennsylvania Avenue, which was the length of two football fields away from the front steps, a long toss for anyone, but which was logical enough if you knew what a great arm Schlesinger had and how he had gripped Vidal by the laces and spiraled him." (More seriously, Schlesinger later said that Vidal had not been forcibly ejected at all.) The two principals perpetuated the comedy in public, on talk shows and in interviews with reporters. Vidal said Capote had "raised lying to an art—a minor art." Capote told David Susskind he was sorry about their falling-out: "Of course, I'm always sad about Gore. Very sad that he has to breathe every day."

Even the depositions for the court had their light moments. Vidal was asked when he had last seen Capote. At a party in the sixties, he said.

Q: What occurred on that occasion?

A: I sat on him.

Q: What do you mean?

A: I didn't have my glasses on and I sat down on what I thought was a stool and it was Capote.

Q: Where was Capote sitting at the time you sat on him?

A: On a smaller stool.

Capote retaliated by pretending to misremember Vidal's first novel, *Williwaw*, as "Willie Wonka," the hero of Roald Dahl's children's story, to convey his sense of Vidal's childishness.

In fact, the comedy was turning into tragic farce for Capote. In 1978 he appeared on a TV talk show clearly drunk and strung out on drugs; the *New York Post* ran a cartoon the next day showing a bum lying in a litter of used syringes and liquor bottles, holding a copy of "Breakfast at the Bowery." The following year would see the climax of his battle with Vidal, and the beginning of the end of everything for Capote. His case for the truth of his story about Vidal's humiliating expulsion from the White House had always depended on Jacqueline Kennedy's sister Lee Radziwill, from whom he said he had heard it. For years he had exploited his Hollywood connections to find movie roles for the beautiful but talentless aristocrat who had hoped to become better known than her famous sister. Now Lee Radziwill, one of his few remaining jet-set friends, had—as he saw it—betrayed him. "I do not recall," she told Vidal's lawyer, "ever discussing with Truman Capote the incident or the evening which I understand is the subject of this lawsuit."

Stunned by Radziwill's disavowal, Capote counterattacked by releasing copies of his and Vidal's legal depositions to *New York* magazine, which ran lengthy excerpts as part of a cover story that pictured Vidal flying out of the White House. Capote had managed to convince himself that the reading public would equate Vidal's testimony with that of the comically deranged Captain Queeg of *The Caine Mutiny*: The transcripts would now "explode and destroy his career. I will have the greatest single revenge in literary history. Nothing equals it. For the rest of his life he'll wake up in the morning and be happy for ten minutes—and then he'll remember what happened on that day in June. The humiliation for him! I love it! I love it! I love it! When he dies, they'll write on his tombstone, 'Here lies Gore Vidal: He Messed Around with T. C.'"

But Capote's position was further weakened when *Playgirl* quickly printed a retraction. Vidal released the magazine from liability and offered to let Capote off the hook if he paid his legal fees of $40,000, plus an additional $10,000. Capote declined the offer; he had reached such a high pitch of emotional distress and anger over what he regarded as Radziwill's betrayal that he was beyond reason. The bitterest blow was delivered by the columnist Liz Smith, whom Capote had called to find out why Radziwill had refused to answer his requests for information about her letter to Vidal's lawyers. "I'm tired of Truman riding on my coattails to fame," she told Smith. "And Liz, what difference does it make? They're just a couple of fags."

Capote struck back at Radziwill in television and newspaper interviews: "I've been in love before with people who were just ghastly. I was in love with her like I would have been in love with anybody." She must have betrayed him, he said, because she was afraid of Vidal; she thought Capote was dying and that her betrayal couldn't really hurt him. "Unfortunately for Princess Radziwill, this fag happens to be alive and well and in New York City." Vidal responded by saying, "This is pathology. Real nut-house stuff." Weary and disgusted, Vidal told a friend late in 1979 that Capote had in a sense achieved his goal: He "has now so muddled things as to make me seem to be his equal: a pair of publicity-mad social-climbers who make it a habit to libel and slander one another and everyone else." He told the same friend that "we are willing to settle for an apology, one-dollar damages, and my legal fees. . . ." Again Capote refused.

Finally, in the fall of 1983, Capote surrendered. Enfeebled by illegal and prescription drugs, alcohol, and debilitation, nearly broke and unable to write, at fifty-nine he was less than a year from his early death. In a short "Dear Gore" letter of legal boilerplate, Capote offers a pro forma apology for "any distress, inconvenience or expense" that Vidal may have experienced as a result of the *Playgirl* interview. Capote, the experienced reporter, falls back on the antique evasion of indiscreet interviewees—he had been misquoted, he tells Vidal, particularly "with regard to any remarks which might cast aspersions upon your character or behavior . . . ," and he promises to keep his mouth shut henceforth. The suit was settled out of court.

Word of Truman Capote's death in August 1984 reached Gore Vidal at his home in Ravello, Italy, a beautiful villa high above the Amalfi Coast. Many years earlier, Capote once said, when they were still young and intermittently civil, Vidal had told him

> how he was going to manage his life. He planned to become the grand old man of American letters, the American Somerset Maugham. He wanted to write popular books, make lots of money, and have a house on the Riviera, just as Maugham did. He always used to say, "Longevity's the answer. If you live long enough, everything will turn your way." I would say, "Gore, you will do it all if you really want to."

And so he had. But hypocrisy never being one of Vidal's vices, nor generosity to a fallen foe one of his virtues, his acidulous reaction to Capote's death is not surprising: It would be, as it had been for Elvis Presley, a "good career move," he said in a letter to Paul Bowles. Capote had assured his immortal fame, Vidal continued. "Since he has told the most extraordinary lies about every famous person of our time, the hacks will have a field-day recording the sorts of lies they usually make up. . . . Well, he is what this vulgar tinny age requires. RIP."

Vidal also dropped a line to Johnny Carson. Capote had died at the Hollywood house of Carson's estranged wife, Joanne. Knowing, Vidal said, that Carson "would be upset by Joanne's coup . . . I promised him that I would die at *his* house. This will even things out."

In the years since his rival's death, Vidal has gone on to publish still more books, notably his memoir, *Palimpsest*, in 1995; a novel, *The Golden Age* (2000), about President Roosevelt and World War II; and a collection of his critical essays in 2001. In terms of sheer quantity, he has far outpaced Capote, as he has almost every one of his contemporaries except John Updike. The praise for his achievements, though not universal, exceeds any ever claimed for Capote. An English observer, Michael Shelden, says

the brilliant, naughty and delightfully condescending Gore Vidal would make an impressive Duke of Pough-keepsie. . . . Denied political office, the great Vidal has done his best to play the benevolent despot in the realm of literary culture. As America's pre-eminent man of letters, he has spent half a century trying to encourage good writers and shame bad ones. To set an example, he has written scores of witty essays and a series of historical novels that Gabriel García Márquez rightly describes as "magnificent." . . . [He is] America's last great man of letters at his aristocratic best.

The noted writer and critic Jonathan Raban, also British, concurs: For him Vidal is a serious writer who

stands for the proud tradition in which the imaginative writer has a place of honor at the table of the big bad world of politics, money, manners and morals. . . . Defending the novel as the civilized and civilizing secular entertainment, wrangling with Jefferson, the Adamses, Lincoln, Grant, Theodore Roosevelt as if they were his obstreperous contemporaries, speaking out for the right of the individual to share his or her bed with whomsoever he or she pleases, damning religion ("The great unmentionable evil at the center of our culture is monotheism"), Mr. Vidal is fearless and cogent. He writes of himself as a "born-again atheist." It's a telling phrase, for he believes in reason (and reason's bright child, wit) with something closely akin to religious fervor: Denouncing the Puritan sky-god, he sounds eerily like Cotton Mather reincarnated with a magnificently un-Puritan sense of humor.

And yet . . . "America's last great man of letters" is not regarded, even by his admirers, as having the stature of Henry James, Thomas Mann, or Edith Wharton, three writers he admires. His fiction, other than *Myra Breckinridge* and *Myron* in an occasional gay studies course (where he is treated as an "iconic figure," according to Fred Kaplan), is not taught in college English or history departments. Jason Epstein, Vidal's Random House publisher and friend, thought Vidal was "not really a novelist, that he had too much ego to be a writer of fiction because he couldn't subordinate himself to other people the way you have to as a novelist. You've got to become the people you impersonate, you have to have the ability to let yourself go a little bit and become the characters. He didn't seem to do that." Truman Capote had said something similar, in talking about *In Cold Blood*. A good reporter had to "empathize with personalities outside his usual imaginative range, mentalities unlike his own, kinds of people he would never have written about had he not been forced by encountering them inside the journalistic situation." The writer of fiction had to do this also, he said, referring now specifically to Vidal, who he said (with his usual hyperbole) "has no talent, except for writing essays. He has no interior sensitivity—he can't put himself into anyone else's place—and except for *Myra Breckinridge*, he never really found his voice. Anybody could have written *Julian* or *Burr*."

Capote exaggerated, but there are other problems with Vidal's historical fiction. These novels are less attempts to re-create and explain the past than to press arguments that only revisionists, conspiracy theorists, and radical leftists find persuasive, as they do Oliver Stone's films. He considers himself a satirist, and "like most satirists . . . a reactionary: I like the old republic, repelled though I am by many of its manifestations now. I see Caesarism as the alternative. . . . Yet under good Caesars we might enjoy a Pax Americana without too much limiting of individual freedom in America." Over the years Vidal has seldom strayed from his underlying conviction that the country turned from being a republic into an empire in the nineteenth century and that, as he said in *Myra Breckinridge*, it is an evil empire: "But then it is our peculiar fate to destroy or change all things we touch since . . . *we* are the constant and compulsive killers of life, the mad dogs of creation. . . . Death and destruction, hate and rage, these are

the most characteristic of human attributes. . . ." Consequently his novels, fact-filled, informative, and entertaining
though they are, consistently invert what has been accepted as
true. The good are diminished, the bad are elevated. Burr
was a misunderstood hero. Washington had a fat behind.
Lincoln had syphilis. And FDR engineered the attack on
Pearl Harbor, as Vidal explains in *The Golden Age*, a novel
that the reviewer for *The New York Times* accurately says
"almost continuously strains credulity."

We know now that Vidal was wrong in saying, after Capote
died, that nobody would read his books: The old gossip is now
boring, but the stories retain their charm and *In Cold Blood* was
unquestionably a milestone in the development of the New
Journalism. It is too soon to say whether Vidal will stand the test
of time as well as Capote does, but we can hazard a guess.
Nearly forty years ago, while he was adapting a novel by John P.
Marquand called *Sincerely, Willis Wayde* for television, Vidal
wrote to John Aldridge that "the only sad aspect of being a hack
is that one is called upon to adapt the work of more successful
hacks." In November 2000, Michael Davie wrote in his *London
Observer* review of *The Golden Age* that "Vidal is not a highbrow
novelist. He is a mixture of the popular writer J. P. Marquand
and the worldly political philosopher Henry Adams, with an
Adams-like understanding of the way politicians think and
operate."

It must have stung Vidal to be compared to Marquand as
much as it pleased him to be thought of as a successor to Henry
Adams. Of course, Adams was a brilliant figure, but he is
remembered for his autobiography, not for his novels. Vidal
similarly is at his best in his critical essays, not in what he
regards as his important work, his fiction. Indeed, there is nothing in Vidal's fiction that bears comparison with the best works
of that "hack," John P. Marquand: *H. M. Pulham, Esquire* and

Wickford Point. It's not, then, that Vidal is an admixture of Adams and Marquand, but that he is almost entirely an aspiring Adams—an often amusingly mean-spirited iconoclast and, as Truman Capote found, a dangerous antagonist, but not the great novelist he wanted to be.

8

Not-So-Dry Bones

TOM WOLFE, JOHN UPDIKE, AND THE PERILS OF
LITERARY AMBITION*

Born in the third decade of his eventful century, he worked for
years on the fringes of the literary establishment as a newspaper
reporter and magazine writer of humorous and satirical stories.
His distinctive style made him a celebrity with the larger public
even before he finally, well into middle age, got around to writing his best novel. The novel was attacked by some as frivolous
and degraded, but its author was, at his core, a stern moralist—
nothing provoked him more than pretension and hypocrisy,
both of which he saw enshrined in the intellectual and artistic
temples of the day. A gifted performer and explainer of his
work, he became something of a dandy in his trademark white
suit, which he wore with as much éclat as he did his irony and
wit. He seldom showed any visible wounds from the assaults of
his enemies, but he was painfully sensitive to slights and jealous
of his hard-won fame—and not always confident that it would
long survive him.

   The writer referred to is our old friend Mark Twain
(1835–1910), the vivid persona that Samuel Clemens created for
himself, and the book is his first fully realized adult novel,
Huckleberry Finn. But it could just as easily be Tom Wolfe, the

*I asked Tom Wolfe and John Updike for their responses to questions I had for them. I
am grateful for their generous responses, and for permission to quote from their letters
to me.—A.A.

late-blooming novelist whose *The Bonfire of the Vanities* was published in 1987. Born in 1931, Wolfe is still very much alive— a good thing too, because he faces more formidable foes in John Updike and Norman Mailer than Twain did at the equivalent point in his career. Granted, Wolfe seeks out controversy as a professional gadfly—he cites with approval Twain's credo, "The last thing in the world I want is not to be noticed." His flamboyance serves, as did Twain's in his time, both to obscure and to highlight the issues raised by his work, especially his more recent novel, *A Man in Full* (1998): Can a popular book be good? Can a satire be moving? Are most novelists saying too little of interest about America, and too much about themselves? Can a journalist, who by definition spends his time on the remains of the day, write fiction that will be read tomorrow?

Wolfe thinks the answer to these questions is yes. He offers his two enormously popular novels as proof positive. Several prominent novelist-critics, among them Updike, Mailer, and John Irving, disagree, particularly with regard to *A Man in Full*—Updike elegantly (Wolfe "fails to be exquisite"); Mailer pedagogically (too much plot, Tom: it's "equal to a drug"); and Irving contemptuously ("journalistic hyperbole disguised as fiction . . . —[all] yak.") All three are in turn ridiculed by Wolfe as "the three stooges," Larry, Curly, and Moe, unable to do what he has done and jealous of his success.

Puckish excess has marked Wolfe's career almost from the beginning. His first book lionized an obscure bunch of California hot-rodders, *The Kandy-Kolored Tangerine-Flake Streamline Baby*, and helped to launch the New Journalism phenomenon in 1965. In 1970 Wolfe's *Radical Chic* mocked Leonard Bernstein and his friends for the party they hosted for the Black Panthers. It "never occurred" to Bernstein, Wolfe said later, "that there could be anything humorous about the spectacle of the Black Panthers outlining their ten-point revolutionary program in his 13-room duplex on Park Avenue." He attacked modern art as a gigantic hoax in *The Painted Word* (1975), which earned him endless opprobrium from defenders of the faith as a Manchurian Candidate mole in the cultural world, seeking to destroy it from within. Undaunted, he did the same for the world of modern architecture a few years later in *From Bauhaus to Our House* (1981). Switching from condemnation of vice to celebration of virtue, he immortalized the original seven Mercury astronauts as American heroes in *The Right Stuff* in 1979. At the end of the fabled decade of excess and greed, in 1987, Wolfe reverted to satire as the engine power for his first novel, *The Bonfire of the Vanities*, as he tracked his arrogant bond salesman, Sherman McCoy, to his comic doom.

Bonfire was a runaway hit, devoured by the public and praised, somewhat surprisingly, by at least some of the critics whom Wolfe assumed he had alienated over the years—not just with his cultural conservatism but with his reiterated charges that the writers of fiction, his contemporaries, were not doing their job. His model for *Bonfire* had been William Makepeace Thackeray's *Vanity Fair*, but the writer with whom he sought comparison was Charles Dickens. The reviewer for *The Christian Science Monitor* thought he had succeeded in his effort to write "a richly textured, contemporary novel whose epicenter is situated in the social concerns that so much of today's minimalist, self-absorbed fiction ignores."

Encouraged by his success, Wolfe boldly staked out his novelistic claim to the inadequately exploited gold mine of contemporary America in a 1989 *Harper's* article, "Stalking the Billion-Footed Beast." The novelists of the past who made a difference in their world, Wolfe said, were those like Dickens, Sinclair Lewis, and Émile Zola—writers who "*assumed* that the novelist had to go beyond his personal experience and head out into society as a reporter." Zola in particular became a legend for his "documenting expeditions to the slums, the coal mines, the races." American literature, pale, introverted, and sickly, needed "a brigade" of Zolas to "head out into this wild, bizarre, unpredictable, hog-stomping Baroque country of ours and reclaim its literary property. . . ." Wolfe said, in effect, don't leave the task to the journalists, who lack the necessary tools of the novelist: Let *me* do it. It would take him nearly ten more years, but by the time *A Man in Full* appeared, Wolfe was satisfied that he had done the right and necessary thing.

Many agreed, not least Michael Lewis in *The New York Times Book Review*. He praised Wolfe's new novel for "passages as powerful and as beautiful as anything written not merely by contemporary American novelists but by any American novelist." All of the reviews, hostile or friendly, noted the epic scope and intent of *A Man in Full*. Set in Atlanta, it is longer, at 742 pages, than the most popular epic about the South, Margaret Mitchell's *Gone with the Wind*. The "man" of the title is the heroically outsized Charlie Croker. A dirt-poor Georgia country boy (for Croker read "cracker") who went to college on a football scholarship, Charlie has parlayed his strength and shrewdness into a business conglomerate based on real estate. He loses his moral bearings and his economic footing in his lust for acquisition and consumption. His loans are recalled by the bank, and its verbal SWAT team of recovery experts, in one of the book's best scenes, gratuitously humiliates him.

Sixty years old, on the edge of bankruptcy, crippled by an old football injury, Charlie receives a tempting offer of redemption. The state university's current football hero is a black thug who may or may not have raped the daughter of Charlie's friend, a local executive. The various power brokers in Atlanta and the state—the black mayor, the white bankers, the university and its athletic program—all want the case to go away, fearing race riots, economic dislocation, and (hardly less important) a losing football season. Charlie must say, at a televised press conference, that he has met the young man, likes him, knows how athletes can be misunderstood. Because of Charlie's endorsement, the impending riots will vanish, local business will resume its placid and profitable path, the bread and circuses will continue at the university. Profoundly grateful for Charlie's civic-mindedness, the bank will back off. His empire will survive and he will continue to prosper.

Enter young Conrad Hensley, a paragon of pluck and luck right out of Horatio Alger—or perhaps an idiot savant like Forrest Gump. Thrown out of work at a Croker warehouse across the continent, in Oakland (the result of Charlie's cost-cutting maneuvers to satisfy the bank), Conrad has been wrongly imprisoned. He is rescued spiritually by reading the teachings of the ancient Roman Stoic, Epictetus, and physically by an earthquake that literally springs him out of jail. No less improbably (the whole escape sequence is reminiscent of the movie version of *The Fugitive*) he ends up working as a nurse's aide to Charlie, who, following a knee replacement, needs not only physical but moral support. Conrad introduces Charlie to the Stoic tenets of self-reliance and integrity. Charlie makes the right decision, exposing the machinations of the establishment at his press conference. He and Conrad ride off into the sunset together, poor but happy, virtuous men in a world of fools and knaves—and soon not even poor, having established a quasi-religion based on Epictetus that is pulling in scads of money.

Assuming that like calls unto like, then the quality of the writers and critics who have taken the trouble to read and comment on Wolfe's book suggests that it has merit, though some simply dismiss it and its author. John Irving, when asked about the dispute between Wolfe and Updike, wondered, wittily enough, how there could be war "between a pawn and a king." Wolfe simply "can't write," Irving said; less wittily, he said that he could at random pick a sentence from Wolfe that "would make me gag . . . If I were teaching fucking freshman English, I couldn't read that sentence and not just carve it up."

Sven Birkerts's review in *Atlantic Unbound* was a considered written response, rather than a conversational one, but it too is hard to take seriously. He had a great time reading *A Man in Full*, Birkerts says—but that's the problem: "if it's too much fun, it can't be art," because "serious art is only enjoyable up to a point, and then it becomes work: perceiving, judging, and knowing." These are "pleasures that push us up against the grain of our ease." Birkerts can't even bring himself to give Wolfe credit for partial success: "A novel either manifests artistic vision or it doesn't." *A Man in Full* is "written for the collective readership, the mass" (those who read *Time* instead of the *Atlantic?*). It lacks the individuality of true art, resembling Hollywood box-office hits such as *Titanic*; it appeals not just to the so-called general reader "but also to what is general (that is, collective) in the reader."

Birkerts's argument tracks back through time to Dwight MacDonald, who drew a distinction between what he called "mass-cult" and "mid-cult" audiences, and, before him, to Russell Lynes's "highbrow," "middlebrow," and "lowbrow" definitions of art and literature. It is rather nice, in fact, to see the case being made so openly for a hierarchical approach to art in the midst of mass popular culture—elitism has its place. But lumping Wolfe with the likes of John Grisham, Robert Ludlum, and other tin ears won't work; even Birkerts's complaint that that there is no psychological equivalent to the precise and sometimes even "brocaded density" of Wolfe's descriptive passages implies mastery of the language. And whatever Wolfe's other flaws may be, they don't include insensitivity to nuances of social conduct and behavior—to what Lionel Trilling called the "hum and buzz of implication"—that are at the heart of the novel of manners.

Norman Mailer's objections to *A Man in Full* were more substantial—and, coming from a writer who had himself excelled first as a novelist and later as a literary journalist, were presumably harder for Wolfe to take. Mailer's first book, *The Naked and the Dead*, published in 1948, remains the benchmark for American novels about World War II. His later fiction, from *Barbary Shore* (1951) through *The Gospel According to the Son* (1997), has not lived up to the promise of that great first novel, but his nonfiction has won him a degree of fame and praise that overshadow Wolfe's. His honors include a National Book Award and the Pulitzer Prize for nonfiction for *The Armies of the Night* in 1969 and another Pulitzer for the fact-based novel *The Executioner's Song* in 1980. His other works (among many) deal with the space program (*Of a Fire on the Moon*, 1970), boxing (*The Fight*, 1975), and the CIA (*Harlot's Ghost*, 1991). Mailer has more than earned the right to be listened to when he speaks about other writers' efforts to describe what is happening in America.

Mailer has gloried in his reputation as the bad-boy brawler of American letters, but he is nearing his eightieth birthday (he was born in 1923), and the last man he punched publicly was Gore Vidal, at a cocktail party in 1974. It may have been his more-in-pity-than-in-pique tone, his lack of personal animus toward a striving colleague who hasn't quite measured up, that irritated Wolfe most about Mailer's long, long critique of *A Man in Full* for *The New York Review of Books*. Or perhaps, as with the Updike review in *The New Yorker*, it's the deceptively generous evenhandedness of the review that makes it all the more devastating.

Mailer begins by recalling his own complaint, in 1965, that America had failed to produce a Tolstoy or a Stendhal to depict and explain its vast complexity—only Theodore Dreiser had tried and he had not even come close. After his "heroic failure," American writers made their own "separate peace," content to play with metaphors and to leave "the task of explaining America" to journalism—in the form of Henry Luce's magazine empire of *Time, Life*, and *Fortune*. Nothing new, then, about the need for the kind of writing that Wolfe thought we needed.

Mailer does not despise *A Man in Full*. He applauds the sub-

tleness with which the black social and political structure of
Atlanta are described; he likes Wolfe's wonderful ear for
accents and dialects; he finds Conrad Hensley an appealing
young man (though he doubts the scene in which Conrad sub-
dues a prison bully); and he praises the coming together of the
various elements of the novel toward the middle as "startlingly
good." Sometimes, as in the prison scenes, Mailer finds that the
writing is so good that it "forces one to contemplate the uncomfortable possibility that Tom Wolfe might yet be seen as our best
writer," certainly in terms of portraying "the surface" of things.

But Wolfe lacks direction—a "compass"—and depth, failing
to go deeply into his characters' minds and hearts. He recalls the
worst aspects of Dickens with his reliance on coincidence and
chance (the earthquake that releases Conrad from jail) and the
abrupt and unpersuasive disposition of all the problems at the
end. His pacing "has gas and runs out of gas, fills up again, goes
dry." Plot twists and complications substitute for character
motivation and depth; the characters reveal nothing significant
about themselves in their many internal monologues, having
"no signature quality of mind." Wolfe can't create "a vital and
interesting woman." And Charlie Croker's moral dilemma—
should he betray a friend and save his empire?—is unpersuasive
and too easily resolved.

Wolfe's flaws as a novelist, Mailer says, derive from his
virtues, which are those of a journalist who must grasp a subject
quickly, describe it compellingly so that a reader will not be
bored, and move on. His earlier success is also a hindrance;
Mailer notes that Wolfe's first novel, *The Bonfire of the Vanities*,
sold three quarters of a million copies in hardback and became
"the literary phenomenon of the Eighties." Now Wolfe obviously wanted to better that performance, which meant, according to Mailer, that he had been deliberately striving to write a
bestseller and, at the same time, a "major novel." For Mailer,
"the real interest is in Wolfe's search for the answer to his own

deep question of motive"—i.e., did he set out to "deal with literary matters or [with] adroit commercial counterfeits?"

Mailer raises the stakes, suggesting that Wolfe was simply selling out. The great lampooner of hypocrisy, Mailer implies, is himself a hypocrite for pretending to be writing anything other than a money-making potboiler. A hypocrite, and maybe a whore: Sometimes reading Wolfe's book is like "making love to a three-hundred-pound woman. Once she gets on top, it's over. Fall in love, or be asphyxiated."

Wolfe is inclined to a more generous reading of Mailer's critique. In response to a personal query for a reaction to the preceding paragraph, he writes, "I don't think Norman was interested so much in challenging my integrity as constructing a rationale for the fact that people stopped reading him after *The Executioner's Song*—which was based totally on Lawrence Schiller's saturation reporting of the Gary Gilmore case. I didn't read 'whore' in Norman's review at all. All I got out of that is the fact that Norman has made love to a lot of three-hundred-pound women. Takes all tastes." In another letter, Wolfe says that he and Mailer often see each other on social occasions, "and he has always been cordial. I'd say the jousting has been *pour le sport.*"

John Updike's remarks in his *New Yorker* review of *A Man in Full* were apparently closer to the bone for Wolfe than Mailer's. His four *Rabbit* novels do exactly what Wolfe claims he is doing—that is, they depict the reality of American life in the twentieth century. But he is almost as well-known for his reviews as he is for his novels. For Michiko Kakutani, Updike is "a major and enduring critical voice; indeed . . . the preeminent critic of his generation," and James A. Schiff compares him with Edmund Wilson for his range and output over the years. Like Wilson, he is famous for his eclecticism: An Updike review might be about a little-known but worthy African novelist (Yambo Ouologuen, Ezekiel Mphahlele, Ousmane); American masters (James, Whitman, Hawthorne); theologians (Kierkegaard, Tillich, Karl Barth); or about books on music, art, anthropology, science . . . virtually nothing fails to excite his interest. Nothing, that is, except most contemporary American literature—for every review of a book by Philip Roth, Anne Tyler, or Saul Bellow there are half a dozen of foreign writers. (In this respect, he is Wilson's polar opposite.)

One reason for Updike's relative inattention to his contemporaries is that he doesn't like the bleakness and insularity of much of their work (an attitude that he shares, interestingly, with Tom Wolfe). Another, more important, reason is that Updike's natural inclination is not to be combative or destructive. He prefers to write about books he likes; his reviews are usually generous and kind—friendly attempts to persuade readers to join him in sharing his pleasure. "Do not accept for review a book you are predisposed to dislike," he says in his self-imposed rules for reviewing: And *never* "try to put the author 'in his place,' making of him a pawn in a contest with other reviewers. Review the book, not the reputation."

At first glance Updike's *New Yorker* review of *A Man in Full* does not seem particularly negative. He notes its "muscularity"—the book is a "burly bruiser," with a "teeming cast of characters." Wolfe manages to wrest some "poetry and thematic harmony out of flat, hostile, usually obscene rap lyrics." He paints an effective "vision of hell" in his jail scenes. His descriptions of black Atlanta are "morally elaborate as well as intensely observant" and reflect "an admirable intention" to describe a part of the black experience in America. Wolfe's treatment of Stoicism and its religious implications is effective, largely because Wolfe seems to be serious about what he is saying.

But . . . the plot is out of control, spreading "like kudzu." The "explosive onomatopoetics" ("Brannnnng! Brannnnng? Brannnnng!" "Scrack crack scrack scraaaccck," "Awriiiighhhh-hht!") remind us constantly of the writer behind them, whose guiding philosophy, his theme, is that "America comes down to noise, trash, and vanity." Charlie Croker is not so much a character as a "specimen under glass," a collection of physical attributes (bull neck, bum knee) who talks funny ("far fat" for *firefight*, "sump'm" for *something*).

Subtract the negatives (plot, theme, character, and language) from the positives (bulk, energy, good intentions, cleverness, and effective nastiness) and what are we left with? A book by "a talented, inventive, philosophical-minded journalist, coming into old age," who "has gone for broke" in an ambitious attempt to be regarded as a writer of literature. He has failed, Updike says, echoing Birkerts: *A Man in Full* is merely "entertainment, not literature, even literature in a modest aspirant form." Not even a good try for a beginner, in other words.

It would seem that Updike bent the first part of his rule—avoid books you are "predisposed to dislike"—in agreeing to review *A Man in Full*. He confesses that he had never been able to read *The Bonfire of the Vanities* "because the blatancy of its icy-hearted satire repelled me." The second part of the rule fares no better—what is his dismissal of Wolfe as an aging journalist who has overreached himself if not putting him "in his place"? The world of literary art is a hierarchy, not a democracy: Journalists are only literary journeymen.

Leaving aside for the moment the merit of Updike's argument, he had some cause for annoyance with Wolfe. Though the two men have never met, their association goes back many years, to March 10, 1964, when Updike received his first National Book Award. Wolfe teasingly described Updike approaching the stage to receive his award for *The Centaur*, wearing.

a pair of 19-month-old loafers. . . . First he squinted at the light through his owl-eyed eye glasses. Then he ducked his head and his great thatchy medieval haircut toward his right shoulder. Then he threw up his left shoulder and his left elbow. Then he bent forward at the waist. And then, before the shirred draperies of the Grand Ballroom and an audience of 1,000 culturati, he went into his Sherwin-Williams blush.

The following year, Wolfe joked that Updike's stories, like most of those in *The New Yorker,* were all about men

who meditate over their wives and their little children with what used to be called "inchoate longings" for something else. The scene is some vague exurb or country place or summer place . . . with Morris chairs, glowing coals, wooden porches . . . leaves falling, buds opening, birdwatcher types of birds, tufted grackles and things, singing, hearts rising and falling, but not far—in short, a great lily-of-the-valley vat full of what Lenin called "bourgeois sentimentality."

Updike has weathered much more pointed attacks (Gore Vidal cites Mailer's gibe that Updike's writing is the kind that "those who know nothing about writing think good") than these mild digs by Tom Wolfe half a lifetime ago; it's unlikely that they could have colored his reading of *A Man in Full.* But the context of the long-ago remarks is something else. In 1965 Wolfe was writing for the recently inaugurated *New York Herald Tribune* weekly supplement, *New York,* under the editorial direction of Clay Felker. Ambitious to undercut and overtake the revered *New Yorker,* Felker assigned Wolfe to do a two-part profile in April 1965, attacking the magazine as stuffy, out-of-touch, and boring under its dull editor, William Shawn. Wolfe leaped joyfully at the task, calling the first installment "Tiny Mummies! The True Story of the Ruler of 43rd Street's Land of the Walking Dead!" The second installment, a playful dissection of the magazine's complicated syntax and involuted style, was called "Lost in the Whichy Thickets."

There was some smoke to Wolfe's fire. Although virtually everyone agreed that the magazine deserved praise for publishing John Hersey's *Hiroshima*, Rachel Carson's *Silent Spring*, and Truman Capote's *In Cold Blood*, many readers also found it too arch, too mannered, too predictable, especially in its arts and literature coverage and in its fiction. Wolfe charged that the magazine had shunned the literary giants of the century such as Hemingway, Faulkner, and Steinbeck, while elevating "tiny giants" such as J. D. Salinger, E. B. White, James Thurber, and A. J. Liebling to Olympian status. It was in this context that he cited the failings of Updike's "tabescent" stories, filled with their "inchoate" longings, clearly implying that he viewed Updike as a pygmy in the making. (Wolfe recycled the unfamiliar *tabescent*, which means "dwindling" or "wasting away," in his 1989 *Harper's* essay, again applying it to Updike.)

"Tiny Mummies" was often funny and entertaining, though as the subtitle suggests it is mostly a demolition job on the "ruler" of Forty-third Street. Like most satire, it also violated some rules of delicacy and good taste—as well as accuracy. Wolfe charged that *The New Yorker*'s myth-making apparatus shrouded its editorial procedures and its editors in a reverential haze—especially its reclusive managing editor, William Shawn, who had replaced the legendary Harold Ross in 1952. As the successor to the great editor who started the magazine, Shawn had a difficult role to play. He was a quiet and private man, lacking Ross's forceful personality and mystique. By his own apparent design, very little was known about his past, and he declined to be interviewed by Wolfe for the story. Wolfe, trying to spoof what he considered Shawn's aura of mystery, claimed that he had discovered that William Shawn had been the original target of Richard Loeb and Nathan Leopold, who kidnapped and murdered Bobby Franks in Chicago in 1924.

The deserved deluge of condemnation that greeted this misguided attempt at satire almost drowned Wolfe's more salient criticisms. Something of the depth of emotion that it stirred in John Updike at the time is suggested by his comment in 2001, in a letter responding to a request for his reaction to Wolfe's articles. "I did resent Wolfe's attack . . . at the time," Updike writes, "and still think it was a crass, philistine, sensational piece of work, casually cruel in its flip judgments and especially cruel to a man, William Shawn, whose whole editorial career was an exemplification of fairness, intelligence, dedication, and modesty."

Despite his resentment at Wolfe's treatment of Shawn, Updike sought to avoid ill feeling on Wolfe's part. His review of *A Man in Full* appeared in the November 26, 1998, issue of *The New Yorker*. A week earlier, on November 18, Updike received a National Book Foundation Medal for "Distinguished Contribution to American Letters." This would be his third National Book Award, the first having come in 1964 for *The Centaur* and the second in 1982, for *Rabbit Is Rich*. In a June 2001 letter to this author, Updike says that he assumed Wolfe would be in the audience that night, "primed to receive the award for *A Man in Full*." (Wolfe did not attend; the award went another novel, Alice McDermott's *Charming Billy*.) Updike regarded his remarks as "a kind of peace offering, or at least noncombative bow, to Wolfe. . . ." This is the context for Wolfe's description cited earlier of Updike's awkward stumbling, his "thatchy medieval haircut" and his "Sherwin-Williams blush." That Updike should begin his acceptance speech by quoting Wolfe's barbed account of his first award does indeed seem generous.

It may have been too late for peace offerings. First Wolfe, apparently outraged at the negative reviews of his book, started calling Updike and Mailer "old bags of bones" in radio and TV interviews. Then he included their defender, John Irving, on his hit list: "I think of the three of them now—because there are three—as Larry, Curly and Moe," Wolfe told Evan Solomon, the host of a Canadian book show, *Hot Type*. "It must gall them a bit that everyone—even them—is talking about me." "By all accounts," noted London's *Sunday Times* with quiet glee a few days later, "America's young rap poets and writers of serial-killer thrillers are perfect pussycats; but steer clear of the old guys."

Wolfe elaborated on his complaints a few months after the reviews in an article that he later included in *Hooking Up* (2000). It is called, rather unpromisingly for those who were hoping for a more measured and thoughtful analysis, "My Three Stooges."

The first few pages are devoted to a summary of the years of labor Wolfe put in gathering material for the book, much of it never used; to the gratifying financial success of the book (1,375,000 hardback copies, including eight printings) and to the good reviews, especially those in *The New York Times* and Paul Gray's laudatory comments in his *Time* cover story. Wolfe displays an almost childlike joy in telling us how he signed more than two thousand books in four hours at a Borders bookstore in Atlanta, and in explaining his delight with his picture on the cover of *Time*, "wearing a white double-breasted suit and vest and a white homburg and holding a pair of white kid gloves in one hand and a white walking stick in the other." The "famous *Time* logo" was modified just for him to be "white against a white background." The caption shouted, "TOM WOLFE WRITES AGAIN." The subtitle read: "The novelist with the white stuff is back with *A Man in Full*. More than a million copies, before anyone has read a word!"

But there was trouble lurking, Wolfe says. In a broadside attack unique "in all the annals of American literature," Updike, Mailer, and Irving "denounced" his novel. Why should these "famous old novelists" bother to "declare a particular new novel anathema"? Because, he answers, they are old and tired and afraid they are about to be replaced.

Wolfe concentrates his fire on the age and supposed infirmities of the "old codgers" Updike and Mailer—Updike was sixty-six, publicly "complaining about his aging bladder," and Mailer was seventy-five, hobbling around with "two canes, one for each rusted-out hip." How could "our two senior citizens have found the energy in their exhausted carcasses" to review a mere novel—and at such length! "Frankly, I was amazed, not that the two of them didn't approve, but that at this stage of their lives they had taken the time. 'My God, those two old piles of bones!' I said to the reporters who began clamoring for interviews. 'They're my age!'"

Tit for tat, perhaps—both writers had alluded to Wolfe's age in their reviews—but not very persuasive. Both Mailer and Updike have been energetic and healthy enough to write many books in recent years. He is on firmer ground with John Irving—though he has to admit that, at fifty-seven, Irving was not exactly "old" (like Wolfe, Irving looks a decade younger than his years). But there is no question that Irving lost his composure when asked about Wolfe's book on *Hot Type,* or that Wolfe thoroughly enjoys himself in recounting the episode: "Irving's face turned red. His sexagenarian jowls shuddered. He began bleeping." (The obscenities were edited out of the videotape Wolfe saw.) "The bleeping concluded with "He's not a writer. . . . You couldn't teach that bleeping bleep to bleeping freshmen in a bleeping freshman English class!'—and on and on in that mode. I don't pretend to be a lip-reader, but it took no particular expertise to decode bleepos that began with such bitterly lower-lip-bitten *f*'s. Evan Solomon kept covering his face with his hand and smiling at the same time, as if to say, 'How can the old coot make such a spectacle of himself—but wow, it's wonderful television!'"

Later, in New York, Solomon asked Wolfe if he felt bad that

"one of the foremost novelists in the United States, John Irving, says you simply can't write." Why should he feel bad, Wolfe responded: "Now I've got all three." "All three?" "Larry, Curly, and Moe. Updike, Mailer, and Irving. My three stooges."

What Wolfe meant, he explained, was that "a stooge is literally a straight man who feeds lines to the lead actor in a play. My three stooges were so upset by *A Man in Full*, they were feeding me lines I couldn't have dreamed up if they had asked me to write the script for them." Why were they upset? Because they saw the handwriting on the wall. It said that *A Man in Full* was the harbinger of "the likely new direction" in fiction, "the intensely realistic novel, based upon reporting, that plunges wholeheartedly into the social reality of America today. . . ." A revolution was under way that "would soon make many prestigious artists, such as our three old novelists, appear effete and irrelevant."

Panic-stricken because their own recent books—Updike's *Toward the End of Time* and *Bech at Bay*, Mailer's *The Gospel According to the Son*, Irving's *A Widow for One Year*—had not been bestsellers, and jealous of Wolfe's astonishing success, they were now trying to deny him admission to the hallowed halls of literature; he was a mere entertainer. Tom Wolfe "no longer belongs to us (if indeed he ever did?)," Mailer had said; Updike said that he appeals to an American public that Updike had elsewhere described as "coarsened in its tastes."

Wolfe moves away from simple ad hominem attacks on his antagonists in the longest part of his essay to make three important points. The first is that more people watch movies than read books, and that talented young people who once would have been writers are now making films. The second is that movies can't explain life as well as books do; *Anna Karenina* has "enough action, suspense, and melodrama" for "ten movies," but no movie version can capture "the play of thoughts and feelings" of the characters or of "Tolstoy's incomparable symphony of status concerns, status competition, and class guilt within Russia's upper orders." The third is that we used to have American writers who knew this (Dreiser, Lewis, John Steinbeck, James Farrell) and we still have some today (the Norman Mailer who wrote *The Naked and the Dead* and *The Executioner's Song* among them). But Mailer and the others have lost their way. He, Tom Wolfe, is trying to show them how to get back on track.

Edmund Wilson once noted that Ernest Hemingway's personal voice when he commented on his relationships with other writers was querulous and unattractive. Mark Twain, whom Wolfe resembles in some flattering ways, could be remarkably mean-spirited, as he was with Bret Harte. Wolfe's pokes at Updike, Mailer, and Irving as "stooges" and out-of-touch failures are inconsistent with the frequent wit and humor of his fiction and nonfiction, and the dignified, even courtly presence often remarked in his interviews, not to mention the thoughtful courtesy of his personal correspondence. Although he has had his supporters, particularly among fellow reporters, Wolfe has opened himself to charges of self-promotion and ambition—and insecurity. He has, mocks Jim Windulf in *The New York Observer*, a "quivering need to be perceived as a great author. For all his bluster and devil-may-care attacks on literary establishments from *The New Yorker* to the American Academy of Arts and Letters, Mr. Wolfe, at age 68, is desperate to be accepted into the literary pantheon. He longs for, lusts for, posterity."

"Quivering" and "desperate" are as accurate in describing Wolfe as "stooges" is in describing his antagonists—mere hyperbole. But we need to step back from the personalities involved. Updike in a personal letter calls this contretemps a "so-called feud"; Wolfe says it has all been "*pour le sport*"; and by comparison with the other quarrels between writers described in this book, this one is far less vituperative, ill-tempered, or personally damaging to those involved. At the same time, it raises legitimate questions, as already noted, about what we expect of novelists in modern America. What should they be writing about, and how?

However these questions are answered, it's fair to say that not many writers' works and reputations survive for more than a generation or two. Many extremely popular and influential masters of social realism such as Lewis, Dreiser, and John Dos Passos created more and better fiction than Wolfe has, and they are little read today. But Wolfe has an additional hurdle if he hopes to achieve posterity. Most of the writers he admires, from Zola and Balzac through Steinbeck and Farrell to his younger contemporaries Pat Conroy and Joseph Wambaugh, are known best for attempting serious, weighty—often ponderous—investigations into not just society but the human soul. Even in Dickens, Lewis, and Mark Twain, it's not their satire that makes them live but the efforts of their great characters, like David Copperfield, Carol Kennicott, and Huckleberry Finn, to make sense of their lives.

Late in Wolfe's novel, Charlie Croker tries to make sense of his life in a moment that suggests emotional depth; he wonders, "Am I like that character in that book—he couldn't remember the name of it—Ivan Something, the one where the man gets a second life—and helplessly repeats the first one?" The apparent reference to Tolstoy's *The Death of Ivan Ilyich*, in which Ivan realizes that his life has been wasted, suggests that Wolfe is aiming at the same sort of soul-shattering revelation achieved by Tolstoy, but the comparison does not work to Wolfe's advantage. As with Sherman McCoy, the self-anointed "master of the universe" in *The Bonfire of the Vanities*, we can be amused and entertained by Wolfe's characters, but we aren't moved to care very much about them or their dilemmas. (In Charlie's case, it also seems unlikely that he would actually read Tolstoy's novella.)

It is here that the most substantial criticism of Wolfe's work comes into play—the assertion by Birkerts in particular, but also by Mailer and Updike, that his novels lack psychological depth. Wolfe's comments on this supposed lack in his letter to the author are worth repeating. "[L]et's take the case of Anna Karenina," he says.

Anna is a not terribly bright or complicated woman who gives up her reputation and social position and, by and by, her son for love. Vronsky is a not terribly bright or complicated man who gives up his reputation and social position and military career for love. Psychologically that's what they are from beginning to end. What gives the book a rich brocade (if we must use an outdated metaphor) is the way in which this drive—love, sex—becomes entangled in the Russian social order of their time. Without that, it would be nothing but a soap opera. For that matter, what would happen if the same story were told against the backdrop of America in the year 2001? There would be no tragic series of events. It would be a society divorce item in the Page Six column of the *New York Post*. Anna would simply head off with Vronsky and probably get custody of the boy, if she wanted it. It's Tolstoy's detailed rendition of the period's social classes and moral and social rules—and that alone—that makes the characters interesting. What would they be without it?

Clearly, Wolfe is not caught up in the psychological obsession, the internal mechanisms of justification and remorse that most readers respond to when reading Anna's story. His métier is a rather cool, even chilly hyper-realism, a frequently grotesque mixture of satire and comedy that, while sometimes brilliant, appeals more to the mind than to the heart.

But it should be noted that Wolfe does not regard his work as either comic or satiric. "As for satire and comedy," he continues in his letter,

> I'm sorry, but not for a moment have I intended to write either one. I wrote both *The Bonfire of the Vanities* and *A Man in Full* as absolutely accurate depictions of our times. How could some of it help but strike people as funny? Just look around you. I have never, ever, thought of anything I've written as satire, in fiction or non-fiction. I realize that the dictionary's definition of satire is rather broad: any writing that treats of human foibles and vices and holds them up to ridicule. But I have always thought of satire as writing that pushes the truth to some ridiculous outer limit. More often than not, I found out later that my measurements of the human condition have been too conservative.

Perhaps Wolfe is joking here, just as he surely is when he calls Updike, Mailer, and Irving "stooges." "Tiny Mummies" is not satire? We need to trust the tale, not the teller, and the reasonable response of careful readers. Certainly college students of literature recognize and admire Wolfe's work as based on admirably and effectively observed fact—but they respond to it primarily as funny exaggeration. It is usually broad enough to reach most readers, but as every teacher of literature knows, comedy and satire are harder to teach than tragedy and melodrama; everyone can feel, but not everyone can think. Wolfe may be thought of as a moralist, which he is, but it is even more to the point to see him as a novelist of ideas.

In a practical sense, writers in this country generally survive after their death—that is, they stay in print—because they are taught in the classroom. Moreover, short books, like small dogs, live longer; Fitzgerald's *The Great Gatsby* and Hemingway's *In Our Time* and *The Sun Also Rises* are taught much more frequently than *Tender Is the Night* and *For Whom the Bell Tolls*, not necessarily because they are better but because shorter books are easier to get students to read and to teach. Tom Wolfe's novels are long and they are—or are seen to be—comic satires. As such, they are not likely to be taught frequently in literature classes, whatever their merits.

In the meantime, we can be grateful to Tom Wolfe for keeping the literary pot bubbling with the questions suggested earlier. He has answered some of them for us. Can a popular book be good? Of course it can; even Updike and Mailer find much of value in *A Man in Full*, and many others think it is a very good, even a great book. If it's a satire, can it move us? Sometimes, as in *Catch-22*, but not, the evidence suggests, in Wolfe's work. Is it true that most novelists say too little of interest about America, and too much about themselves? Not really, as the evidence of Mailer and others indicates, but it's a good talking point and a useful stick for beating young writers with. Finally, can journalists write great fiction? Yes; witness the work of Whitman, Dreiser, Hemingway, Stephen Crane, and Mark Twain.

And has Tom Wolfe joined this elite club? Not yet; not quite; but he's only seventy years old, after all . . . his self-described old bones are now at work on a novel about the university in America, and if that doesn't take him over the top, nothing will.

Notes

Preface

xi **Reviewers on writers:** Roger Rosenblatt, "Why Writers Attack Writers," *Time*, 24 Jan. 2000 (online); Walter Kirn, "Remember When Books Mattered?" *The New York Times Book Review*, 4 Feb. 2001: 8; Judith Shulevitz, "The Best Revenge," *The New York Times Book Review*, 17 June 2001 (online).

1. Partners No More: Mark Twain and Bret Harte

1. **Harte background:** Marilyn Duckett, *Mark Twain and Bret Harte* (Norman, Okla.: University of Oklahoma Press, 1964), 8–14.
2. **Indian massacre:** Gary Scharnhorst, *Bret Harte: Opening the American Literary West* (Norman, Okla.: University of Oklahoma Press, 2000), 13–14. The episode occurred 26 Feb. 1860, on an island in Humboldt Bay, near Arcata, when more than sixty Wiyot Indians, mostly women and children, were murdered by white settlers. Harte's uncompromising condemnation of the massacre, and his gruesomely effective description of what he saw when he went to the scene, nearly cost him his life. Many years later he commented scornfully on "the old story of our Anglo Saxon civilized aggression" and its "desire to 'improve' people off the face of the earth with a gun. . . ."

   Harte publications: *Atlantic* story: Scharnhorst, 20; *Californian* publications: Scharnhorst, 25. His short story "The Legend of Monte del Diablo" appeared in the October 1863 issue of the *Atlantic*, preceding Thoreau's essay "Life Without Principle."

3. **Harte manner:** Francis Murphy, "The End of a Friendship: Two Unpublished Letters from Twain to Howells About Bret Harte," *The New England Quarterly* 58, no. 1 (March 1985): 87–91.

   Harte and Twain meeting: T. Edgar Pemberton, *The Life of Bret Harte* (New York: Dodd, Mead, 1903), 74–75.

   Twain's military service: Mark Twain, "Private History of a Campaign That Failed," in *The Portable Mark Twain*, ed. Bernard DeVoto (New York: Penguin, 1977), 139–140.

4. **Frog story:** "The Notorious Jumping Frog of Calaveras County," in *The Portable Mark Twain*, 41. ("Notorious" later was changed to the more familiar "celebrated.")

   Harte on Twain's "Jumping Frog": Pemberton, 74–75.

5. **Harte influence:** Henry Seidel Canby, "The Luck of Bret Harte," *Saturday Review of Literature* II (17 Apr. 1916): 717.

   Harte on Twain's qualities: Duckett, 28, citing George R. Stewart and Edwin S. Fussell, eds. *San Francisco in 1866, by Bret Harte: Being Letters to the Springfield Republican* (San Francisco: The Book Club of California, 1951), 83.

6. **Twain debt to Harte:** *Mark Twain's Letters,* vol. I, ed. Albert Bigelow Paine (New York: Harper & Brothers, 1950): I, 182–183; to Thomas Bailey Aldrich, dated 28 Jan. 1870. It should be noted that the sentence in which Twain acknowledges his debt to Harte begins: "But I do hate to be accused of plagiarizing Bret Harte, who trimmed and trained me . . . ," and that in this same letter Twain says, "Bret broke off our friendship a year ago without any cause or provocation that I am aware of."

   Twain's competitiveness, rivalry with Harte: Van Wyck Brooks, *The Ordeal of Mark Twain* (New York: Meridian Books, 1955; originally published 1920) 135, *Mark Twain's Letters* I: 102; to Mrs. Jane Clemens and Mrs. Moffett (Twain's mother and sister), dated 20 Jan. 1866, and Duckett, 63, citing Twain's 11 March 1871 letter to Orion Clemens.

7. **Twain's rage:** Hamlin Hill, *God's Fool* (New York: Harper & Row, 1973), Introduction, xxiii–xxiv. Duckett, 293, describes Hamlin Garland's 1895 interviews with Twain and Harte, when both writers were in London but did not meet. Twain told Garland with "cold malignity" that he was keeping a diary to be published after his death in which he would settle accounts with all who had offended him—including Harte, Duckett infers from Garland's account.

8–9. **"Plain Language from Truthful James" and Twain and Howells quotes:** Scharnhorst, 52, 63.

9. **Emerson visit:** Scharnhorst, 86.

   Harte and literary establishment: Bernard DeVoto, *Mark Twain's America* (Boston: Houghton Mifflin, 1932), 191–192; Scharnhorst, 67.

10. **Harte as lecturer:** Scharnhorst, 104, 107.

    Harte and money problems: Scharnhorst, 77, 100.

11. **Twain's Hartford house:** Duckett, 92. A National Historic Landmark, the Mark Twain House in Hartford is beautifully restored and open to the public.

12. **Twain irritation with Harte's remarks:** *Mark Twain in Eruption*, 278–279.
    Two Men of Sandy Bar: Scharnhorst, 122.

13. *Ah Sin* **collaboration:** Scharnhorst, 126–127, Albert Bigelow Paine, *Mark Twain: A Biography* (New York: Harper & Brothers, 1912), 587.

    Twain's misanthropy: "Mark Twain Returns," *Atlantic* July–August 2000, 49–81, including Twain's "A Murder, a Mystery, and a Marriage," 54–64, and Roy Blount's Foreword, 49–53, and Afterword, 67–81. Twain described this short piece as a "skeleton novelette," the first part of an intended collaboration for the *Atlantic* in March 1876, between himself, James Russell Lowell, Henry James (astonishingly!)—and Bret Harte. Nothing came of the idea and the story remained in Twain's files, unpublished until now. It is an ill-tempered and hopeless mess, as Blount says, of interest here primarily because its bitterly sarcastic tone suggests Twain's state of mind while he was trying to work with Harte.

14. **Harte as "gentle, trustful":** Duckett, 335, citing Harte, "Jeffrey Briggs' Love Story," *Writings* III: 258.

    Harte letter to Twain: Duckett, 135–136; this was the first publication of the letter.

    Twain reaction to Harte letter, Parsloe snub: Duckett, 141, 143; Harte telegram: Scharnhorst, 128.

15. *Ah Sin* **reception:** Scharnhorst, 129.

15–17. **Twain opposition to Harte appointment:** Scharnhorst, 134–135.

16. **Howells to Hayes on Harte:** Scharnhorst, 138.

17. **Twain's "black frost":** George McMichael, *Concise Anthology of American Literature*, 2nd ed. (New York: Macmillan, 1985), Introduction, "Whittier Birthday Dinner Speech," 1111.

    Twain to Howells: Henry Nash Smith and William M. Gibson with Frederick Anderson, eds., *Mark Twain–Howells Letters* I (Cambridge: Belknap Press of Harvard University Press, 1960), 235–236.

18. **Harte's dismissal:** Scharnhorst, 78.

    Harte and Van de Velde: Scharnhorst, 199.

Harte's English successes: Duckett, 308.

19. Harte's Jewish ancestry: Scharnhorst, 4.

Harte's alleged homosexuality: Duckett, 10, 173; Scharnhorst, 238; Axel Nissen, *Bret Harte: Prince and Pauper* (Jackson, Miss.: University of Mississippi Press, 2000).

Twain on Harte: *Twain-Howells Letters* I: (3 Aug. 1877), 192; (15 Apr. 1879), 261; (23 Mar. 1882), 396.

20. Twain's reaction to Harte's death: Duckett, 303, citing DeLancey Ferguson, *Mark Twain: Man and Legend* (Indianapolis: Bobbs, Merrill, 1943), 187–188.

Twain's dream: *Twain-Howells Letters* II: (4 Dec. 1903) 775.

Twain linked with Harte: *Mark Twain in Eruption,* ed. Bernard DeVoto (New York: Harper & Brothers, 1940), 219.

Man without a country: *Mark Twain in Eruption*, 286.

21. "The damned human race": *Mark Twain in Eruption*, 372.

22. Harte on Twain as "sick man": Duckett, 336.

Harte and partners: Duckett, citing *The Writings of Bret Harte, 1896–1914* II (Boston: Houghton Mifflin), xxiv.

2. THE BOY WITH THE INTERESTED EYES: ERNEST HEMINGWAY AND GERTRUDE STEIN

23. Mother Goose: John Malcolm Brinnin, *The Third Rose: Gertrude Stein and Her World* (Reading, Mass.: Addison-Wesley, 1987; originally published Boston: Atlantic Monthly Press, 1959), 287.

MacLeish: John Raeburn, *Fame Became of Him: Hemingway as Public Writer* (Bloomington, Ind.: Indiana University Press, 1984), 1. Raeburn's title and the description of Hemingway come from MacLeish's poem "Years of the Dog," in which the poet asks "what became" of the young Hemingway, and answers, "Fame became of him." Archibald MacLeish, *Collected Poems* (Boston: Houghton Mifflin Company, 1963), 376–377.

24. Stein descriptions: Ernest Hemingway, *A Moveable Feast* (New York: Charles Scribner's Sons, 1964), 13–14.

Stein as "Jewish patriarch": Brinnin, 277.

Stein and Toklas: *A Moveable Feast*, 14.

25. Stein ego: Brinnin, 272.

James Joyce: *Ernest Hemingway: Selected Letters*, ed. Carlos Baker (New York: Charles Scribner's Sons, 1981), 87.

Ezra Pound: Gertrude Stein, *The Autobiography of Alice B. Toklas*, in

Selected Writings of Gertrude Stein, ed. Carl Van Vechten (New York: Random House, 1962), 189.

William Carlos Williams: Stein, *Autobiography*, 274.

26. **Stein style:** Stein, *Selected Writings*: Carl Van Vechten, "A Stein Song," xxiii; *Autobiography*, 198

Kazin and Gold objections: *Hemingway: The Critical Heritage*, ed. Jeffrey Meyers (London: Routledge & Kegan Paul, 1982), 229.

Stein and *Three Lives*: *Autobiography*, 63–64.

27. **Stein as genius:** *Autobiography*, 5.

Stein and Sherwood Anderson: *Autobiography*, 185.

28. **Hadley and friend on Hemingway:** Carlos Baker, *Ernest Hemingway: A Life Story* (New York: Charles Scribner's Sons, 1969), 78, 79.

29. **Anderson letters:** Baker, *Life Story*, 83; James R. Mellow, *Hemingway: A Life Without Consequences* (Boston: Houghton Mifflin, 1992), 149.

Hemingway to Anderson: Baker, *Life Story*, 162.

Stein to Anderson: Sherwood Anderson and Gertrude Stein, *Sherwood Anderson/Gertrude Stein*, ed. Ray Lewis White (Chapel Hill: University of North Carolina Press, 1972), 18.

Stein advice to Hemingway: *Autobiography*, 201.

Stein on instruction: *Autobiography*, 76.

30. **"Remarks are not literature":** *Autobiography*, 270.

Stein and bullfighting: Robert McAlmon and Kay Boyle, *Being Geniuses Together: 1920–1930* (San Francisco: North Point Press, 1984), 161.

Hemingway to Stein: Baker, *Letters*, 79; letter dated (18 Feb. 1923).

31. **Hemingway praise of Stein:** Mellow, *Hemingway: A Life Without Consequences*, 219, citing review of *Geography and Plays*, Paris edition of *Chicago Tribune*, 5 March 1923.

Stein review of Hemingway: Mellow, *Hemingway: A Life Without Consequences*, 246.

32. **Stein quote:** Gertrude Stein, *The Making of Americans* (New York: Something Else Press, 1966), 1.

Stein influence on Hemingway style: Stein, *The Making of Americans*, 218; Mellow, *Hemingway: A Life Without Consequences*, 251.

Rosenfeld review: Mellow, *Hemingway: A Life Without Consequences*, 315.

33. **Wilson review:** Reprinted in *The Shores of Light* (New York: Noonday Press, 1952), as "Emergence of Ernest Hemingway," 120.

34. **Anderson parody:** Ernest Hemingway, *The Torrents of Spring* (New York: Charles Scribner's Sons, 1972; originally published 1926), 8.

35. **Dos Passos rebuke:** John Dos Passos, *The Fourteenth Chronicle: Letters and Diaries of John Dos Passos*, ed. Townsend Ludington (Boston: Gambit, 1973), 158.

Anderson response to parody: Brinnin, 255.

Hemingway intent with *Torrents*: Baker, *Letters*, 174; Mellow, *Hemingway: A Life Without Consequences*, 381, citing Hemingway to Pound, dated 30 Nov. 1925 (Yale Collection of American Literature, Beinecke Rare Book and Manuscript Library, Yale University).

36. **Expatriates:** Ernest Hemingway, *The Sun Also Rises* (New York: Charles Scribner's Sons, 1926), 115.

38. **"Poor Scott Fitzgerald":** Scott Donaldson, *Hemingway vs. Fitzgerald. The Rise and Fall of a Literary Friendship* (Woodstock, N.Y.: Overlook Press), 1999, citing August 1936 *Esquire* version of the story; Hemingway changed the name to "Julian" in the final version.

Attacks on Hemingway by Broun, Fadiman: Raeburn, 64.

Attack by Lewis: Baker, *Letters*, 264, note 2.

Attack by Woolf: Meyers, *Hemingway: The Critical Heritage*, 196–197; Raeburn, 34.

Attack by Eastman: Raeburn, 60.

39. **Hemingway to Smith:** Baker, *Letters*, 242, letter dated c. 21 Jan. 1927.

Hemingway responses to critics: Raeburn, 34.

Wilson criticism of Hemingway persona: quoted in Raeburn, 70.

40. **Critical reception of *Autobiography:*** James R. Mellow, *Charmed Circle: Gertrude Stein & Company* (New York: Praeger, 1974), 356–357, 20–21.

40–42. **Stein comments on Hemingway:** *Autobiography*, 200–207.

42. **Effect of Stein attack on Hemingway:** Jeffrey Meyers, *Hemingway: A Biography* (New York: Harper & Row, 1985), 81.

42–46. **Hemingway response to Stein attack:** For a full discussion, see Kirk Curnutt, " 'In the Temps de Gertrude': Hemingway, Stein, and the Scene of Instruction at 27, Rue de Fleurus," in J. Gerald Kennedy and Jackson R. Bryer, eds., *French Connections* (New York: St. Martin's Press, 1998), 122–139.

42. **Stein as "goofy":** Baker, *Letters*, 395.

Stein as "a woman who isn't a woman": Ernest Hemingway, *By-Line: Ernest Hemingway* (New York: Charles Scribner's Sons, 1967), 28.

Stein and "female": Baker, *Letters*, 423–424.

Hemingway refuses Gingrich offer to attack Stein: Baker, *Letters*, 411.

43. **Stein no longer the writer:** Michael Reynolds, *Hemingway: The American Homecoming* (New York: Norton, 1999), 84.

Stein as "literary mother" of Hemingway: Michael Reynolds, *Hemingway: The Final Years* (New York: Norton, 1999), 146.

43. Hemingway on Stein instruction, first meeting: *Moveable Feast*, 11–21 inclusive; see 13, 14, 17, 18, 19.

44. Lost Generation: *Moveable Feast*, 29, Brinnin, 233 (for Stein's hotel version).

45. Cowley on Lost Generation: Malcolm Cowley, *Exile's Return* (New York: Viking Press, 1969; originally published in 1934), 3.

Hemingway on Stein and Lost Generation: *Moveable Feast*, 30–31.

46. Hemingway final visit to Stein apartment: *Moveable Feast*, 117, 118–119.

47. Hemingway marketing: Donaldson, 300.

48. Stewart on Hemingway and friendship: Donald Ogden Stewart, "An Interview," in *Hemingway-Fitzgerald Annual, 1973* (Washington: NCR Microcard Editions, 1974), 85.

3. The Slap Heard 'Round the World: Sinclair Lewis, Theodore Dreiser, and the Nobel Prize

49. Lewis appearance: Thompson cited in Vincent Sheean, *Dorothy and Red* (Boston: Houghton Mifflin, 1963), 347; Bacon cited in Mark Schorer, *Sinclair Lewis: An American Life* (New York: McGraw-Hill, 1961), 502; Sheean in Sheean, 10; Cowley in Schorer, 316.

50. Mencken and Lewis: Schorer, 284. Mark Schorer notes that Nathan was sometimes unreliable as a storyteller, but Mencken's own account of meeting that "idiot" Lewis is very similar to Nathan's.

Main Street and Babbitt success: James D. Hart, *The Popular Book: A History of America's Literary Taste* (Berkeley: University of California Press, 1963; London: Oxford Press, 1950), 236.

51. Babbitt definition: *The American Heritage Dictionary of the English Language*, 1967 edition.

52. Nobel Prize speech: Sheldon Grebstein, *Sinclair Lewis* (New York: Twayne, 1962), 120–121.

53. Whitman: "Time will put him above all other American poets up to now," Dreiser said of Whitman in 1901. Richard Lingeman, *Theodore Dreiser: An American Journey* (New York: John Wiley & Sons, 1993), 186.

Dreiser as reporter: Richard Lingeman, "The Titan," *American Heritage* 44, no. 1 (Feb./Mar. 1993): 74–75.

55. Dreiser "Immoral!" protest: Lingeman, "The Titan," 73.

Dreiser advice to contributor: W. A. Swanberg, *Dreiser* (New York: Scribner's, 1965), 126.

56. **Lengel and Dreiser:** Swanberg, 126.

   "Blazing with sex": Daniel Aaron, "Brother Theodore: Review of Richard Lingeman, *Theodore Dreiser: An American Journey, 1908–1945,* Volume II," *The New Republic* 203, no. 30 (1990), 34.

   Dreiser self-description: Lingeman, 62.

   Fornication: Aaron, 34.

57. **"Editors Who Write":** Schorer, 179.

   "vescits": This is Lewis's neologism; he was probably imitating the Yiddish pronunciation of *waistcoats.*

   Thelma Cudlipp, Dreiser dismissal: Swanberg, 131; Aaron, 34.

58. *Our Mr. Wrenn* **request:** James M. Hutchisson and Stephen R. Pastore, "Sinclair Lewis and Theodore Dreiser: New Letters and a Reexamination of Their Relationship," *American Literary Realism* 32, no. 1 (Fall 1999): 73. The authors explain that the letters were "purchased in 1997 by a rare book dealer" who gave them permission to examine and publish the documents, 71.

   Cowley on Lewis career: Malcolm Cowley, "The Last Flight from Main Street," in *Sinclair Lewis: A Collection of Critical Essays, Twentieth Century Views* (Englewood Cliffs, N.J.: Prentice-Hall, 1962), 144 (originally published *New York Times,* 25 Mar. 1951).

   Dreiser in Greenwich Village: H. L. Mencken, *My Life as Author and Editor* (New York: Alfred A. Knopf, 1993), 152, 217.

59. **Schorer on Thompson:** Schorer, 487.

   Dreiser's "dizzy ride": Mencken, 339.

60. **Dreiser flirtation with Thompson:** Lingeman, 433.

   Thompson letter to Lewis: Sheean, 60.

   Dreiser "seething with dislike": Mencken, 152.

61. *American Tragedy* **discussion:** Hutchisson and Pastore, 75–77.

   Lewis in Moscow: Schorer, 495.

62. **Plagiarism charge:** Peter Kurth, *American Cassandra: The Life of Dorothy Thompson* (Boston: Little, Brown, 1990), 143; Swanberg, 344.

63. **Dreiser Nobel ambitions, plans:** Rolf Lunden, "Theodore Dreiser and the Nobel Prize," *American Literature* (May 1978): 218–219.

64. **Lewis Nobel ambitions:** Schorer, 525.

   Nobel committee recommendations: Lunden, 221–222.

   Reasons for Lewis award: Lunden, 223.

65. *Time Magazine* **on** *Elmer Gantry:* Schorer, 476.

   Writers' reactions to prize: Schorer, 560.

66. **Dreiser reaction to loss:** Lunden, 227.

Lewis letter to Dreiser: Hutchisson and Pastore, 78–79.

67–69. Slapping incident: Schorer, 561–564: Swanberg, 372–373; *New York Times,* 21 March 1931, 11.

70. Depression and writers' mood: Malcolm Cowley, *Exile's Return* (New York: Viking Penguin, 1976), 306.

Public reaction to slap: Swanberg, 373; Schorer, 563.

Wolfe and Lewis: Schorer, 558.

71. Thompson and Sheean on Lewis: Sheean, 7, 347.

Arrowsmith dispute: Swanberg, 373.

Lewis American Academy activity, letter to Mrs. Dreiser: Hutchisson and Pastore, 79.

72. "Ambitious young man": Lingeman, "The Titan," 80.

Kazin appraisal: "Dreiser, The Esthetic of Realism," in *Contemporaries* (Boston and Toronto: Little, Brown, 1962), 94–95.

73. Dorothy Parker on Dreiser: *Twentieth-Century Literary Criticism* 10 (Detroit: The Gale Group, 1976), 174.

Lewis centenary, reputation: Jonathan Yardley, "Sinclair Lewis: Forgotten Satirist," *Washington Post* (11 Feb. 1985) http://web.lexis-nexis.com/universe.

74. Scholarship: See Jackson R. Bryer, ed., *Sixteen Modern American Authors: Volume 2: A Survey of Research and Criticism Since 1972* (Durham and London: Duke University Press, 1990). James L. W. West edited the Dreiser section, pages 120–153.

75. Schorer view of Lewis: Schorer, 813.

Vidal on Schorer: "The Romance of Sinclair Lewis," in *The Last Empire: Essays 1992–2000* (New York: Doubleday, 2001), 47.

New Lewis biography: Richard Lingeman, *Sinclair Lewis: Rebel from Main Street* (New York: Random House, 2002). In a 1995 comment for the Sinclair Lewis Society newsletter (http://lilt.ilstu.edu/separry/nbiol.html), Lingeman says that "Schorer did not fully interpret Lewis' personal relations with his wives and friends, particularly Dorothy Thompson; nor did he adequately place him in the context of his times; nor fully appreciate him as a satirist and political and social critic. Lastly, though, God knows, Lewis's life was often sad and self-destructive, he was a funny man, as well as a trenchant critic of American flaws, which he knew as well as a rejected lover knows his mistress's body."

4. Not Always a "Pleasant Tussle": The Difficult Friendship of Edmund Wilson and Vladimir Nabokov

In addition to the sources identified below, I wish to thank Gayla Diment for sending me her paper, "From Kafka's Castle to Axel's Castle: Nabokov vs. Wilson as Critics of Modernism," *Cycnos Nice, France* 12, no. 2 (1995): 83–92. Also helpful were Brian Walter, "Many a Pleasant Tussle: Edmund Wilson and the Nabokovian Aesthetic," *Nabokov Studies* 3 (1966): 77–87, and Jeffrey Meyers, "The Bulldog and the Butterfly: The Friendship of Edmund Wilson and Vladimir Nabokov," *The American Scholar* 63, no. 3 (1994): 379–390; the substance and detail of this article are developed more fully in Meyers's biography of Wilson.

77. **Nabokov New York arrival:** Brian Boyd, *Vladimir Nabokov: The American Years* (Princeton, N.J.: Princeton University Press, 1991), 11–12.

79. **Nabokov job search:** Andrew Field, *VN: The Life and Art of Vladimir Nabokov* (New York: Crown Publishers, 1986), 32.

   Weeks on Nabokov: Cited in Boyd, 26.

80. **Burke on Wilson:** Paul Jay, ed., *The Selected Correspondence of Kenneth Burke and Malcolm Cowley, 1915–1981* (New York: Viking, 1988), 381.

80–82. **Wilson quotes:** Mencken: "Marxism and Literature," in *The Triple Thinkers* (New York: Harcourt, Brace, revised and enlarged edition, 1948), 439; Corbière: "T. S Eliot," in *Axel's Castle: A Study in the Imaginative Literature of 1870–1920* (New York: Charles Scribner's Sons, 1931), 94;

   Reviewer's task: "The Literary Worker's Polonius," in *The Shores of Light* (New York: Farrar, Straus and Giroux, 1952), 605; *The Sun Also Rises*: "The Sportsman's Tragedy," in *The Shores of Light*, 343.

83. **Wilson appearance:** Field, *VN: The Life and Art*, 233; Jeffrey Meyers, *Edmund Wilson: A Biography* (Boston and New York: Houghton Mifflin, 1995), 45. Meyers thinks the "plump Roman emperor" quotation is from Tom Matthews, an editorial assistant to Wilson at *The New Republic*. McCarthy, *The Groves of Academe* (New York: Signet, 1963; originally published 1951 by Harcourt, Brace & World), 13–14.

   Kazin on Wilson: Alfred Kazin, *New York Jew* (New York: Vintage, 1978), 65, 67.

84. **Wilson as minotaur:** Meyers, 233.

   Wilson printed card: Meyers, 248–249.

Wilson as magician: Meyers, 296.

Wilson as tenderhearted: Meyers, 297, 233.

85–86. **Pushkin:** Edmund Wilson, "My Fifty Years with Dictionaries and Grammars," in *The Bit Between My Teeth* (New York: Farrar, Straus and Giroux, 1965), 157; Simon Karlinsky, ed., *The Nabokov-Wilson Letters: Correspondence Between Vladimir Nabokov and Edmund Wilson, 1940–1971* (New York : Harper and Row, 1979), 9 May 1959, 243 (Wilson on *Madame Bovary,* 9 May 1959); Edmund Wilson, "In Honor of Pushkin," in *The Triple Thinkers* (New York: Harcourt, 1938), 32–33.

86. **Wilson on genius:** Meyers, 348.

Levin friendship: Boyd, 47, citing Levin interview in Field, *VN: The Life and Art,* 262.

86–87. **Wilson and Nabokov mutual fondness:** Boyd, 26, 49.

87–88. **Correspondence on writers:** Karlinsky, Wilson on Fielding (16 May 1953), 282; 25 May 1950, 247; Wilson on Dickens (18 Nov. 1950), 253.

88–89. **Nabokov literary opinions** (James et al.): Karlinsky, 25 Jan. 1947, 182; 15 May 1959, 246; 1 Nov. 1948, 210, 213; 27 Nov. 1946, 175.

89–91. **Political disagreements:** Edmund Wilson, "Marxism and Literature," in *The Triple Thinkers* (New York: Harcourt, Brace, revised and enlarged edition, 1948), 200; Karlinsky, 23 Feb. 1948, 195; Karlinsky, note 10, p. 221; Karlinsky, 4 Jan. 1949, 220; Nabokov's reference is to Wilson commenting in an essay on Henry James that, following the revolution, Americans had been "stimulated much like the Russians of the first few years of the Soviet regime—to lay the foundation for a new humanity. . . ." Karlinsky, 182–183; 9 Feb. 1947, 185.

91–92. **Nabokov as teacher:** Field, *VN: The Life and Art,* 273, 274; Vladimir Nabokov, *Strong Opinions* (New York: McGraw-Hill, 1973), 128; Vladimir Nabokov, *Lectures on Literature,* ed. Fredson Bowers (New York: Harcourt Brace Jovanovich/Bruccoli Clark, 1980), 5, 124.

92. **Nabokov on Gogol:** Alfred Appel Jr., "Remembering Nabokov," in Peter Quennell, ed., *Vladimir Nabokov: A Tribute* (London: Weidenfeld & Nicolson, 1979), 16–17.

93. **Nabokov appeal for students, fatigue with teaching:** Field, *VN: The Life and Art,* 225, 227, 224; Karlinsky, 24 Jan. 1952, 270.

93–94. *Lolita* **preparation:** Karlinsky, 1 June 1948, 202, Note 1; Boyd, 211.

95. *Lolita* **intended as tragedy:** Karlinsky, 30 July 1954, 285; Field, *VN: The Life and Art,* 310.

Wilson on *Lolita:* Karlinsky, 8 March 1945, 165; 30 Nov. 1954, 288–289; 30 Nov. 1954, 280.

96. **Wilson and** *Fanny Hill,* **Lolita success:** Field, *VN: The Life and Art*, 313, Boyd, 387.

   Wilson jealousy, praise for Pasternak: Gennady Barabtalo, *Aerial View* (New York: Peter Lang, 1993), 274; V. S. Pritchett, "Difficult Friends," *The New York Times Book Review*, 10 June 1979: 7:1; Stacy Schiff, *Vera* (New York: Modern Library Paperback Edition, 1999), 244, 243.

97. **Wilson tax and teaching problems:** Meyers, 382, 388, 389.

98. **Nabokov on Onegin completion:** Karlinsky, 15 Feb. 1958, 321.

98–100. **Nabokov on translation challenges:** Alexander Pushkin: *Eugene Onegin: A Novel in Verse*, trans. Vladimir Nabokov, 4 vols. (New York: Pantheon Books, 1964), I, i, x; II, 29–35; the Deutsch citation is from Alexander Pushkin, *Eugene Onegin: A Novel in Verse*, trans. Babette Deutsch (New York: Heritage Press, 1943).

98, 100–102. **Wilson NYRB review:** reprinted in Edmund Wilson, "The Strange Case of Pushkin and Nabokov," in *A Window on Russia* (New York: Farrar, Straus and Giroux, 1972), 2; Wilson on Onegin as murderer: "In Honor of Pushkin: I: 'Evgeni Onegin,' " in *The Triple Thinkers* (New York: Harcourt, Brace and Company, 1938), 55–56; Nabokov on "only logical course": *Eugene Onegin*, III, 16.

102. **Meyers on Wilson motive:** Meyers, 20, 442–443.

103. **Nabokov "first reply":** "Reply to My Critics," in *Strong Opinions*, 264.

   Wilson visit in Montreux: Field, *VN: The Life and Art*, 358; Meyers, 435.

   Lowell support for Wilson: Field, *VN: The Life and Art*, 358.

   Wilson "hubris": Clarence Brown, "Pluck and Polemics," *Partisan Review* 40 (February 1973), 313.

103–104. **Nabokov "final salvo":** "Reply to My Critics," in *Strong Opinions*, 248, 251, 358, 262.

105. **"dear friend":** Boyd, 496.

   "Reply" conclusion: *Strong Opinions*, 263.

106. **Updike's "The Cuckoo and the Rooster":** reprinted in his collection *Hugging the Shore: Essays and Criticism* (New York: Alfred Knopf, 1983), 216–222.

   Wilson on Nabokov as "admirable person": *Upstate*, 162.

   Nabokov on Wilson competition: Boyd, 494, citing unpublished note to Andrew Field, 31 Aug. 1973.

107. **Nabokov dream and letter, Wilson reply:** Karlinsky, 2 Mar. 1973, 3 Mar. 1973, 332–333.

   Nabokov on "agony": Karlinsky, "Introduction," 2.

5. THE BATTLE OF THE "TWO CULTURES": C. P. SNOW AND F. R. LEAVIS

109. **Rede Lecture:** C. P. Snow, *The Two Cultures*, ed. Stepan Collini (Cambridge: Cambridge University Press, 1959; Canto edition, 1993), 3.

110. **Vitamin A experiment:** Philip Snow, *Stranger and Brother: A Portrait of C. P. Snow* (New York: Charles Scribner's Sons, 1982), 9.

   Snow's *The Masters:* Geoffrey Heptonstall, "The Two Cultures" (book reviews), *Contemporary Review* (May 1994), 264.

   Kazin on Snow: Alfred Kazin, "A Brilliant Boy from the Mid-lands (1959)," in *Contemporaries* (Boston: Atlantic–Little, Brown, 1962), 171.

111. **Snow appearance:** John Halperin, *C. P. Snow: An Oral Biography* (New York: St. Martin's Press, 1983), Introduction, xiii.

112. **Snow on his qualifications:** *The Two Cultures*, 1.

113. **Snow on definitions of cultures, representative qualities:** *The Two Cultures*, 4, 5, 7, 14–15.

114. **On peasants:** "The Two Cultures: A Second Look," in *The Two Cultures* (Canto edition, 1983), 87, citing Lawrence, "Dana's *Two Years Before the Mast*," in *Studies in Classic American Literature* (New York: Doublday Anchor, 1951), 127–129.

   On Emerson et al.: *The Two Cultures*, 25.

   Snow on obligations to the poor: "The Two Cultures," *The New Statesman* (6 Oct. 1956), 41; *The Two Cultures*, 25, 46.

115. **Leavis background:** Ian MacKillop, "F. R. Leavis: A Personal View," 1995: "Ian MacKillop's Web Pages" www.shef.ac.uk/uni/academic/D-H/el/imk/index.html.

116. **Leavis description:** John Harvey, "Leavis: An Appreciation," in Denys Thompson, ed., *The Leavises: Recollections and Impressions* (Cambridge: Cambridge University Press, 1984), 175, 176; MacKillop, citing *The Sunday Telegraph* (London), n.d.

   Leavis as combative: Jonathan Mirsky, "On Noel Annan (1916–2000)," *The New York Review of Books* (13 Apr. 2000), 6; Frederick Crews, "Another Book to Cross Off Your List," *The Pooh Perplex: A Freshman Casebook* (New York: E. P. Dutton, 1963), 100.

   "They can all go to hell": Crews, 100.

117. **Leavis on *Scrutiny*:** Allen Massie, "Review of [Ian MacKillop's] *F. R. Leavis: A Literary Biography*," *The Daily Telegraph* (London) 27 Jan. 1996: 7.

118. **Steiner and Priestley on Leavis:** Cited in *Contemporary Authors Online*, "F(rank) R(aymond) Leavis 1895–1978" (Detroit: The Gale Group, 2000).

120. **Wells on James:** H. G. Lovatt, *H. G. Wells: His Turbulent Life and Times* (New York: Atheneum, 1971), 254.

  Leavis on Wells: F. R. Leavis, "Babbitt Buys the World," *Scrutiny* I (1932): 80, 82, and "The Literary Mind," *Scrutiny* I (1932): 30.

120. **Snow on Wells:** C. P. Snow, "H. G. Wells and Ourselves," *The Cambridge Review* 56 (19 Oct. and 30 Nov. 1934); 27–28, 148.

122. **Kennedy quote:** Philip Snow, *Stranger and Brother*, 117.

  Snow praise: Burnett, from *Encounter* and other periodicals, 200–201.

  Incendiary: D. Graham Burnett, "A View from the Bridge: The Two Cultures Debate, Its Legacy, and the History of Science," *Daedalus* 128, no. 2 (Spring 1999): 200.

122. **Marginal note:** Burnett, 205

122–124. **Leavis on Snow:** "Two Cultures? The Significance of Lord Snow," in *Nor Shall My Sword: Discourses on Pluralism, Compassion and Social Hope* (London: Chatto & Windus, 1972), 42, 43, 44, 45, 47, 50, 52, 54, 57, 60.

124. **Summary of responses to Leavis attack:** John Naughton, "A Clash Along the Great Rift," *The Observer Review Page Online: The Guardian Online*, (9 July 1995); John Wain, "A Certain Judo Demonstration," *The Hudson Review* (Summer 1962): 253; Frederick Raphael, "When the English Don Went Nuclear," *The Independent* (London), 24 Mar. 1994, 3; Melvyn Bragg, "Whose Side Are You On?," *The Observer Review Page Online: The Guardian Online*, 7 Mar. 1999, 1; Roger Kimball, "The Two Cultures Today," *The New Criterion* 14, no. 5 (Jan. 1996): online at www.newcriterion.com; Geoffrey Heptonstall, *Contemporary Review*, "The Two Cultures: A Second Look at Snow," 264 (May 1994), 35, n. 10 and 49.

124–125. **Defenses of Snow:** Wain, 253; Burnett, 254; Kimball.

125. ***New Republic* attack:** Hilary Corke, "The Dog That Didn't Bark," *The New Republic* (Apr. 13, 1963), 22, 27, 30.

126. **Snow evaluation:** "C. P. Snow," in *Contemporary Authors Online Source Database: Contemporary Authors* (Detroit: The Gale Group, 2000).

  Snow on lasting contributions: C. P. Snow, "The Case of Leavis and the Serious Case," in *Public Affairs* (New York: Scribner's, 1971), 95.

126–127. **Snow's reputation:** Heptonstall; Jonathan Rees, "Will the Sectarian War of Arts and Science Ever End?," *The Independent* (London), 13 Mar. 1999, 7; Graham Farmelo, "The Clash of the Two Cultures: Is Science Still at War with the Arts?," *The Daily Telegraph* (London), 10 Mar. 1999, 14.

128. **Snow on nostalgia:** Snow, *The Two Cultures*, 17–20.
      Blake poem: Preface to "Milton."
129. **Leftist intellectuals:** Rees.
      Snow's ideas: Collini, "Introduction," *The Two Cultures*, xxix.
131. **Leavis reputation:** MacKillop.
132. **Pop culture:** Kimball.

6. "Now There's a Play": Lillian Hellman and Mary McCarthy

135. **"Now There's a Play":** The phrase is William Wright's, from his article "Why Lillian Hellman Remains Fascinating," *The New York Times, 3 Nov. 1996, 2:9.

    "icon": Wayne Warga, "Hellman at 75: Fragile but Furious," in Jackson R. Bryer, *Conversations with Lillian Hellman* (Jackson and London: University Press of Mississippi, 1986), 274

137. **Will Rogers:** Carol Gelderman, *Mary McCarthy: A Life* (New York: St. Martin's Press, 1988), 74.

137–139. **Hellman HUAC:** Lillian Hellman, *Scoundrel Time* (Boston, Toronto: Little, Brown, 1976), 110–111, 114.

139. **Bentley play and "the letter":** William Wright, *Lillian Hellman: The Image, the Woman* (New York: Simon & Schuster, 1986), 381.

    Hellman heroism: Peter Feibleman, *Lilly: Reminiscences of Lillian Hellman* (New York: William Morrow, 1988), 54.

140. **Old age:** Feibleman, 232.

140–141. **McCarthy on Hellman:** Gelderman, 336.

141. **Hellman on McCarthy;** John Phillips and Anne Hollander, "The Art of the Theater I: Lillian Hellman—An Interview," from *Paris Review* 33 (Winter-Spring 1962), in Bryer, 60, 64–95.

    McCarthy appearance: MacDonald cited in Gelderman, 184; Randall Jarrell, from his 1952 novel *Pictures from an Institution*, which caricatures McCarthy as "Gertrude Johnson," cited in Larissa MacFarquhar, "Group Therapy," *The New York Times Book Review*, 26 March 2000, 8.

142. **Mailer on McCarthy:** cited in Michiko Kakutani, "Hellman-McCarthy Libel Suit Stirs Old Antagonisms," *The New York Times, 19 March 1980.

    McCarthy "compulsion" and comments: Gelderman, xiv.

    "bitch": MacFarquhar.

    "grand old lady": Carol Brightman, "With Malice Toward One," in

Writing Dangerously: A Critical Biography of Mary McCarthy (New York: Clarkson Potter, 1992), 599.

   Cavett: Brightman, 599–600; Gelderman, 334.

143. **McCarthy reaction to suit:** Herbert Mitgang, "Miss Hellman Suing a Critic for 2.25 Million," *The New York Times*, 16 Feb. 1980, 12.

   McCarthy and Wilson: Ryan, 254.

   Kazin on McCarthy: MacFarquhar.

   McCarthy as satirist: MacFarquhar; as conscience: John Hersey, "Lillian Hellman," *New Republic*, 18 Sept. 1976, 25.

145. **Offense fund:** Wright, 400.

   "dying old lady": Frances Kiernan, *Seeing Mary Plain: A Life of Mary McCarthy* (New York: W. W. Norton, 2000), 687.

   "lying": Gelderman, 342.

   "bankrupting": Brightman, 611.

   "By suing McCarthy . . ." Wright, 395.

146. **"Intellectual dishonesty":** Wright, 390.

147. **Letter about Hellman at Sarah Lawrence:** Gelderman, 334.

   Cowley and Hellman linked: Brightman, 604.

148. **Howe quote:** Gelderman, 333.

   Scoundrel Time: Brightman, 604, Gelderman, 335.

   Deposition: Brightman, 602.

149. **Baer decision:** Brightman, 638.

150. **Mailer, Rahv:** Brightman, 616–618.

151. **Kazin et al. criticism of Hellman:** Brightman, 606.

   Hellman on memory: Janet Chusmir, "Lillian Hellman on Lillian Hellman" (1974), in Bryer, 164; Christine Doudna, "A Still Unfinished Woman: A Conversation with Lillian Hellman" (1976), in Bryer, 195, 199–200.

152. **HUAC and Rauh:** Brightman, 604.

   letter to HUAC: Brightman, 606. The letter was found by Carl Rollyson in the course of research for his book *Lillian Hellman: Her Legend and Her Legacy* (New York: St. Martin's Press, 1988).

   Schwabacher: Brightman, 614–615.

153. **Spender:** Kiernan, 682.

   McCracken: *Commentary*, 43.

   Brightman conclusion: 614.

154. **McCarthy on Hellman death:** CBS Interview, 1985, cited in Brightman, 38; Michiko Kakutani, "It Is Easy to Picture Mary McCarthy," *The New York Times Magazine*, Sunday, 29 Mar. 1987, 60.

McCarthy reputation: Kakutani, *The New York Times Magazine*, Sunday, 29 Mar. 1987, 60.

154–155. **high estimation and negative criticism:** Cited in Bryan Ryan and Jean W. Ross, "Mary (Therese) McCarthy," in *Contemporary Authors* (Detroit: Gale Research Company, 1986), 252.

155. **"viperously clever":** MacFarquhar.

literal truth: Norman, "Lillian Hellman's Gift to a Young Playwright," *The New York Times*, 27 Aug. 1984, 7:7.

156. **truth and irony:** Jeanne Braham, *Crucial Conversations: Interpreting Contemporary American Literary Autobiographies by Women* (New York: Teacher's College Press, 1995), 28, 46.

Adams: Timothy Dow Adams, "Lillian Hellman: 'Are You Now or Were You Ever?'" in *Telling Lies in Modern American Autobiographies* (Chapel Hill: University of North Carolina Press, 1998), 128, 131, 134, 135.

"final judgment": Katherine Lederer, "An Ironic Vision" in Lillian Hellman, 1979, cited in Harold Bloom, ed., *Women Memoirists* (New York: Chelsea House Publishers, 1998), 87, 88.

157. **Wright summary:** William Wright, "Why Lillian Hellman Remains Fascinating," *The New York Times*, 3 Nov. 1996, 2:9.

7. *Les Enfants Terribles:* Truman Capote and Gore Vidal

159-160. **Nin on Vidal:** Anaïs Nin, *The Diary of Anaïs Nin* (New York: Harcourt Brace Jovanovich, 1971), 104.

160. **Nin and Capote-Vidal meeting:** Nin, 111; Gerald Clarke, *Capote: A Biography* (New York: Simon & Schuster, 1988), 139.

161. **Capote appearance:** Clarke, 71.

Marvell poem: Clarke, 108.

162. **Barth:** George Plimpton, *Truman Capote* (New York: Doubleday, 1997), 242.

Kerouac: Janet Winn, "Capote, Mailer and Miss Parker," *The New Republic*, 9 Feb. 1959, 27–28.

Cowley on "homosexual": *The Literary Situation* (New York: Viking Press, Compass Books Edition, 1958), 211.

Mann praise: Fred Kaplan, *Gore Vidal: A Biography* (New York: Doubleday, 1999), 258.

Nin dislike: Nin, 106.

163. Willingham quote: Kaplan, 276.

"fairy Huckleberry Finn": Clarke, 158.

Connolly quote: Cyril Connolly, *Ideas and Places* (New York: Harper & Brothers, 1953), 130.

Life picture: Kaplan, 239.

Vidal to Aldridge: Kaplan, 276.

164. Vidal on Capote's fiction: Kaplan, 292.

Williams and quarrel: Clarke, 141, 142.

Capote discipline: Clarke, 223.

165. "The Headless Hawk": Truman Capote, *Selected Writings* (New York: Modern Library, 1963), 31, 36.

"A Diamond Guitar": Capote, *Selected Writings*, 123.

"The Muses Are Heard": Capote, *Selected Writings*, 293.

165–166. *Porgy and Bess:* Capote, *Selected Writings*, 289.

166–167. Capote reporting techniques: Clarke, 294.

Brando and Wally Cox: Capote, 440.

Brando anger: Joshua Logan, *Movie Stars, Real People, and Me* (New York: Delacorte, 1978), 120.

167. Knickerbocker review: "One Night on a Kansas Farm," *The New York Times*, 16 Jan. 1966.

"Capote watched them hanged": According to Clarke (354), Capote called a friend after the execution "to describe the terrible scene he had witnessed."

168. Capote on "violent America": quoted in George Garrett, "Then and Now: *In Cold Blood* Revisited," *Virginia Quarterly Review* 172 (Summer 1996): online.

Capote on technique: Clarke, 357, citing Gloria Steinem, "A Visit with Truman Capote," *Glamour*, April 1966.

169. Garrett criticism: Garrett, 7.

Farmers and TV: Clarke, 324.

170. "Intellectuals": George Plimpton, *Truman Capote* (New York: Doubleday, 1997), 241.

Small Planet influence: Gore Vidal, *Palimpsest: A Memoir* (New York: Random House, 1995), 286.

171. Vidal vanity: Kaplan, 456, 556.

172. Vidal-Capote in Rome: Kaplan, 564–565.

Capote on Vidal: Clarke, 140–141.

172–173. Capote and Jacqueline Kennedy: Clarke, 270; Plimpton, 295.

174. **"Shut a Final Door":** Capote, 196.

Playgirl interview: Richard Zoerink, "Truman Capote Talks About His Crowd," *Playgirl*, September 1975, 54.

174–175. **Vidal on RFK encounter:** Plimpton, 378.

"Attacking an elf": Susan Barnes, "Gore Vidal," *Miami Herald*, 25 Nov. 1973.

176. **Vidal suit:** Clarke, 489.

176. **Vidal *Esquire* article:** Kaplan, 519.

177. **Vidal and Nureyev on RFK:** Vidal, *Palimpsest*, 363.

Plimpton parody: Plimpton, 380.

Capote on Vidal: Kaplan, 700.

178. **Capote cartoon:** Clarke, 513.

Radziwill denial: Anthony Haden-Guest, "The Vidal-Capote Papers: A Tempest in Camelot," *New York*, 11 June 1979, 56.

179. **Capote anger:** Clarke, 517.

Radziwill "fags": Liz Smith, *New York Daily News*, 23 Sept. 1979, E1.

Deposition: Clarke, 481.

Capote on Radziwill: Sally Quinn, "In Hot Blood," *The Washington Post*, 6 June 1979, E1.

Vidal on "pathology": Sally Quinn, "Hot Blood—and Gore, Chapter Two," *The Washington Post*, 7 June 1979, C7.

180. **Vidal willingness to settle suit:** Kaplan, 706.

Capote apology: Clarke, 520.

Vidal ambition: Clarke, 140–141.

181. **Vidal reaction to Capote death:** Kaplan, 707.

181–182. **Praise for Vidal:** Michael Shelden, "The Good, the Great—and Gore," *The Daily Telegraph* (London), 2 Nov. 1998, online; Jonathan Raban, "Gore Vidal Romps Through History, Stirring Up Controversies Along the Way," *The Baltimore Sun*, 6 June 1993, online.

182–183. **Vidal limitations:** Kaplan, 771; Lloyd Chiasson and others, "Truman Capote," in *Dictionary of Literary Biography*, 185: *American Literary Journalists, 1945–1995, First Series*, ed. Arthur J. Kaul (Detroit: The Gale Group, A Bruccoli Clark Layman Book, Source Database: Dictionary of Literary Biography, 1997), 29–39; Clarke, 140–141.

183. **Vidal as satirist:** Kaplan, 509.

183–184. **Vidal on U.S. failures:** Gore Vidal, *Myra Breckinridge* (New York: Little, Brown, 1968), 142.

184. **Golden Age flaws:** Andrew Sullivan, "The Greatest Generation (Revised)," *The New York Times Book Review*, 1 Oct. 2000, 14.

184–185. **Vidal on Marquand:** Kaplan, 381.
   Vidal compared to Marquand: Michael Davie, "The Golden Age,"
   The Observer: online 1 Nov. 2000.

8. Not-So-Dry Bones: Tom Wolfe, John Updike, and the Perils of Literary Ambition

188. **Twain quote:** Geordie Greig, "Ahead of His Time," *The Sunday Times*
   (London) online: 30 May 1999.
   Wolfe critics: John Updike, "Awriiiighhhhhhhhht!" (Review of *A
   Man in Full*), *The New Yorker*, 26 Nov. 1998, 101; Norman Mailer, "Man
   Half Full," *The New York Review of Books*, 17 Dec. 1998, 20; Craig Offman, "John Irving Blasts Tom Wolfe, Wolfe Blasts Back," *Salon:* online
   21 Dec. 1999.
   Radical Chic: William McKeen, *Tom Wolfe* (New York: Twayne,
   1995), 78.
   ***Christian Science Monitor* praise:** McKeen, 125 n. 19.
189. **"Billion-Footed Beast":** *Harper's*, November 1989, 45.
190. **Michael Lewis praise:** *The New York Times Book Review* 28 Oct. 1998, 1.
191. **Irving attack:** Offman, *Salon:* online 21 Dec. 1999.
191–192. **Birkerts criticism:** "That's Entertainment," *Atlantic Unbound:*
   online 2 Dec 1998.
192. **Mailer criticism:** Mailer, 8–10.
195. **Wolfe response:** Letters from Tom Wolfe to Anthony Arthur, 3 May and
   1 June 2001.
195–196. **Updike reputation as critic:** James A. Schiff, *John Updike Revisited*
   (New York: Twayne, 1998), 17, 174.
196. **Updike's rules for criticism:** *Picked-Up Pieces* (New York: Alfred A.
   Knopf, 1975), Introduction, xvii.
196–197. **Updike review comments:** 99–102.
197. **Wolfe description of Updike:** cited in John Updike, "Of Prizes and
   Print: Remarks Delivered on the Occasion of His Receiving the 1998
   National Book Foundation Medal for Distinguished Contribution to
   American Letters" (New York: Alfred A. Knopf, 1998), 8–9. My thanks
   to John Updike for calling this speech to my attention.
198. **Wolfe parody of Updike story:** "Tiny Mummies . . .", in *Hooking Up*
   (New York: Farrar, Straus and Giroux, 2000), 279.
   Vidal on Updike: "Rabbit's Own Burrow," in *The Last Empire: Essays
   1992–2000* (New York: Doubleday), 104. Vidal's attack is more political

than literary; he regards Updike as "a born reactionary," 110, who is ignorant of "history and politics and of people unlike himself," 108, apparently because Updike was ambivalent about the Vietnam War and because he once reproached Vidal as someone who, in Vidal's words, 87, did "not sufficiently love the good, the nice America. . . ."

200. **Reaction to Wolfe attack on Shawn:** McKeen, 55, John Updike letter to Anthony Arthur (2 June 2001). Russell Baker, "The Love Boat," *The New York Review of Book*, 23 March 2000, 4–6, reviews six books by former *New Yorker* writers, most of them dealing with Shawn and his years as editor from 1952 to 1987. Baker's comments indicate that the great majority of those who knew Shawn agree with Updike's appraisal of him.

　　Updike "peace offering": John Updike letter to Anthony Arthur, 2 June 2001.

201. **Wolfe *Hot Type* comments:** Offman, "Tom Wolfe Calls Irving, Mailer, and Updike 'the Three Stooges,' " *Salon*: online 21 Jan. 2000, 2.

　　"steer clear" advice: Anonymous, "Feuding in American Fiction." *The Sunday Times:* online 30 Jan. 2000.

　　***Man in Full* favorable reaction cited:** "My Three Stooges," in *Hooking Up* (New York: Farrar, Straus and Giroux, 2000), 145–171, 149–150.

201–202. **"famous old novelists":** ibid., 151–152.

　　Irving television interview: ibid., 154.

203. **"stooges" explanation:** ibid., 152, 154.

　　Wolfe a "mere entertainer": ibid., 154, 158.

　　Anna Karenina: ibid., 170.

204. **Windulf:** "It's Tom Wolfe Versus the 'Three Stooges.' " *The New York Observer*: online 27 Feb. 2000, 2.

　　Updike on "so-called feud": John Updike letter to Anthony Arthur, 2 June 2001.

205. **Croker and "Ivan Ilyich":** *A Man in Full* (New York: Farrar, Straus and Giroux, 1998), 671.

206. **Wolfe on psychological "brocade" and on satire and comedy:** Tom Wolfe letter to Anthony Arthur, 3 May 2001.

Index

Adams, Henry, 184–85
Adams, J. Donald, 67
Adams, Timothy Dow, 156
Adventure Magazine, 57
Aldridge, John, 163, 184
Alger, Horatio, 73
American Academy of Arts and Letters, 71, 204
American life, novelists' depiction of, 73, 168, 189–90, 193, 203–4
American literature, 5, 205–8
  criticized for irrelevance, 189–90, 193, 196
Anarchists' Ball, 58
Anderson, Sherwood, 25, 27–29, 33–34, 41, 45, 52, 64
  Hemingway's parody of, 34–35
  Winesburg, Ohio, 27
Annan, Noel, 116
antifascists (Communist), 146–48
anti-Semitism, 19
Arnold, Matthew, xi, 80, 118
  feud with Huxley, 118–19, 120
Atlantic Monthly, 2, 8, 10
Auchincloss, Hugh, 161
Auden, W. H., 86, 162
Austria, 136, 152
autobiographical theory, 156
Avedon, Richard, 163

Bacon, Peggy, 49
Baer, Harold, Jr., 149
Balzac, Honoré de, 54, 205
Barry, Dave, 6

Barth, John, 162
Beach, Sylvia, 28, 38
Beat writers, 162
Bentley, Eric, *Are You Now or Have You Ever Been*, 139
Berlin, Isaiah, 86
Bernstein, Leonard, 146, 188
Bierce, Ambrose, 3, 5
Birkerts, Sven, 191–92, 206
Black Panthers, 188
Blake, William, 117, 128
Bliss, Elisha, 13–14
Boni & Liveright, 34
books, popular, 188, 208
Boston, literary, 9
Bouvier, Jacqueline, 161, 172–73
Bowles, Paul, 162, 181
Boyd, Brian, 94, 103
Boyd, Ernest, 65
Braham, Jeanne, 156
Brando, Marlon, 166–67
Braque, Georges, 24
Brecht, Bertolt, 78, 128
Breen, Robert, 166
Brightman, Carol, 152–53
Brinnin, John Malcolm, 25
Brisbane, Arthur, 67, 68
Broun, Heywood, 38, 67, 68
Bryer, Jackson R., *Sixteen Modern American Authors*, 46–47, 74
Buckley, William F., Jr., 176
Burke, Kenneth, 80
Burnett, D. Graham, 122
Butterick magazines, 55–57

Buttinger, Joseph, 152
Byron, Lord, 38
  Don Juan, 98

Caldwell, Zoe, 157
California, 5
Californian, 2, 5, 11
Cambridge University, 115, 117, 125,
  132–33
camp literature, 161
Candide (musical), 141
canon, the, 131–33
Capote, Truman, 154, 160–69, 173–81
  "Breakfast at Tiffany's," 165, 168
  character and appearance, 160
  "A Christmas Memory," 165
  critical reputation, 167, 184
  decline and death of, 178–81
  "A Diamond Guitar," 165
  feud with Vidal, 174–81
  "The Headless Hawk," 165
  In Cold Blood, 164, 165, 166–69, 173,
    183, 184, 199
  Kennedy association, 173–74
  "La Côte Basque, 1965," 174
  meets Vidal, 160
  "Miriam," 164–65, 168
  "The Muses Are Heard," 165–66
  Other Voices, Other Rooms, 162–63
  Playgirl interview, and remarks about
    Vidal, 174–80
  "Shut a Final Door," 174
  writing style, 161–66
Carlyle, Thomas, 168
Carson, Joanne, 181
Carson, Johnny, 181
Carson, Rachel, Silent Spring, 199
Cather, Willa, 35
Cavett, Dick, 140–43, 148
censorship, 55
Chagall, Marc, 78
characters, in great novels, 205–6
Chinese immigration, 8, 12
Christian fundamentalists, 130–31
Civil War, American, 3–4
Clarke, Gerald, 160, 164
classical education, 118–19
Clemens, Orion, 4
Clemens, Samuel. See Twain, Mark
Clinton, Hillary, 175
Clutter family, 167–69
Cobb, Irwin S., 67, 68

Cocteau, Jean, 24
Cold War, 121–22, 137, 165
Collini, Stepan, 129
Communism, 59–60, 61, 74, 89–90, 136,
  146
  sympathy for, 90, 137, 146–48
Connolly, Cyril, 163
Conrad, Joseph, 52, 117
Conroy, Pat, 205
Coolidge, Calvin, 65
Cooper, Gary, 37
Copland, Aaron, 146
Corbière, Tristan, 81
Corke, Hilary, 125
Coward, Noël, 162
Cowley, Malcolm, 49, 58, 90, 147, 150, 162
  Exile's Return, 45, 69–70
Cox, Wally, 167
Cozzens, James Gould, Guard of Honor,
  162
Crane, Stephen, 159, 170, 208
Crews, Frederick, The Pooh Perplex,
  116–18
criticism. See literary criticism; reviewers
Cudlipp, Thelma, 57
culture
  national, 131
  popular, 131–32, 192
Cummings, E. E., 30
Curnutt, Kirk, 42, 43

Dahl, Roald, 178
Daily News, 164
Dana, Richard Henry, 9
Davie, Michael, 184
Davis, Robert Gorham, 110
Dawkins, Richard, 130
de Kruif, Paul, 71
The Delineator, 55–57
Depression, the, 69–70, 137–38
DeVoto, Bernard, 9, 20
Dickens, Charles, 88, 91, 189, 194, 205
  Bleak House, 88
Dos Passos, John, 35, 48, 90, 136, 147, 205
Dostoyevsky, F., 7, 102, 106
Doubleday, Frank, 55
Dreiser, Helen, 71
Dreiser, Theodore, 52–75, 159, 193, 204
  An American Tragedy, 55, 58, 60–61, 64,
    65, 72
  character and appearance, 56–57
  critical reputation, 72–75, 205

Dreiser Looks at Russia, 59, 61–62
feud with Lewis, 60–72
The Financier, 57
The Genius, 57–58
The Hand of the Potter, 58
Jennie Gerhardt, 57
praised by Lewis, 52–53
in Russia, 59–60
Sister Carrie, 53, 54–55
slaps Lewis, 68–69
The Titan, 57
writing style, 74, 204, 208
Dresser, Paul, 53
Duckett, Marilyn, 13–14

Eastman, Max, 38, 120
Einstein, Albert, 78
"electronic brain called Charlie," 123
Elias, Robert, 75
Eliot, George, 117
Eliot, T. S., 24, 25, 28, 80, 89, 113, 116
    "The Hollow Men," 113
    The Waste Land, 25
Ellis, Havelock, 19, 93
Emerson, Ralph Waldo, 9, 16–17, 114,
    127
Epstein, Jason, 182
Esquire, 38, 43
"every word is a lie," 143, 149

Fadiman, Clifton, 38
Farrell, James, 204, 205
Fascists, 147
Faulkner, William, 47, 86, 88, 89, 170, 199
    Light in August, 89
    The Sound and the Fury, 159
Feibleman, Peter, *Cakewalk*, 157
Feiffer, Jules, 139
Felker, Clay, 198
Fenwick, Elizabeth, 163
Fiedler, Leslie, 162
Fielding, Henry, *Tom Jones*, 88
Fifth Amendment, 138
First Amendment, 149
Fitzgerald, F. Scott, 34, 38, 43, 46, 48, 82,
    86, 159
    The Great Gatsby, 207
    Tender Is the Night, 208
Foote, Shelby, 168
Ford, Ford Madox, 28, 31, 41, 43, 45
Franco, Francisco, 136, 147
Franks, Bobby, 199

Frémont, Jessie Benton, 2
French Revolution, 89
Freud, Sigmund, 104
    Art and Neurosis, xiv
Freudian criticism, 74, 105
Frost, Robert, 65, 128

Gable, Clark, 37
Galsworthy, John, *The Forsyte Saga*, 118
García Márquez, Gabriel, 181
Gardiner, Muriel, 152–53, 157
    Code Name Mary, 152
Garrett, George, 169
Garroway, Dave, 171
gay literary scene, 162–63
gay studies, 182
Gelderman, Carol, 140, 142
German-Soviet pact (1939), 146
Germany, Nazi, 128–29, 131
Gillette, Chester, 72
Gilmore, Gary, 195
Gingrich, Arnold, 38, 42
Girodias, Maurice, 94
Goethe, J. W. von, 38
Gogol, Nikolai, 92–93
Gold, Michael, 26
Goldman, Emma, 58
"a good career move," 181
Gore, Thomas P., 159
gossip, 173–74
Gould, Stephen Jay, 130
Grant, Ulysses S., 21
Gray, Paul, 201
Great Tradition, the, 133
Greenwich Village, 58, 160
Grey, Zane, 73
Grisham, John, 192
Griswold, Anna, 2

Halperin, John, 111
Hammett, Dashiell, 135–36, 138, 146
    The Thin Man, 136
Harcourt, 51
Hart, James D., 51
Harte, Bret, 1–22
    Ah Sin (play written with Twain),
        12–15
    career and appearance, 1–3, 15–18
    character and appearance, 10–11, 13
    critical reputation, 8–10
    feud with Twain, 15–20, 204
    Gabriel Conroy, 13

Harte, Bret (*continued*)
"The Luck of Roaring Camp," 2, 20
"The Outcasts of Poker Flat," 2–3
"Plain Language from Truthful
   James," 8–9, 12
"Tennessee's Partner," 3, 22
Two Men of Sandy Bar, 12–13
writing style, 2–3, 6, 8–9, 18–20, 22
Hawking, Stephen, 130
Hawthorne, Nathaniel, 16
   The Scarlet Letter, 61
Hayes, Rutherford B., 15–17
Heggen, Thomas, 163
   Mr. Roberts, 159
Heller, Joseph, *Catch-22*, 208
Hellman, Lillian, 90, 135–57
   The Children's Hour, 135
   critical reputation, 135, 155–57
   feud with McCarthy, 140–57
   HUAC testimony, 137–40, 152
   The Little Foxes, 135
   Pentimento, 137, 149, 152
   Scoundrel Time, 139, 148, 149, 151
   sues McCarthy for libel, 143–53
   Toys in the Attic, 135
   Watch on the Rhine, 135
   writing style, 140–41, 155–56
Hemingway, Ernest, 6, 7, 23–48, 52, 65,
   82, 86, 88, 136, 199
   "Big Two-Hearted River," 30
   character and appearance, 28, 47–48,
      204
   "A Clean, Well-Lighted Place," 37
   critical reputation, 32–33, 37–39, 46–47
   Death in the Afternoon, 37
   A Farewell to Arms, 29, 36–37, 47
   feud with Stein, 35–46
   For Whom the Bell Tolls, 47, 208
   Green Hills of Africa, 37, 42
   "Hills Like White Elephants," 37
   In Our Time, 29, 32, 33–34, 47, 207
   meets Gertrude Stein, 23, 29
   A Moveable Feast, 29–30, 43–46, 47
   The Old Man and the Sea, 47
   parodies of Anderson and Stein, 34–36
   "The Snows of Kilimanjaro," 38
   "Summer People," 32
   The Sun Also Rises, 29, 32, 34, 36, 44,
      45, 47, 82, 207
   Three Stories & Ten Poems, 31, 33
   The Torrents of Spring, 34–35
   Winner Take Nothing, 37

writing style, 29–33, 37–39, 46–47, 159,
   168, 208
Hemingway, Hadley Richardson, 24, 28,
   29, 37
Heptonstall, Geoffrey, 110, 124
Hersey, John, 140, 145, 150, 168
   Hiroshima, 199
Hickok, Dick, 167, 169
highbrow, middlebrow, and lowbrow, 192
Hill, Hamlin, 7
Hiss, Alger, 137
Hitler, 78, 90, 129, 142, 146, 147
Holbrook, Hal, 7
Holmes, Oliver Wendell, Sr., 9
homosexual themes, 162–63
Hook, Sidney, 151, 156
Hopkins, Gerard Manley, 117, 121
House Committee on Un-American
   Activities (HUAC), 137–40, 148, 152
"how does it feel to be an enfant terrible,"
   160
Howe, Irving, 72, 148, 150
Howells, William Dean, 7, 8, 9–10,
   15–17, 19, 20, 52
Hutchinson, James F., 66
Huxley, T. H., 132
   feud with Arnold, 118–19, 120

Indian massacres (by whites), 2
Industrial Revolution, 114–15, 118,
   127–28
intellectuals, 170
   leftist, 146–48
   literary, 112–15, 129
interviewers/ing, 166–67
Irving, John
   feud with Wolfe, 188, 191, 201–8
   A Widow for One Year, 203
Irving, Washington, 16
Isherwood, Christopher, 162
"isn't writing—it's typing," 162

James, Henry, 52, 88–89, 150, 170, 182
   feud with Wells, 119–20
   The Portrait of a Lady, 119
   The Turn of the Screw, 119
   What Maisie Knew, 88–89
   writing style, 119–20
Jarrell, Randall, 142
Johnson, Pamela Hansford, 112
Johnson, Paul, xi–xii
Johnson, Samuel, 80, 112

Johnston, Jimmy, 70
Jones, James, *From Here to Eternity*, 159
journalists, xiii, 28–29, 53–54, 183, 188, 193, 194, 208
literary, 165–66
See also New Journalism
Joyce, James, 25, 28, 30, 80, 91, 98, 116
Ulysses, 25
Julia (film), 137
"Julia" (Hellman character), 136–37, 146, 152–53

Kafka, Franz, 91
Kakutani, Michiko, 154, 195
Kaplan, Fred, 182
Kaplan, Justin, *Mr. Clemens and Mark Twain*, 7
Karl, Frederick, 110
Karlinsky, Simon, 87
Kazan, Elia, 138
Kazin, Alfred, 26, 72, 83, 110–11, 142, 144, 151, 156
Keillor, Garrison, 6
Kendall, W. A., 11
Kennedy, Ethel, 176
Kennedy, John F., 122, 171, 172–73, 176–77
Kennedy, Robert F., 173, 175, 176–77
Kennedy family, 142, 161, 172–79
Kerouac, Jack, 162
On the Road, 162
Khrushchev, Nikita, 151
Kimball, Roger, 132
Kirn, Walter, xi
Knickerbocker, Conrad, 167
Kramer, Hilton, 151
Kubrick, Stanley, 96

Lamb, Charles, 20
Langdon, Olivia, 11–12, 21
Lawrence, D. H., 31, 113–14, 116–17
Leavis, F[rank]. R[aymond]., 115–33
critical writings, 120–21
feud with Snow, 121–33
The Great Tradition, 117
New Bearings in English Poetry, 116
Nor Shall My Sword, 128
Richmond College lecture on "Two Cultures," 122–25
teaching career, 115–16
See also Scrutiny

Leavis, Q. D. "Queenie," 117
Lederer, Katherine, 156
Lengel, William, 56, 67, 68–69
Lenin, 80, 90
Leopold, Nathan, 199
Levin, Harry and Elena, 86
Lewis, Michael, 190
Lewis, Sinclair, 31, 35, 49–53, 55, 57–75, 189
Arrowsmith, 50, 52, 71
Babbitt, 50, 51, 58, 64
character and appearance, 49–51
critical reputation, 65–66, 73–75, 204, 205
Dodsworth, 58, 59, 61, 63
Elmer Gantry, 50, 58, 65
feud with Dreiser, 60–72
The Job, 58
Main Street, 50, 51, 52, 58, 64
Nobel Prize, 51–52, 63–69
Our Mr. Wrenn, 58
praised Dreiser, 52–53
public speaking by, 66–67
in Russia, 59–60
writing style, 73–74, 205
Lewis, Wyndham, 38, 113
libel, 144
liberals, American, 146–48
Liebling, A. J., 199
Lilly and Dash (TV program), 157
Lingeman, Richard, 53, 72, 75
Sinclair Lewis: Rebel from Main Street, 75
literary biography, xii, 75
literary criticism, 106, 117–18, 131–33, 140, 155–57
literary intellectuals, 112–15, 129
literary journalism, 165–66
literary modernism, 26, 32
literature
compared to science, 126
modern, pessimism of, 127–28
value of, 118, 131–33
Liveright, Horace, 35
Loeb, Richard, 199
Logan, Joshua, 167
Lolita (movie), 96
London, Ephraim, 145, 148
Long, Ray, 67
Longfellow, Henry Wadsworth, 9
"Excelsior," 15
Lord, Walter, 168

"lost generation," 44–45, 82
Lowell, James Russell, 9, 16–17
Lowell, Robert, 103
Luce, Henry, 193
Luddites, 114, 127
Ludlum, Robert, 192
Lunden, Rolf, 64
Lynes, Russell, 192
Lyons, Leonard, 166

MacDonald, Dwight, 141, 192
MacFarquhar, Larissa, 144, 155
Machiavelli, 159
MacKillop, Ian, 115, 131
MacLeish, Archibald, 23, 136, 212
Mailer, Norman, 142, 154, 168, 198
  Advertisements for Myself, 163
  "Appeal to Lillian Hellman and Mary
    McCarthy," 150
  The Armies of the Night, 193
  Barbary Shore, 193
  The Executioner's Song, 193, 195, 204
  feud with Wolfe, 188, 192–95, 200–208
  The Fight, 193
  The Gospel According to the Son, 193,
    203
  Harlot's Ghost, 193
  The Naked and the Dead, 159, 162,
    192–93, 204
  Of a Fire on the Moon, 193
  punches Vidal, 176, 193
Malraux, André, 86, 88, 89
  Man's Fate, 89
Mann, Thomas, 78, 106, 128, 162, 182
Marquand, John P., 184–85
  H. M. Pulham, Esquire, 184
  Sincerely, Willis Wayde, 184
  Wickford Point, 185
Marshall, George C., 137
Marvell, Andrew, 39
  "The Picture of Little T.C. in a
    Prospect of Flowers," 161
Marx, Leo, The Machine in the Garden,
  127
mass-cult and mid-cult, 192
Matisse, Henri, 24
Matthiessen, F. O., 146
McAlmon, Robert, 25, 30
McCarthy, Joseph, 137
McCarthy, Mary, 83, 84, 87, 156
  character and appearance, 141–42
  critical reputation, 154–55

critical writings, 140–41
  on Dick Cavett show, 140–43
  feud with Hellman, 140–57
  The Group, 154
  The Groves of Academe, 83
  Mary McCarthy's Theatre Chronicles,
    1937–1962, 155
  The Mask of State: Watergate Portraits,
    154
  The Stones of Florence, 154
  Venice Observed, 154
  writing style, 144, 154–55
McCracken, Samuel, 153
McCullers, Carson, 164
McDermott, Alice, Charming Billy, 200
Mencken, H. L., 31, 50–51, 56, 58–59, 60,
  80–81
Meyers, Jeffrey, 42, 43, 84, 86, 102, 106
Miller, Arthur, 138
  The Crucible, 138
Miller, Henry, 160
Mitchell, Margaret, Gone with the Wind,
  190
Mitgang, Herbert, 143
Modernism, 80, 113, 116
Moers, Ellen, 74
Moorehead, Alan, 168
Morris, William, 114
Morrow, William, 58
Moscow Trials, 146
movies, 203
multiculturalism, 131–32
Mumford, Lewis, 65
Mussolini, Benito, 147
"my three stooges," 188, 201, 203

Nabokov, Vera, 77
Nabokov, Vladimir, 77–79, 86–107
  arrival in U.S., 77–78
  Bend Sinister, 90
  character and appearance, 78–79
  The Gift, 79
  Lolita, 78, 93–96
  Pushkin translation, 98–105
  retires to Switzerland, 97–98
  as teacher, 91–93
  writing style, 98
Nathan, George Jean, 50–51
National Book Award, 193, 197, 200
Nazis, 78, 128–29, 131, 136, 147
New Criticism, xii, 73–74
New Humanists, 39

New Journalism, 154, 166–69, 184, 188
New York magazine, 198
The New Yorker, 160–61, 167
    Wolfe's profile of, 198–200, 204
New York Herald Tribune, 198
New York Post, 178
Nin, Anaïs, 159–60, 162
Nissen, Axel, *Bret Harte: Prince and Pauper*, 19
Nobel, Alfred, 64
Nobel Prize for Literature, 50, 51–52, 61, 63–69
Norman, Marsha, 155
North Star (film), 138, 141
novelists
    criticized for irrelevance (Wolfe), 189–90
    depiction of life by, 73, 189–90, 193, 203–4
    modern American, 205–8
novels
    "nonfiction," 168
    power of, 203, 205–6
Nureyev, Rudolf, 177

"old bags of bones," 200, 202
Olympia Press, 94
O'Neill, Eugene, 52
    The Iceman Cometh, 140
O'Sullivan, Benjamin, 148
Overland Monthly, 5, 8, 11

Paar, Jack, 171
Paley, Bill and Babe, 174
Paris, avant-garde in, 24
Parker, Dorothy, 73
Parsloe, James, 13, 14
Pasternak, Boris, *Dr. Zhivago*, 96–97
Pastore, Stephen R., 66
Pegler, Westbrook, 70
Perkins, Maxwell, 34, 38, 42
Picasso, Pablo, 23, 25, 27
Pilnyak, Boris, 67–68
plagiarism, 62
Playgirl, 174, 179
Plimpton, George, 150, 176, 177
Plutarch, 168
Podhoretz, Norman, 150
Poirier, Richard, 150
political correctness, 131
popular books, value of, 188, 208
popular culture, 131–32, 192

Porgy and Bess, 165–66
pornography, 93–96
Porter, Katherine Anne, 24
postmodernism, 74
Pound, Ezra, 24, 25, 28, 35, 43, 113
Presley, Elvis, 181
Priestley, J. B., 118
Pritchett, V. S., 96
progress, belief in, 128
Proust, Marcel, 52, 80
Pulitzer Prize, 52, 193
Pushkin, Alexander, 85–86, 88, 103
    Eugene Onegin, 85–86, 98–105
Putnam, G. P., 94
Pynchon, Thomas, *Gravity's Rainbow*, 130

Raban, Jonathan, 182
race, creed, and gender politics, 131
Radziwill, Lee, 174, 178–79
Rahv, Philip, 150
Random House, 182
Rascoe, Burton, 67
Rauh, Joseph, 152
realistic novels, 203
Rees, Jonathan, 129
Resistance (World War II), 136, 152
reviewers/reviewing, 81–82, 196
Reynolds, Michael, 43
Rogers, Will, 137–38
Romantics, 89, 127, 128
Roosevelt, Eleanor, 171
"rose is a rose," 26
Rosenberg case, 137
Rosenblatt, Roger, xi
Rosenfeld, Paul, 32
Ross, Harold, 161, 199
Rostow, Eugene, 65
Rovere, Richard and Eleanor, 171
Ruskin, John, 114
Russell, Bertrand, 24
Russia, 104. *See also* Soviet Union
Russian language, 103–4
Russian Revolution, 80, 89
Rutherford, Ernest, 110, 113, 126

Salinger, J. D., 199
salons, 24–25, 160
San Francisco, 1
Sartre, Jean-Paul, 89, 102
satire, 144, 197, 207, 208
Sayonara (film), 167

Scharnhorst, Gary, 9, 12, 15, 19
Schiff, James A., 195
Schiff, Stacy, 96–97
Schiller, Lawrence, 195
Schlesinger, Arthur, Jr., 175, 177
Schorer, Mark, 70–71, 75, 164, 217
Schwabacher, Karl, 152–53
science education, 118–19, 121–22
scientists
  and social issues, 128–29
  vs. writers, 109, 112–15, 128–29
Scribner's, 34–35
Scrutiny, 117, 120, 124
Second Law of Thermodynamics, 113,
  130
Seigneaux, Hydeline de, 18
sex, writing about, 93–96
Shakespeare, William, 126
Shakespeare & Company, 28, 38
Shaw, George Bernard, 63
Shaw, Irwin, *The Young Lions*, 159, 162
Shawn, William, 198–200
Sheean, Vincent, 49, 71
Shelden, Michael, 181
Shulevitz, Judith, xi
Simpson, Eileen, 142
Smith, Chard Powers, 39
Smith, Liz, 179
Smith, Perry, 167, 169
Snow, C[harles]. P[ercy]., 109–15, 120,
  121–31
  character and appearance, 111
  Corridors of Power, 110, 126
  critical reputation, 110–11, 127
  Death Under Sail, 110
  essays, 121, 129–30
  feud with Leavis, 121–33
  The Masters, 110, 126
  Rede lecture "The Two Cultures," 109,
    112–15, 121–24, 129–30
  The Search, 110
  Strangers and Brothers series, 110–11,
    126
  writing style, 110–11, 126–27
Solomon, Evan, 201, 202–3
Sontag, Susan, 150
Soviet Union
  in the Cold War, 121, 137
  crimes of, 89–90
  sympathy for, 79, 138
  visits to, 59–60, 61, 85, 89–90, 136,
    165–66

Spanish-American War, 21
Spanish Loyalists, 136, 147
Spencer, Herbert, 54
Spender, Stephen, 153
Sputnik, 121
Stafford, Jean, 163
Stalin, 89–90, 137, 146, 151
Stalinists (American), 146–48
Stallings, Lawrence, 67
Stark, Bruce, 47
Stein, Gertrude, 23–48, 160
  Autobiography of Alice B. Toklas, 26,
    40–42, 46
  feud with Hemingway, 35–46
  Hemingway's parody of, 35–36
  home at 27, rue de Fleurus, 24–25,
    40, 45–46
  The Making of Americans, 31–32, 41,
    44, 45–46
  "Melanctha," 26
  Tender Buttons, 26
  Three Lives, 26–27, 33
  writing style, 31–32
Stein, Leo, 24
Steinbeck, John, 199, 204, 205
Steiner, George, 118
Stendhal, 193
Sterne, Laurence, *Tristam Shandy*,
  88
Stevenson, Robert Lewis, 7
Stewart, Donald Ogden, 48
Stokes Publishers, 58
Strachey, Lytton, 168
Strater, Mike, 35
Styron, William, 140
Sully Prudhomme, René, 52
Sumner, John, 58
Susskind, David, 171, 177
Swanberg, W. A., 57, 75
Swift, Jonathan, 144

teaching, university, 91
technocrats, 120, 132–33
television, Golden Age of, 170
Thackeray, William Makepeace, 20
  Vanity Fair, 189
Thale, Jerome, 110
Third World, 129
Thompson, Dorothy, 49, 59–62, 71
  The New Russia, 61–62
Thoreau, Henry David, 114
Thurber, James, 199